Distant Cycles

❄

Distant Cycles

Schubert and the Conceiving of Song

Richard Kramer

❄

The University of Chicago Press
Chicago and London

Richard Kramer is dean of humanities and fine arts and professor of music at the State University of New York at Stony Brook.

The University of Chicago Press, Chicago 60637
The University of Chicago Press, Ltd., London

Printed in the United States of America
03 02 01 00 99 98 97 96 95 94 1 2 3 4 5
ISBN: 0-226-45234-4 (cloth)
0-226-45235-2 (paper)

A publishing subvention from the American Musicological Society is gratefully acknowledged.

Kramer, Richard.
Distant cycles : Schubert and the conceiving of song / Richard Kramer.
p. cm.
Includes bibliographical references and indexes.
1. Schubert, Franz, 1797–1828. Song cycles. 2. Schubert, Franz, 1797–1828—Manuscripts.
3. Song cycles—History and criticism. I. Title.
ML410.S3K775 1994
782.4'7'092—dc20 93-39891 CIP MN

♾ The paper used in this publication meets the minimum requirements of the American National Standard for Information Sciences—Permanence of Paper for Printed Library Materials, ANSI Z39.48-1984.

For Martha

To devour one's own legs for hunger is not the worst that can happen to a being cursed with the gift of song. There are human crickets who must eat their own hearts in order to sing.

Lafcadio Hearn, "Kusa-Hibari"

Contents

Acknowledgments

This work could not have been written without the help of the curators of the great Schubert collections in Europe and the United States. For allowing me access to their precious archives, I am deeply indebted to Otto Biba, of the Gesellschaft der Musikfreunde in Vienna; to Ernst Hilmar, of the Stadtbibliothek in Vienna; to Erling Lomnäs, for providing valuable and detailed information on the autograph manuscript of *Abendröte* in the collection of the Stiftelsen Musikkulturens främjande in Stockholm; to Charles E. Pierce, Jr., director of the Pierpont Morgan Library in New York City; and to the librarians at the Sächsische Landesbibliothek in Dresden and the Staatsbibliothek Preußischer Kulturbesitz in the former West Berlin. Walther Dürr, of the Internationalen Schubert-Gesellschaft at Tübingen, was most generous in his replies to my many questions about manuscripts now in private collections, and I am further indebted to him for his forthright exchange of ideas on topics central to this book. Robert Winter shared his expert reading of the watermarks of a good many papers inaccessible to me. Kristina Muxfeldt helped track down arcana in the Viennese archives and at the Schiller-Museum in Marbach am Neckar. Kip Montgomery prepared the index.

Two chapters were published previously: chapter 4, as "Distant Cycles: Schubert, Goethe and the *Entfernte*" (*Journal of Musicology*, vol. 6, no. 1 [Winter 1988]: 3–21, © 1988 by the Regents of the University of California), and chapter 6, as "Schubert's Heine" (*19th Century Music*, vol. 8, no. 3 [Spring 1985]: 213–25, © 1985 by the Regents of the University of California). I am grateful to the University of California Press for granting permission to publish them here in revised form. Much of an earlier version of chapter 2 formed the basis of a lecture for the first of the Schubertiaden at the 92d Street Y (New York City) in January 1988; Joseph Horowitz proposed the topic of the talk, and I am indebted to him for that.

Books of this kind do not get very far without the free and vigorous exchange of ideas among colleagues, students, and teachers. I think warmly of Siegmund Levarie, whose probing analyses of *Die schöne Müllerin*—more than thirty years ago!—remain with me still. Kristina Muxfeldt and Greg Vitercik enlivened many a Stony Brook seminar on these songs and have now written fine Schubert studies of their own, from which I have learned much. To Charles Rosen I owe some of the ideas woven into the study of *Die Götter*

Griechenlands (D. 677)—and no doubt much else gleaned in stimulating impromptu excursions through this inexhaustible repertory.

In the decade or more during which the inchoate first thoughts of these distant cycles took hold and grew, I was sustained through the spirited support of my wife, Martha Calhoun, whose three professional lives—as musician, as literary critic, and as attorney-at-law—fittingly served the arguments of this book.

Stony Brook, New York

I

Introduction

❄

1

In Search of Song

Preamble

What does Schubert want from poetry? This may seem a strange entry into the topic, but to address the question in earnest is to take hold of the problem in a fresh way. In these opening reflections, intended as they are to warm to the main themes of the book, I endeavor to suggest that to understand the phenomenon of Schubert song, we are obliged to return to the moment at which song is conceived. If, in a literal sense, we can do no such thing, the instinct runs deep in all performance, all reading, to bring us closer to this arcane matrix of thought from which song is born.

We are driven back to the autographs. They tell us a great deal—of the minutiae that register decision making, certainly, but also, and more significantly, of those plain facts that have been muted in the subsequent process, the steps toward publication by which the song was made presentable for public consumption.

In the midst of this process, the songs were often transposed. Is something lost in the transposition? Unquestionably. What is lost is of the essence and has to do with this ineffable moment at which poem and music are fused in the composer's mind. The process toward publication does further damage to the bold yet fragile configurations through which sets of poems are put into music, for the evidence is everywhere that the song was conceived in a context. Returned to its milieu, construed as the participant in some greater narrative unfolding, the single song seems now less coherent, more vulnerable as a thing in itself. How to verify that it is textually genuine? And what, precisely, is this narrative context? How is it constituted? Answers to these questions are sought in the studies that follow.

This, it will be clear, is not a monograph on Schubert's song cycles. Rather, it is an inquiry into something more elemental, an attempt to tease out from the songs a primary instinct toward cyclic process. The reader will wonder how it is that two chapters are given to *Winterreise* while *Die schöne Müllerin* is accorded only the occasional aside. That is in part because the autograph score of the latter has not survived—the evidence preliminary to such inquiry is missing—and in part because its agency as song cycle is simply not in doubt. The former, on the other hand, is burdened with all those problems described above. Its published form conceals a complexity of conception that its storied autograph masks and unmasks.

I

Ever tinkering with his songs, fitting and refitting them for publication, Schubert bequeathed a legacy riddled in aesthetic contradiction, taxing even to the most assiduous students of his music. The rift between the composer in Schubert and the merchant in him—between the private Schubert, lost in the work at hand, and the Schubert who tenders this work to the public—is often palpable, acutely felt in the repertory of songs, where the genre itself seems to encourage blithe disregard for the fundamental axioms by which textual authority is commonly established. The very idea of the song both as something self-contained and, often enough, as an aspect of some complex weave of poems conceived together is an invitation to textual distortion of a more subtle kind. Understandably, it is the composer himself—but the composer who, for motives not readily apparent, now removes his songs from the context in which they were conceived—to whom later editors have turned for guidance.

In the history of Lied, the art and manner of publication has traditionally been central to the enterprise. Max Friedlaender's *Das deutsche Lied im 18. Jahrhundert*, the exhaustive bibliographic history, reconstructs this rich chronicle of publication.[1] The dissemination of the repertory was early on coupled with an aggressive publication program, for this was a genre with appeal to a broad clientele, both literary and musical, and requiring only the most modest musical competence. From Sperontes's *Singende Muse an der Pleisse* (1736) through two undistinguished volumes of settings titled *Schiller's Ode an die Freude* (1799–1800), the poet dominates in collaborations of modest and didactic tone. Something of the aesthetic is captured in the famous preface to *Lieder im Volkston*, where Johann Abraham Peter Schulz urges "a striking similarity between the musical and the poetic. . . ; a melody whose progression never raises itself above the course of the text, nor sinks beneath it, and whose declamation and meter cling to the words like a garment the body; and which in addition flows forth in altogether singable intervals in a range suitable to all voices and in the simplest possible harmonies." Through all this, the Lied achieves the "appearance of the unsought, the artless, the familiar—achieves, in a word, the *Volkston.*" The ultimate goal, yet more modest, is simply "to make good Lied texts generally known."[2]

A few years earlier, Johann Friedrich Reichardt sent a collection of *Oden und Lieder* (Berlin, 1780) into the world with "Some Good Advice Instead of

1. Max Friedlaender, *Das deutsche Lied im 18. Jahrhundert: Quellen und Studien*, 2 vols. (Stuttgart and Berlin, 1902; reprint, Hildesheim, 1962).

2. Johann Abraham Peter Schulz, *Lieder im Volkston*, 2d ed. (Berlin, 1785). For a reprint of Schulz's text, see Friedlaender, *Das deutsche Lied*, 1, pt. 1: 256–57. (Unless an English-language source is given, all translations from the German are mine.)

a Preface" ("Auch ein guter Rath statt der Vorrede"): the singer—not at once distinguishable from the composer himself—is admonished to *read* the poem before he can hope to render it in song. (There will be more to say about this in chapter 2.) Forty years later, the goals were no longer quite so modest; even the trace of *Volkston*, whether muted or pronounced, acquired an ironic aftertaste. The collaborative enterprise, now internalized and imaginary, lost its innocence.

By April 1821, Schubert had composed well over four hundred songs. A very few had appeared in print, but there had been no substantial commercial publication. The famous manuscript of Goethe settings sent by Spaun to the poet in April 1816 was to have been the first of eight volumes devoted to the Classical poets in a series very likely modeled on those published by Breitkopf and Härtel of Lieder by Zumsteeg (1800–1805) and Reichardt (1809–11).[3] Nothing came of it. But, by 1821, a demand for Schubert's songs had begun to make itself felt. At first, and for roughly two years, publications were decidedly retrospective. The inclination to include earlier songs in the published collections continued right through until the end of Schubert's life. Opus 108, which Leidesdorf brought out toward the end of January 1829—perhaps the last publication over which Schubert is believed to have exercised some control—contains three songs: *Über Wildemann* (E. Schulze; D. 884); *Todesmusik* (Schober; D. 758), a transposition, slightly revised, of a song composed in 1822; and *Die Erscheinung* (Kosegarten; D. 229), a strophic Lied in the old-fashioned sense, composed in 1815, and first published in an *Album musicale* by Sauer and Leidesdorf in 1824. *Todesmusik*, Walther Dürr reminds us, evokes the mystical ceremonial round described in Schubert's troubled narrative "Mein Traum," written some months earlier, in July 1822. Perhaps not coincidentally, a copy of the narrative in Schober's hand was known to exist.[4]

Scholars and musicians of high standing have argued strenuously for the transposition of Schubert's songs, in the name of convenience for the performer, and on the evidence that Schubert himself sanctioned such transposition. Whatever Schubert's motives, we must contend with the sense in which the three songs of op. 108 constitute a single work—were meant to be sung as a group. But decisions taken in the mapping of a strategy for publication do not always illuminate—indeed seem intentionally to impede—deeper inquiries into Schubert's music. Transposing *Todesmusik* up a semitone from G♭ is to deprive it of an aspect of its meaning. By 1824, G♭—the key itself—had acquired a certain cachet in Schubert's music (a point further explored below). If the transposition to G does nothing for the song or the singer, it pointedly accords better with the keys of *Über Wildemann* (D minor) and *Die*

3. See the letter of 17 April 1816 from Spaun to Goethe, given in Otto Erich Deutsch, *Schubert: A Documentary Biography* (New York, 1947), 56–58; and *Franz Schubert: Die Dokumente seines Lebens* (Kassel, 1964), 40–41.

4. See Deutsch, *Documentary Biography*, 226–28, and *Dokumente*, 158–59.

Erscheinung (E major), and this we may take as evidence that Schubert felt the sacrifice justified for the sake of some tonal constellation within op. 108. But *Die Erscheinung*, an ingratiating fairy tale *im Volkston*, does not sing well after *Über Wildemann* (which carries the stormy oppositions of *Rastlose Liebe* a notch higher) and the elegiac *Todesmusik*. Its *Ton*—the innocence of those touching Kosegarten songs from 1815—seems misplaced, is poorly matched to the internal agonies (a composer much wiser, if not appreciably older, and no longer innocent) in these songs that now precede it. Perhaps Schubert had in mind a singer's encore, conjuring some past evening of music making with friends. *An Sylvia*, following on *Vor meiner Wiege* at the end of op. 106, makes a similarly vacuous impression that diminishes both songs, just as the beguiling *Fischerweise* at the end of op. 96 answers poorly to the profundities of *Wandrers Nachtlied* ("Über allen Gipfeln ist Ruh").

If op. 108 illuminates something of Schubert's perspective on his own work, perhaps even his sense of the market (however he may have perceived it), it unwittingly obscures a deeper aspect of his art. To probe beneath the surface of *Todesmusik* means to put out of mind the new trappings with which Schubert thought to release it in 1828—or at any rate to understand these for what they are. For Lieder perhaps more so than for works of another genre, and for Schubert's Lieder in the extreme, to establish a text means to return it to an environment that clarifies its genesis: the conceiving of the song, as an instance among the conceiving of other songs, figures in the decoding of its meanings. The more that publication obscures this genesis, the more urgent the task of textual clarification. The need is particularly acute in a genre where the creation of one work seems to follow on another with only the faintest articulation.

It is not always the isolated poem that prompts Schubert to compose, but often rather a series of poems from a single collection. Here again, retrospective publication can deceive. Opus 92, a striking case, offers three songs by Goethe. The third is *Geistes-Gruß* (D. 142), a very early song that exists in six "versions." The three measures of tremolo in the piano at the outset, new to this sixth version, must date from 1828. Joseph Kerman read the harmonic significance of those measures as a thumbprint of style increasingly common in Schubert's final years. In this instance, publication provoked some telling changes. "*Geistes-Gruß*," in Kerman's words, "was transformed as few works ever were in their revisions."[5] The published song is not quite the one offered to Goethe in 1816.

Opus 92 opens with *Der Musensohn*, touched up and transposed for publication in 1828. The autograph of the original version shows it to have been one of four Goethe poems set down in the order in which Schubert refers to them in a letter to Spaun of 7 December 1822: "Auch habe ich einige neue

5. Joseph Kerman, "A Romantic Detail in Schubert's *Schwanengesang*," *Musical Quarterly* 48 (January 1962): 41 (reprinted, slightly revised, in *Schubert: Critical and Analytical Studies*, ed. Walter Frisch [Lincoln, Nebr., and London, 1986], 54–55).

Lieder von Göthe componirt, als: Der Musensohn, die Entfernte, am Flusse, u. Willkommen und Abschied" (I have also set several new songs by Goethe: Der Musensohn, an die Entfernte, am Flusse, and Willkommen und Abschied).[6] Allusions, poignant and suggestive, resonate from song to song and even in the implicit tale that the poems seem to tell when they are read in just this order. Their implications are pursued in chapter 4. Opus 92 serves as evidence that by 1828 such cyclic intimations, pronounced and veiled as they may have been in 1822, were no longer what Schubert valued in these songs. Schubert, now the entrepreneur, expropriates the works of his Muse; the songs are repackaged with an ear tuned to some public response.

Whatever its merits in Schubert's mind, op. 92 points up the historical convolutions to which a privileging of the print *as work* in some textually authoritative sense must lead, for, in spite of all the details that "improve" *Geistes-Gruß* for publication—even allowing that its original notation encouraged a freedom of declamation now forfeited in Schubert's endeavor to control all gesture—the song nevertheless belongs to the history of Schubert's earliest encounters with Goethe's poetry. That immanent quality is lost in the new company of op. 92. The encounter of 1822 was a more sophisticated enterprise, shared among a coterie of artists and intellectuals for whom Goethe was a figure of both adoration and dispute. If Schubert later saw no contradiction in pairing *Geistes-Gruß* with *Der Musensohn* (sandwiching *Auf dem See*, from yet another Goethe phase, in between), this must not dissuade us from hearing each as an expression of its own time, with attendant limits of style. It is sobering to think that this *Geistes-Gruß* of op. 92, a song reheard after the experience of *Winterreise* and in the midst of the final Lieder, was born in the spirit of those Goethean declamations that Reichardt had been publishing at the turn of the century.

If op. 108 holds claim as the final publication over which Schubert may have exercised some control, the so-called *Schwanengesang* was the first—and in many ways the most problematic—of a notorious series of song publications that would appear soon after his death and over which he can have held only a posthumous, sometimes even mythic, influence.[7] Yet the publication of seven songs on texts by Rellstab and six by Heine together in a single, incongruous opus, preposterous as this may seem on its face, takes its justification from Schubert's autograph. Here, too, the pressure toward publication is clearly in conflict with what any commonsense reading of the *Schwanengesang* will convey: there are two sets of songs here, each with its own partly inscrutable history. A chapter is devoted to each of them in an effort to reclaim an original sense of *work* that is concealed in the *Schwanengesang*.

6. See Deutsch, *Documentary Biography*, 248, and *Dokumente*, 173.

7. The classic study of the problem is Maurice J. E. Brown, "The Posthumous Publication of the Songs," in his *Essays on Schubert* (London and New York, 1966), 267–90.

II

The studies that follow, each in its own way, are driven by what has been called the "Suche nach dem verlorenen Werk"—the quest to find again the sense of the work whose integrity has been effaced through the inevitable distortions of time and, so to speak, the elements.[8] The concept itself seems a natural corollary to one prominent vein of Romantic expression, where the work itself, as though embarrassed by an eccentric genetic code, now and again vanishes from view, victimized by the fragile new forms that gave it life in the first place.

Six chapters inquire into the nature of cyclic process. The shadowy history of *cycle* as a term to describe some quality innate in a set of songs—or of certain purely instrumental works, with or without poetic implications—must not slow us here. The two chapters on *Winterreise*, a work that neither Müller nor Schubert ever called *cycle*, assume nothing about the conventions of the genre but seek out the signs of such genre defining in the work itself—a work that, all of criticism would agree, has a good deal to tell us about the nature of song cycle.

The poems by Goethe, Heine, Müller, Rellstab, and Friedrich Schlegel that are the subject of these essays confronted Schubert with five species of poetic discourse, each posing a problem of its own in the construction of narrative. The properties of narrative are in each case essential and self-evident, even if the poems taken together do not necessarily "tell a story" in the conventional sense. It is precisely this conventional sense of narrative that sets the Müller cycles apart.

The claims for narrative as an essence—*the* essence without which song cycle fails—are worth some reflection. When the term is used (as I am using it here) to describe a sequence of songs that evince the property of narrative in this essential sense, *cycle* means no reference to geometric design, to that circularity without beginning or end, whose end is its beginning. The return of the beginning—or, in the case of Schumann's *Dichterliebe*, of a middle—at the end is indeed characteristic of two of the celebrated song cycles in the literature. In Beethoven's *An die ferne Geliebte*, the songs are themselves the message, the singing of them enacting a kind of surrogate sexuality:

> Und du singst, was ich gesungen,
> Was mir aus der vollen Brust
> Ohne Kunstgepräng erklungen,
> Nur der Sehnsucht sich bewußt:
>
> Dann vor diesen Liedern weichet,
> Was geschieden uns so weit,
> Und ein liebend Herz erreichet,
> Was ein liebend Herz geweiht.

8. I borrow the phrase from Klaus Kropfinger, "Das Gespaltene Werk: Beethovens Streichquartett Op. 130/133," in *Beiträge zu Beethovens Kammermusik: Symposion Bonn 1984*, ed. Sieghard Brandenburg and Helmut Loos (Munich, 1987), 297. Kropfinger's phrase (as he admitted in a private communication) is a play on the title of Proust's *A la recherche du temps perdue*, a point happily lost in translation.

(And when you sing what I have sung, what sounded from my full breast without artifice, and conscious only of its longing: then that which has separated us will vanish before these songs, and a loving heart will receive what a loving heart has consecrated.)

These final quatrains in the last poem in Jeitteles's cycle inspire a return, but only in a metaphoric sense. The music of the first song, made to stand for the symbolic music between the two lovers, must be heard again, where it now stands as well for the consummation of this love that is sung about. Tellingly, this cycle that most nearly mirrors the figural notion of circle is the one least driven by the narrative impulse—no story is told, no past recapitulated. Space and landscape are its controlling media; the passage of time is minimal, unarticulated, barely perceived. *An die ferne Geliebte*, the work commonly taken to define the genre in its pure, most elemental state, stands ironically at the periphery of it. Schubert's concept of cycle, and the sense of narrativity that drives it, is of a different order.

The postlude at the end of Schumann's *Dichterliebe* engages similarly in reminiscence, an engagement that the music imposes on the poetry: surely nothing in "Die alten, bösen Lieder"—the last of the sixty-five poems in Heine's *Heimkehr*—means to conjure the whispered, sensory discourse of the flowers in "Am leuchtenden Sommermorgen," *after* the poem, where the music—the *composer's* voice—suggests a nuance in the psychological movement of the narrative. The lover has listened. The healing begins. It is this moment—a musical one—that is recalled at the end of the cycle. There is nothing circular about it. The repetition is a metaphor. In the deep structure of the poetic plot—as distinct from the internal, oneiric sense of the music—the repetition has no genuine significance, even if the structure of the music suggests the contrary. The sense of return is illusory.

I have gone on at length about this in the hopes that it may set in clearer perspective the issues raised below in the chapter on Schubert's culling, similarly reductionist, of some Heine poems of his own. The narrative impulse, immanent in the evocative traces of "story" in Heine's *Heimkehr*, is made rather more explicit, less evasive, in the very act by which Schubert isolates a single episode. The multivalence of Heine's sprawling canvas is boiled down; personae and their contexts are reduced to a scenario limited in action and time. A simple story is told.

"Narrative is a place where sequence and language, among other things, intersect to form a discursive code."[9] Succinctly, the literary semiotician Robert Scholes cuts through to the essence hinted at above. To understand narrative as an aspect of language in its structural sense is to admit music into that definition and, further, to consider how it is that music, usurping the *linguistic* element in song, may be said to participate in narrative discourse,

9. Robert Scholes, "Language, Narrative, and Anti-Narrative," *Critical Inquiry* 7, no. 1 (Autumn 1980): 204. Scholes's essay is among three "Afterthoughts on Narrative" that form the appendix to a volume of studies on narrative theory.

and even to control the discourse in some way not given to the verbal languages themselves. In narrative theory, the distinction between the story and the telling of it—between narrative and discourse—is commonly conceded. The narrative, in this formulation, is objective, standing hierarchically above the discourse by which, in some subjective mode, the events of the story are represented.

Literary theory has much to offer. Hayden White, led to speak of "*narrativizing* discourse," isolates some lines by Emile Benveniste: "There is no longer a 'narrator.' The events are chronologically recorded as they appear on the horizon of the story. Here no one speaks. The events seem to tell themselves."[10] This, too, provides an insight into the process, into the mechanics of narrative at the core of song cycle. Schubert's music only begins in the linguistic abstraction suggested by Scholes. Redolent of verbal language in its metaphoric richness, its locutions not only suggest temporal sequencing and the grammatical sinews of language but evoke images, concepts, even psychological states of being.

Students of narrative theory, following Gérard Genette, recognize the need to distinguish the essential strata in the composition of narrative: separating out the continuum of events from the narrative that poetry makes of it and, further, from the discourse that conveys this construct.[11] These moments in a continuum, a fictive background somewhat akin to the raw data, the phenomena from which historical narrative is shaped, may be said to constitute a narrative at another level. In historical writing, the decisions by which such data are entered into the narrative of history have an aesthetic root. The writing of history makes history over in the image of fiction—the invention of its author, an artifact for critical scrutiny.[12] In poetry and in fiction, such events that might be likened to the phenomena behind historical writing are left to the imagination, but, even in this imagined existence, they figure no less prominently in the silent dialogue between the past and its representation. In the discourse of Romantic poetry, such dialogue is yet more elusive. And, because Romantic poetry tells often enough of erotic adventure, the sequence of events that it mirrors is a fabrication to be reconstructed, very often from the faintest allusions, from traces that reside in the telling.

How, precisely, Schubert's music engages in the dialectic with poetry

10. Hayden White, "The Value of Narrativity in the Representation of Reality," *Critical Inquiry* 7, no. 1 (Autumn 1980): 7 (slightly emended). White here cites Emile Benveniste as he is quoted by Gérard Genette in "Boundaries of Narrative," *New Literary History* 8, no. 1 (Fall 1976): 9.

11. I am indebted here to the lucid account of narrative structure in Gérard Genette's *Narrative Discourse: An Essay in Method*, trans. Jane E. Lewin (Ithaca, N.Y., 1980), esp. 25–32.

12. "This value attached to narrativity in the representation of real events arises out of a desire to have real events display the coherence, integrity, fullness, and closure of an image of life that is and can only be imaginary," as Hayden White puts it ("The Value of Narrativity," 27). This is the desire at the beginning of fiction itself, and we may further surmise that, in his cullings from the poets, Schubert is acting on it when, consciously or not, he imposes his own perception of "coherence, integrity, fullness, and closure" on poems that, in their original state, do not display these properties quite so neatly. This impulse in Schubert is taken for granted in the arguments that follow.

through which narrative in its deep sense is unfolded in a discursive language is a problem much exercised in the essays that follow. Something of this complex play of narrative layering is manifest in the setting of *Willkommen und Abschied*, a poem whose ballad-like voice introduces yet another mode of narrative (and the one through which the term is commonly understood). Here, for once, a story is actually told, a sequence of events recounted.

Even the idiosyncratic manner in which the poems in each group are internally arranged is itself an expression of what Dietrich Berke has aptly called Schubert's "zyklische Verfahrensweise," an expression perhaps best rendered as Schubert's "propensity to cycle making."[13] In placing *Willkommen und Abschied* at the end of a group of four Goethe settings, Schubert imposes a narrative construct on the set: a story told in the conventional discourse of poetic narrative is positioned for its revelatory effect. The events of which it tells are suggestive. Intuitively, we are led to recognize them beneath the lyrical effusions of *An die Entfernte* and *Am Flusse*. Here again, the authority of Schubert's autograph is paramount. It does not matter that Goethe intended no such correlation between these poems. It matters only that, by its nature as the defining text, Schubert' autograph imposes a relationship. And because this text was dismembered, a casualty in the process of publication, it needs to be reconstructed, its authority resurrected.

Finally, Schubert's sporadic engagement, between 1819 and 1823, with Friedrich Schlegel's "Gedichtzyklus" *Abendröte* is taken as an inducement to some theorizing on the composing of songs intended to congeal into something resembling a cycle. The obstacles to the process, manifest in the nature of the Schlegel group and of what might be called the Romantic sublime, tell us much about Schubert and his poets—his poetics, even—and more generally about the nature of the bond, this most intimate of aesthetic couplings, between composer-poet and poet-singer.

III

Responding to the troubling dichotomy in the transmission of the songs during Schubert's lifetime, the editorial board of the *Neue Ausgabe sämtlicher Werke* has chosen to publish the songs in two discrete series.[14] In the first of them, those songs are offered that appeared in authorized printed editions during Schubert's lifetime or in the months shortly after his death; the print is taken as the textual document of primary weight. The second series comprises all the other songs, given in the chronological order proposed (too often on insufficient evidence) in O. E. Deutsch's thematic catalog.[15]

13. See Dietrich Berke, "Schuberts Liedentwurf 'Abend' D 645 und dessen textliche Voraussetzungen," in *Schubert-Kongreß Wien 1978: Bericht*, ed. Otto Brusatti (Graz, 1979), esp. 307.

14. See the general preface to *Franz Schubert: Neue Ausgabe sämtlicher Werke* (hereafter *NGA*) (Kassel, Basel, and London, 1964–), ser. 4 (*Lieder*, ed. Walther Dürr), vol. 5a, pp. xi–xii.

15. See O. E. Deutsch, *Franz Schubert: Thematisches Verzeichnis seiner Werke in chronologischer Folge* (Kassel, 1978).

To hold to Schubert's publication program, Walther Dürr suggests, "avoids a danger that grows from every chronological order: namely, that the work of art appear, not primarily as a thing in itself, but as a representative of a stage in the development of, or even in function of, a later work."[16] But we are forever setting works of art in contexts and yet construing them as things in themselves; this oscillation between critical modes is a necessary condition for the reading or art. The genesis of a song inhabits a delicate matrix. Favoring a vertical axis—the subordination of earlier versions to a published "Fassung letzter Hand" (an authoritative "final" version)—costs us the vista that might convey something of the spontaneity of its conception. And it commits the sin that Dürr is at pains to avoid, for the elevation of the published version of a song submerges in its wake all other versions, even distinctly unique settings of the same poem, now relegated, in the plan of the *Neue Ausgabe*, to a volume of "alternative versions": lower species, so to speak, in an evolutionary tale.

The very notion of *variant* is a vexing one in the repertory of Schubert's songs, for it is inevitably drawn into the broader phenomenon of multiple settings. At the one extreme are instances of revision (as the term is commonly understood), where a text is shown to have been altered in the interests of improvement, either in grammatical detail or in matters of substance. Here again, the issue is bound in with the definition of text, for it is not always entirely clear whether—the intentions of the composer aside— a revision is to be understood as the repudiation of an earlier form of the text (often enough this is clearly the case) or, rather, as a text distinct from but neither better nor worse than its parent, even if Schubert had convinced himself that the revision was to be preferred.

At the other extreme are those instances in which Schubert composed different music to one and the same poem. On the face of it, there is no compelling reason to understand the relationship between these settings as that of variant to prototype. Even the temporal relationship that necessarily obtains—the one setting having been composed before the other—may deceive, for, by the axioms of text definition, the two settings are discrete and unrelated. That one was composed before the other is irrelevant to the *meaning* of the song. Yet some impalpable inner voice does indeed make itself felt among settings related in this way. Surely one task of criticism is to hold these two views of the thing in suspension—to seek an understanding of the paradox that resides in them.

The inquiry in chapter 2 is essentially this, for the four settings of Schiller's *Der Jüngling am Bache*, stretching from 1812 to the publication of op. 87 in 1827, test the limits of the problem in the extreme. Even here, processes of narrative discourse are germane, although in yet another sense. For it is proposed that, when Schubert returns again to a poem set earlier, a phenomenon that might be called *narrative memory* sets in: in effect, the new setting is a rehearing, a rehearsing, another singing of a song held faintly in memory.

16. See *NGA*, ser. 4, vol. 5a, p. xii.

An extreme case of such a phenomenon is on display in the two settings of Schiller's *Gruppe aus dem Tartarus*, the astonishing music of which provokes some final thoughts on the matter in a chapter devoted to the aesthetics of revision.

IV

The transposition of *Todesmusik* in op. 108 up from the spectral G♭ in which it had been conceived aggravates another of those classic issues in Schubert criticism. The privilege of pitch as an absolute—as a "trace" inherent in the song—plays into each of the following essays, so a brief reflection on the nature of the problem is in order here. It is not simply that the choice of key is a compositional act no less essential than any other aspect of the music—for it might be argued that thoughts of key and mode are prior even to the concretization of idea into music, not the other way round. We are coming to realize (in ways quite beyond what the contemporary lexicographers had in mind) that, in the early nineteenth century, a hermeneutics of key had begun to formulate itself. G♭ major, a key that seems to have struck terror in the ears of the eighteenth century (when performance in a tuning of equal temperament could evidently not be assumed), had now begun to acquire a special place in the language of music.[17] B minor, too—as is argued in the essay on the Rellstab songs—is a key freighted with its own tropes and allusions, and nowhere more so than in Schubert's music, where it seems to call forth a language of its own, profound and at the edge of despair.

Thoughts of G♭ inevitably lead to the earliest of Schubert's songs set in a key beyond the orthodox scope of three flats. *Nähe des Geliebten*, composed in February 1815, is emphatically in G♭.[18] Still, and in spite of its sublime parsimony, it does not exactly begin there. The opening measures makes a point of "finding" G♭ (see ex. 1.1). They have a poetic mission as well. Why G♭? And why is G♭ to be revealed as though through some reflective process of mind? Before we can attempt to answer these questions, some preliminary harmonic parsing is in order, for the commonly held view about the structure of these measures—and particularly about the sense of the C♭ in the bass at m. 2 both as a root and, in its subsequent motion, as an appoggiatura in the manner of an augmented sixth—is not convincing.[19] And, because the reading of the harmony has everything to do with the poetic significance of the opening phrase, it will be good to consider this C♭ with fresh ears.

17. The topic is richly engaged in Hugh Macdonald's aptly titled " 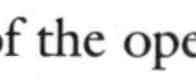 ," *19th Century Music* 11 (Spring 1988): 221–37.

18. "Perhaps the earliest example of a piece of music wholly in G♭," Macdonald is led to propose (ibid., 225). For a fine study of the song and its antecedents, both poetic and musical, see Walter Frisch, "Schubert's *Nähe des Geliebten* (D. 162): Transformation of the *Volkston*," in *Schubert: Critical and Analytical Studies*, 175–99.

19. I have in mind the analysis shown in Frisch, "Schubert's *Nähe des Geliebten*," 188, but only because there is so much else in Frisch's reading to recommend it.

Example 1.1 *Nähe des Geliebten* (D. 162), opening measures

In any such parsing, the appeal must be to the sense of an underlying root motion, and in this case that motion is both elusive and implicity powerful, suggesting something like the construct shown in example 1.2. The harmony

Example 1.2 *Nähe des Geliebten*, opening measures, harmonic abstraction

at the beginning of m.2 is the problem, for the C♭ does indeed suggest the behavior of an upper neighbor to B♭. But is that the case? Here, a note missing in the alto is telling. The B♭ in the alto in m. 1 has no issue. The voice is temporarily abandoned. This is not to say that it loses its status, for the ear, compensating, takes up its cause: the B♭ continues to sound in the mind. Now a dissonance against the C♭ in the bass, it is forced to mute resolution down to A♭—silent, understood, and therefore of greater consequence. The *appearance* of a triad on C♭ is deceptive: the true harmony is in effect an incomplete dissonant seventh chord whose understood root is A♭. The urgency of an A♭ here is programmed in the root motion, descending by fifths, initiated in m. 1: B♭-E♭-A♭.

A seventh chord of this kind, positioned in a circle of fifths, will be familiar to students of Rameau. Its root—the silent, understood A♭ in this instance—is ambiguous and dependent on context, for it is the minor seventh that often trades with Rameau's *sixte ajoutée*, and in either case always signifies the subdominant region. The point is that this seemingly innocent harmony on C♭ has an important mission. G♭ is quietly established, without anyone realizing it. Even the dominant has its place in the unfolding, for, while D♭ itself is never sounded as a root, its position on the second half of the measure is so secure that the D♮ is heard as E𝄫—a minor ninth wanting resolution to the root. And the A♮ on the last beat will be heard as a passing altered fifth. To boot, the G♭ in the soprano—which the voice will appropriate in its breathtaking entrance—must be understood as an anticipation. Yet this penultimate harmony has a double message. A classic "German" augmented sixth, its C♭ poises for resolution *down* to B♭, promoting the return of the opening chord as the true dominant (see the parenthetical harmonies marked X in ex. 1.2). So the sounding of G♭ in m. 3 is both inevitable and shocking.

What does all this have to do with *meaning*? Schubert's harmonies, whether in this early example or in those final excursions in the songs of the *Schwanengesang*, are always persuasive as harmonic constructs in some fundamental theoretical program, even when they are at their most exotic and remote. The harmonic license of which Schubert was often enough accused in the 1820s must be understood—as must all art—in its dialectic between the eccentric and original, on the one hand, and the conventional. Eccentricity that cannot be understood to be grounded in some coherent language is without expressive meaning.

The sounding of G♭, positioned at the end of a labyrinth, is therefore all the more prized. In the quest for G♭ is lodged an aspect of meaning in the song—perhaps even its essence. Is there some analogue here to those gambits in which the piano seizes on some concrete poetic image that captures an essence of the poem? In *Erlkönig* and *Gretchen am Spinnrade* (to cite only the most familiar instances), the image is at once literal and pictorial, an element of the poetic background. And, in both cases, by force of repetition, the image is made an obsession, finally internalized. The opening measures of *Nähe des Geliebten* similarly grasp a detail in the poem. But which one? The rising of the sun that is implied in the first strophe, it is sometimes claimed. But this is only the pictorial "cover." There must be more to it than that.

What is characteristic of both those other settings is the sense in which the piano can be said to choreograph an entrance for a protagonist. Before he speaks a word, the narrator in *Erlkönig* can actually squint out on the heath, and everyone will know what he has in view. Gretchen is preoccupied, and the ennui of the incessant spinning wheel suggested in the opening measures establishes a foil for that. The opening measures of *Nähe des Geliebten* are yet more profound in that they mimic a process of mind: the poet conjuring up the image of the distant beloved. "Ich *denke* dein . . . ," he sings, but only after a difficult groping through the labyrinth, at once obscure (through all those devious chromatic alterations) and on target (assured in its secure root motion). This process of mind—the gradual fixing of an image of the beloved—is played out in the four strophes of the poem, where the progression is from the abstract to the concrete, from the lover beheld in the distance of the mind to a coming, finally, into physical contact: "denke" (what can it mean to *think* of a lover?), "sehe" (her image is now in focus), "höre" (the physiological act of hearing, the acoustic imprint of her voice), and, finally (and euphemistically), "Ich bin bei dir." But the final quatrain shows the progression to have been illusory, for the line goes, "Ich bin bei dir, du seyst auch noch so ferne, du bist mir nah" (for while you are yet so distant, I am with you, and you are near me). Here, in the seizing of the familiar trope, the paradox of the distant lover brought closer through erotic fantasy is the gist of the poem. And here the significance of G♭ comes clear, for G♭ had come to embody a special quality of distance—a veiled distance that heightens the erotic, even when it sounds in the midst of some purely instrumental work. Invariably, the exposition in the first movement of the posthumous Sonata in B♭ springs to mind, together with its contemporary, *Ihr Bild*. In *Nähe des Geliebten*, the searching for G♭ and the finding of it at the outset of the song constitute yet another play on this paradoxical *jeu*: a motion from what is in absolute terms the "nearer" harmony, rooted on B♭, to a resolution at the more remote, just as the harmony on B♭ is perceived as the more remote in the limiting context of the song.[20]

If this mode of understanding has any merit, it will be plain why transposition—and here I mean the concept that in equal temperament any key is as good as any other—is pernicious to the meaning of the song. The argument does not hinge on some empirically demonstrable difference in the quality of the keys. Much nonsense has been written on that score. Rather, it has its roots in the perception that, even in its nomenclature, tone acquires meaning, as do the simplest words of normal discourse, through usage. It is the *illusion* of "being in G♭" that must be valued here, even when the tuning of the piano is shown to be a semitone or more away from Schubert's. And that is why the transposition of *Todesmusik* to G major must be read as an emendation in the direction of the conventional, even if we understand the arguments that might have persuaded Schubert in its favor.[21] More than that, some essence of the

20. Its opening harmony is suggestive in another way. A second setting of the poem by Johann Friedrich Reichardt, published in the Goethe volume of 1809 by Breitkopf and Härtel, begins with this harmony and in precisely the same disposition. Reichardt's song clings to B♭ major, but its opening phrases stake out a modest chromatic ascent to F; Schubert's prologue takes it the next step, to G♭. That Schubert knew this volume, and much Reichardt besides, is fairly well agreed. Reichardt's song can be seen in *Goethes Lieder, Oden, Balladen und Romanzen mit Musik*, ed. Walter Salmen, Das Erbe deutscher Musik, vol. 58 (Munich, 1964), 22.

21. The instance calls to mind the case, still more extreme, of the G♭ Impromptu, op. 90, no. 3, which, together with no. 4, was withheld from publication until 1857. "Im ganzen Takt und in G dur umzuschreiben" (to be rewritten in measures of whole notes and in G major), Haslinger

work is now lost and must be reclaimed—again, the “Suche nach dem verlorenen Werk.”

V

July 1815 was something of a Kosegarten month for Schubert. The yield was thirteen songs—a fourteenth (the earliest of the set) dates from 25 June, and another seven date from 19 October. Perhaps the finest of the lot is *Die Mondnacht* (D. 238), a strophic elegy whose measured, hushed, neoclassical tone is draped finally in an image, unabashedly erotic, whose language calls to mind the Wagner of *Tristan*:[22]

> Dich umringend, von dir umrungen,
> Dich umschlingend, von dir umschlungen,
> Gar in Eins mit dir geeint—
> Schon’, ach schone den Wonneversunknen.
> Himmel und Erde verschwinden dem Trunknen.

(Enfolding you, enfolded by you, embracing you, embraced by you, fully joined in unity with you . . . Save, oh save those sunk in bliss! Heaven and earth vanish to the enraptured.)

Five months after *Nähe des Geliebten*, Schubert confronts a compositional problem of very similar thrust. Goethe’s trim Lied, scraped clean of rhetorical excess, distilled from a considerable lineage of antecedents, inspired Schubert to a similar economy of language. The response to Kosegarten’s ode is palpably different, yet the two settings engage in similar tactics. The key, first of all, is striking. An instance of it that is very nearly unique in all of Schubert, F♯ major suggests a point still more remote in his tonal galaxy.[23] To claim it as an enharmonic equivalent to G♭ is to miss all the subtle ways in which the two keys set off waves of different meaning.[24] Not the least of them, G♭ seems al-

---

inscribed in Schubert’s autograph, and it was not until its publication in the *Gesamtausgabe* in 1894 that the matter was set right (see, e.g., Deutsch, *Thematisches Verzeichnis*, 567). For Macdonald (“ ,” 225), the work signifies “the breakthrough toward a new concept of the key,” and he notes the irony that “this seminal piece remained hidden for thirty years.” It had to wait another thirty to be revealed as a work in G-*flat*.

22. I am anticipated in this thought by Alfred Heuß (“Ein trunkenes Jünglingslied von Franz Schubert,” *Zeitschrift für Musik* 95 [November 1928]: 619–24, 679–82), who speaks of a “crescendo” in the poem from the “Naturbetrachtung der ersten Strophe sich zu der trunkenen ‘Tristan’-Sprache der letzten Strophe”—from the observation of nature in the first strophe to the intoxicated “Tristan” language of the last (p. 621).

23. *Berthas Lied in der Nacht* (D. 653), Schubert’s only setting to a poem by Grillparzer, begins in E♭ minor, but this is as the opening music in a *scena*. The “aria” is in F♯ major. Composed in February 1819, in among the Schlegel settings, the song will come up again in the final chapter.

24. For Macdonald (“ ,” 222), “F♯ major never carried the same sense of remoteness as G♭ for the reason that it was widely seen as akin to F♯ minor, a common enough key in Classical parlance . . . whereas [in the eighteenth century] G♭ had no approach route of this kind.”

ways to convey some lingering sense of "♭VI" (*Ihr Bild* again), always on the brink of resolution, even dissolution. F♯ major has none of this.

Die Mondnacht, too, approaches its tonic from a distance—moves toward its remote tonic from a place of greater familiarity. Again, the concise phrases of *Nähe des Geliebten* give way here to a rather more Classical posture. The tonicization of F♯ is deliberately postponed until deep into the strophe: the identity of B major as the tonic is so strong that even the emphatic E♯s in m. 9 suggest deflections away, toward the dominant of B. Then, at m. 11, the scene changes (see ex. 1.3). The piano begins its throb (another echo of *Nähe des Geliebten*); the palpitations grow in intensity (a long crescendo helps) to the climactic *fortissimo* at mm. 23 and 24, where, finally, F♯ is sounded as the unequivocal tonic. If the measured phrases that set the first three lines of the poem (mm. 5–10) are appropriate, in their neutrality, to all four strophes, the same cannot be claimed for the music that follows m. 10.

Example 1.3 *Die Mondnacht* (D. 238), mm. 11–18

The music that begins at m. 11 forecasts an erotic climax that is realized only in the language of the fourth strophe. Still, the sense of the earlier strophes is not contradicted in this music, for, in each of them, a similar crescendo in tone is plotted out, formalized in the shift of meter from simple trochees to something resembling those complex Aesclepiad verses in the neoclassical odes of Klopstock and Hölty. Schubert's response is tuned to the urgency of the language. The decorum of the meter is forfeited:

Strophe	Line	
2	7	Sprenge die Brust nicht, mächtiges Sehnen;
	8	Löschet die Wehmuth, labende Thränen.
3	7	Solches, ach, wähn' ich, kühlte das Sehnen,
	8	Löschte die Wehmuth, mit köstliche Thränen.
4	7	Schon', ach schone den Wonneversunknen.
	8	Himmel und Erde verschwinden dem Trunknen.

(2:7–8: Powerful longing, do not burst my heart! Soothing tears, quench my sorrow. 3:7–8: A soul such as this, I sense, would cool my longing, and quench my grief with precious tears. 4:7–8: Save, oh save those sunk in bliss! Heaven and earth vanish to the enraptured.)

Composed on 25 July, *Die Mondnacht* was followed two days later by a pair of songs in E major. *Huldigung* (D. 240) and *Alles um Liebe* (D. 241) are twins. To sing them one after the other is to be convinced that the B♯ in the bass with which the second song begins is meant to echo the telling gesture at the climactic moment in the first (see ex. 1.4). The networking of these songs—all fourteen from this summer's engagement with Kosegarten—is complex and slippery in the manuscript transmission. In the main, each song is written out twice and, in the second, cleaner writing, very often grouped differently than in the first. In the earlier autograph, *Die Mondnacht* was grouped with *Das Abendrot* (D. 236—a part song) and *Abends unter der Linde* (the *second* version, D. 237), hinting that the three were conceived as a modest Trilogy to Night.[25] Yet it is with the following two songs that *Die Mondnacht* seems, on purely internal grounds, in closer rapport. The opening phrases of *Huldigung* issue quite innocently from the climactic pitches—the end rhymes in the final couplet—in *Die Mondnacht.*

But in Schubert's clean copy, *Huldigung* and *Alles um Liebe*, both in E major, are grouped with two songs composed three weeks earlier: *Von Ida* (D. 228), in F minor, and *Die Erscheinung*, again in E.[26] In this context, *Die*

25. Offered for sale by Sotheby's on 6 December 1991, the autograph is described in the auction catalog (*Fine Printed and Manuscript Music including the Mannheim Collection* [n.p., n.d.], 32–33) showing a facsimile of the first page of *Die Mondnacht*, the date of which is clearly inscribed "25 July 1815" (not "26," as is claimed here). The manuscript went unsold.

26. Heuß ("Ein trunkenes Jünglingslied," 621) argues for a similar grouping. "Es scheint auch beinahe, als gehörten die drei Lieder [*Die Erscheinung*, *Die Täuschung*, and *Die Mondnacht*], zu denen man, aber doch in einem gewissen Abstand, die mendelssohnisch angehauchte

Erscheinung sustains the pastoral tone of the set and the continuity of a poet's voice—and closes off a miniscule tonal plan: E major, E major, F minor, E major. Some fourteen years later, published as op. 108, *Die Erscheinung* was again positioned to close off a group, but now it is dwarfed in the company of *Über Wildemann* and *Todesmusik*. To return it to its more congenial Kosegarten companions of July 1815 is to return to it its authenticity—the aura of authorship that is bound up in the verification of text.

To seek authenticity in some larger reconstruction of the Kosegarten settings is an exercise in futility. The very act of reconstituting little groups of them in the writing out of fair copies, following only days (or weeks) on their conception, collapses this distinction between a "cyclic" instinct and a contrary, retrospective editorial process in which such primary instincts are forgotten. What was to be gained from this shuffling and reshuffling of the Kosegarten songs? Perhaps we may read in it the symptom of a cyclic tendency that was doomed to failure. The Kosegarten poems are lyrics of the idyllic kind; no story, no narrative thread can be teased out of them.

Still, Schubert is drawn to the problem. The Kosegarten songs enjoy a common language, even a distinct dialect. That Schubert should have wanted to exploit their common inflections in agglomerates that fuse well together seems beyond dispute; perhaps he had already in mind that series of volumes, each dedicated to the settings of one of the Classical poets, that he hoped would interest Breitkopf and Härtel. Conversely, to speak here of incipient song cycle, stressing the concept to its limits, means only to suggest that in his reading of Kosegarten, Schubert caught in his music the accents of a poetic dialect.

In the studies that follow, I examine this inclination to reinforce a narrative thread in musical dialects true to the poetry. Whatever the merits of Kosegarten's poetry, its language, its neoclassical conceits, are very much of the eighteenth century. With the poetry of Goethe and Schiller and of the newer Romantics, Schubert engages poetic languages in closer aesthetic sympathy with his own. The cyclic enterprise is carried forth more boldly, even in its failures. But the impulse that drives it was there from the beginning.

'Huldigung' . . . rechnen könnte, zyklusartig zusammen und wir werden nachher noch davon zu sprechen haben, ob diese drei Lieder nicht am besten nacheinander vorzutragen wären, in welchem Falle, die nachgewiesenen Mängel der beiden ersten Lieder durch das dritte mit dem nun wirklich eintretenden Ereignis einer geradezu trunkenen Ekstase in den Hintergrund treten; sie bedeuten in diesem Fall den Untergrund für das dritte" (It appears even as though these three songs [*Die Erscheinung*, *Die Täuschung*, and *Die Mondnacht*]—to which one might add the Mendelssohnian *Huldigung* [D. 240], but at a certain distance— belong together, cycle-like [*zyklusartig*], and we will accordingly have to consider whether these three songs ought not to be performed consecutively, in which case, the evident imperfections of the first two songs recede into the background through the third, now actually an intercession of a sheerly intoxicating ecstasy. In this instance, the two signify the subsoil for the third). My sympathies for the proposal aside, Schubert's manuscripts do not support such a grouping. The autograph containing the "erste Niederschrift" of *Von Ida* and *Die Erscheinung* was offered for sale as well by Sotheby's on 6 December 1991. *Die Erscheinung* is shown in the catalog in facsimile (p. 40).

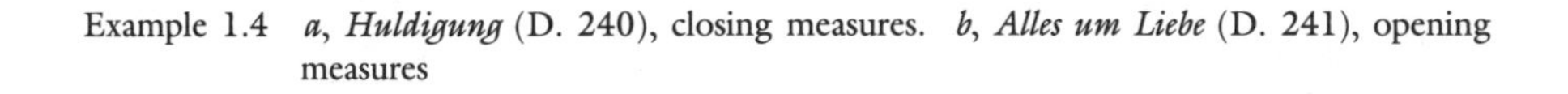
Example 1.4 *a*, *Huldigung* (D. 240), closing measures. *b*, *Alles um Liebe* (D. 241), opening measures

II

Strophe, Variant, Version

❋

2

Der Jüngling am Bache: Schubert at the Source

In *The Singer of Tales*, Albert Lord, contemplating the transmission of text in the earliest epics, conjures these striking thoughts on the beginnings of narrative song:

> The art of narrative song was perfected long before the advent of writing. . . . When writing was introduced, epic singers, even the most brilliant among them, did not realize its "possibilities" and did not rush to avail themselves of it. Perhaps they were wiser than we, because one cannot write song.
>
> Each performance is the specific song, and at the same time it is the generic song. The song we are listening to is "the song"; for each performance is more than a performance; it is a re-creation.
>
> Our concept of "the original," of "the song," simply makes no sense in oral tradition. . . . The first singing in oral tradition does not coincide with this concept of the "original." . . . It follows, then, that we cannot correctly speak of a "variant," since there is no "original" to be varied! Yet songs are related to one another in varying degrees; not, however, in the relationship of variant to original. . . . Our greatest error is to attempt to make "scientifically" rigid a phenomenon that is fluid.[1]

Lord is concerned to understand the instance of the earliest writing down of the Homeric epics, as the fixing of the text in our limited sense. Is this fixing of text—the authority of the *written* word—to be privileged in some ontological sense above the flow of unwritten, and consequently unverifiable, instances of the work that must otherwise be held to constitute its text according to the laws implicit in an oral tradition?

Clearly, what Lord has to say about Homer cannot be taken to apply paradigmatically to the process behind multiple and variant settings in Schubert. Yet these striking thoughts on the origins of song and the nature of what might be called *differences* in its subsequent singings might suggest that, in the categorical way in which we have come to hold the relationship between two or more settings of the same poem as so many variants toward a "Fassung letzter Hand," toward the priority of a Final Version, we may

1. Albert B. Lord, *The Singer of Tales* (Cambridge, Mass., 1960; reprint, New York, 1978), 101, 124.

perhaps have been led to misconstrue something essential in the process of composition itself, even in our valuing of the earlier stages in the process. What I mean to get at is better exemplified than described. Schubert's four settings of Schiller's *Der Jüngling am Bache* constitute as idiosyncratic a sample as we are likely to find, exercising all those multifarious issues that play into a theory of text.

I

Each of Schubert's four settings has survived in an authoritative written document: the first three in autograph, the fourth in an authorized publication:

1. *D. 30.* An autograph dated 24 September 1812 preserves what must be an earliest setting, in F major, and "through-composed" after a fashion.[2] It is an ambitious setting, sometimes claimed as the earliest song to establish firm footing in the Schubert canon.

2. *D. 192.* The autograph of a second setting is dated 15 May 1815, a day on which he returned as well to the setting of Schiller's *Des Mädchens Klage.*[3] The song, in F minor now, is set strophically, even while it retains some of the thematic material of the earlier setting.

3. *D. 638 a.* The autograph of a third setting is dated April 1819, a month during which Schubert seems to have composed no other song.[4] Again strophic, and now in D minor, only the faintest echo of earlier settings is perceptible.

4. *D. 638 b.* A setting in C minor—*essentially* a transposition of the setting in D minor, but with telling differences—was published in 1827 as op. 87 (originally "op. 84") along with *Der Unglückliche* and *Hoffnung.* Neither autograph nor authentic manuscript copy of the song in this final redaction has survived, and we cannot know, therefore, whether the alterations that distinguish it from the setting of 1819 date from close to the time of publication, or (following a suggestion in the *New Grove Schubert*) "ca. 1819."

Schiller's poem has its own convoluted history. First published in 1804, then taken up in the authorized collection of *Gedichte* in 1805, it was actually written a few years earlier for *Der Parasit*, a translation from the French of Picard's *Médiocre et rampant, ou Le moyen de parvenir.*[5] Decidedly not a trans-

2. Vienna Stadtbibliothek, MH 3838/c.

3. Vienna Stadtbibliothek, MH 74/c, in a manuscript together with *Des Mädchens Klage* (D. 191), and two Hölty settings (D. 193 and D. 194). The two poems are often taken to be companion pieces (see *Schillers lyrische Gedichte*, ed. Heinrich Düntzer [Leipzig, 1874], 2:51; and *Schillers sämliche Werke: Säkular-Ausgabe*, vol. 1, *Gedichte I*, ed. Eduard von der Hellen [Stuttgart and Berlin, n.d.], 301).

4. Vienna Stadtbibliothek, MH 115/c.

5. *Der Parasit oder die Kunst sein Glück zu machen* is a free prose translation prepared in 1803 from Picard's comedy *Médiocre et rampant, ou Le moyen de parvenir.* For the text, and a note on it, see, e.g. Friedrich Schiller, *Sämtliche Werke*, vol. 3, *Gedichte, Erzählungen, Übersetzungen*, ed. Helmut Koopman (Munich, 1981), 959–1026, 1220.

lation from Picard but rather a fresh replacement for a troubadour song by Lanvin, Schiller's poem has a part to play in the action. A *Romanze* sung by Charlotte, to whom it is offered as a slightly veiled marriage proposal, its guileless sentiment must speak through the false intrigue around it. It succeeds:

> *Madame Belmont.* Wie rührend der Schluß ist!—Das liebe Kind ist ganz davon bewegt worden. [How touching are the closing lines. The dear child is quite moved by them.]
>
> *Charlotte.* Ja, es mag es gemacht haben wer will, es ist aus einem Herzen geflossen, das die Liebe kennt! [Yes, whoever may have composed it, it flows from a heart that understands love!]

Grandmother Belmont, especially moved by this final quatrain, sings it again:

> Horch, der Hain erschallt von Liedern,
> Und die Quelle rieselt klar!
> Raum ist in der kleinsten Hütte
> Für ein glücklich liebend Paar.

> (Hark, the wood resounds with song, and the brook ripples limpidly, There is room in the tiniest cottage for a happy, loving couple.)

"Schön! Himmlisch! dem widerstehe wer kann!" chirps Madame Belmont. "Selicour, es bleibt dabey! Sie heirathen meine Charlotte!" (Beautiful! Heavenly! Who can resist! Selicour, it is clear: You shall marry my Charlotte!) There is much unraveling of plot before the devious Selicour, having falsely represented himself as the author, is uncovered. "Das Gespinst der Lüge umstrickt den Besten, der Redliche kann nicht durchdringen, die kriechende Mittelmäßigkeit kommt weiter, als das geflügelte Talent, der Schein regiert die Welt, und die Gerechtigkeit ist nur auf der Bühne" (The web of lies ensnares the best of us; the honest cannot penetrate it; fawning mediocrity gets farther than winged talent; appearances rule the world, and justice conquers only on the stage), are the Minister Narbonne's sardonic closing lines. The poem is a Lied, if not in the absolutely strictest sense. Music is implicit in its conception. Cast in the language of pure expression, the authenticity of its sentiment in the end "certifies" Charlotte's true lover and uncovers deceit.

Of Schubert's settings, only the earliest of them takes this final quatrain in its naive sense—sings it in a manner that would have moved Charlotte and enchanted Madame Belmont. It is precisely in the evocative setting of these lines—"Horch, der Hain erschallt von Liedern"—that a music redolent of the naive in Schubert is sprung loose. A veiled, distant epilogue, suggestive of those imagined Lieder invoked in the poem itself, this is the strain that returns when we try to capture the song in memory. This sense of the thing is underscored in the part writing, for the bass sounds its deepest F at "Horch" (m. 79), and then not again. All the rest has the feel of afterbeat, of *Nachhall.*

This separating off of the final quatrain as an echo—Madame Belmont savoring the lines a second time—is in concept antithetical to a strophic setting.

To put it another way, in a strictly strophic setting, this final quatrain would have been sung to a music fit equally for the expression of these passionate lines in the third strophe—

Sehnend breit ich meine Arme
Nach dem teuren Schattenbild . . .

(Lovingly I stretch out my arms to the beloved silhouette.)

—and to their analogues, similarly distinct in expression, in strophes 1 and 2. Finding a music dispassionate enough to serve all four strophes is precisely the self-effacing, repressive exercise through which the Lied composer was obliged to display his sensitivity to the diction and structure of the poem. This, at any rate, is how his profession was understood in eighteenth-century Berlin (and Leipzig and Hamburg), if not quite so attentively in Vienna.

In 1812, Schubert's strategy seems more closely tuned to Mozart's; indeed, two of Mozart's best songs—*Abendempfindung an Laura* and *An Chloe*—reverberate now and again in these pages. The shadow of the obligatory strophic setting hovers over the song: each strophe begins with essentially the same music. But then the inflections at mid-strophe each set off some characteristic digression. Even in this, the impulse is Mozartean, for that is how it goes in *An Chloe*, and very nearly in the *Abendempfindung*. We may even be led to recall another Viennese model, Gluck's austere setting of the Klopstock ode *Der Jüngling*, in which the voice is held rigorously to one and the same rhythmic declamation through all four strophes while the music elaborates a dramatic sonata-like scenario.

In the aesthetics of eighteenth-century song, the ode was held as a Lied of a higher order, where the demands of a strophic setting are most severely tested. And the Klopstock odes, many of them modeled on the classical meters of Greek antiquity, were held highest of all.[6] The publication of a collection of settings of a number of them in 1776 was taken as the occasion for a stiff lecture by that sternest of critics, Johann Nikolaus Forkel, on the innate difficulties in translating the highest thoughts of the greatest poets to music: "When one considers that the noble strain of these excellent poems imposes on the musician who wants to accommodate them to musical dress the obligation to fly along at the same altitude, then one scarcely need mention the other nearly insurmountable obstacles that the form, the meter, and often the whole singular and unusual construction of this great poet provokes, to give an accurate concept of the enormity of the undertaking."[7] Forkel limits the at-

6. The evidence is everywhere, but perhaps no more succinctly expressed than in Georg Sulzer, *Allgemeine Theorie der schönen Künste*, new enlarged 2d ed. (Leipzig, 1792–94), in the article "Ode," where Klopstock is "placed at the side of Homer and Pindar" (3:549).

7. "Wenn man auch bedenkt, daß blos schon der hohe Schwung dieser vortrefliche Gedichte, dem Tonkünstler, der ihnen ein musikalisches Gewand anpassen will, die Pflicht auferlegt, ihnen in eben der Höhe nachzufliegen, und nicht etwa in einer himmelweiten Entfernung von ihnen, nur auf der Erde im Staube nachzukriechen, so braucht man der übrigen fast ebenfalls unüberstei-

tack to those measurable, grammatical aspects in which these settings can be shown to be incompetent. His victim was Christian Gottlob Neefe, later Beethoven's teacher in Bonn. It is tempting to ponder whether Beethoven and his compatriots—or, for that matter, Neefe himself, a teacher whose integrity Beethoven continued to admire in later years—may have taken Forkel's hectoring to heart, for Beethoven was himself plagued—nowhere more clearly than in the four attempts to set Goethe's *Nur wer die Sehnsucht kennt*—by these hard precepts that were at the seat of an aesthetics of Lied.[8]

In an essay published in 1782—an apologia for his own Klopstock settings—Johann Friedrich Reichardt expressed similar thoughts:

> Most difficult of all is to find in a single melody a true declamation for all the strophes of one and the same ode. And for odes that have a unity of feeling, there can be only one single melody if its impression is to penetrate. If this must now apply to several strophes of such greatly various paragraphs and phrase structure, one must often exhaust all harmonic, melodic, and rhythmic artifice, in order to conquer and conceal the ambiguities in significance, at least with regard to its comprehensible performance, at this cadence, in this phrase, in that "Rhythmus." At the same time, it is doubly urgent that he who wishes to sing the ode well must first understand how to read it.[9]

And in a piece of "good advice," as he called it, in place of a preface to a collection of *Oden und Lieder*, published in 1780, Reichardt spoke again about the reading of poems:

> My melodies arise always from a repeated reading of the poem itself; save that I then seek to repeat it with small variants, and don't write it down until I feel and recognize that the grammatical, logical, "pathetic," and musical accent are bound together so well that the melody speaks correctly and sings agreeably—and this not only for a single strophe, but for all. If one is to feel and recognize this as well

glichen Schwierigkeiten, die die Form, das Metrum, und öfters die ganz eigene und ungewöhnliche Construction dieses großen Dichters verursacht, kaum zu erwähnen" (Johann Nicolaus Forkel, *Musikalisch-kritische Bibliothek* [Gotha, 1778; reprint, Hildesheim, 1964], 1:211).

8. For an appreciation of Beethoven's four settings, see Paul Mies, "'Sehnsucht von Göthe und Beethoven,'" in *Beethoven-Jahrbuch*, vol. 2, ed. Paul Mies and Joseph Schmidt-Görg (Bonn, 1956), 112–19 (reprinted with the facsimile of Beethoven's autograph [Bonn, 1970]; the facsimile was itself reprinted, now without Mies's essay, but with "einer Studie von Helga Lühning" [Bonn, 1986]).

9. "Das Schwerste: In einer Melodie für alle Strophen die ganze Ode wahr zu deklamiren. *Eine* melodie muss es seyn bey Oden, die Einheit der Empfindung haben, wenn der Eindruck der Eine treffende tiefeindringende seyn soll. Daß diese nun für mehrere Strophen von so sehr verschiedenen Abschnitten und Einschnitten passen soll—da erschöpft man oft alle harmonische melodische und rhythmische Kunstgriffe, um in dieser Kadenz, in jenem Einschnitte, in jenem Rhythmus doppelte Bedeutung, wenigstens für den verständigen Vortrag mannichfaltige Bedeutung, hineinzulegen und zu verbergen. Dabey wird das nun aber zu einem doppelt wichtigen Bedürfnis, daß der, der die Ode gut singen will, sie auch erst zu lesen ganz verstehe" (Johann Friederich Reichardt, *Musikalisches Kunstmagazin*, vol. 1 [Berlin: "Im Verlag des Verfassers" (by the author), 1782; reprint, Hildesheim: George Olms, 1969], 62).

in performance, the singer must read the words first completely through, and read until he feels that he is reading with true expression. Then he can sing.[10]

Reading the poem well is again the central message in a most intriguing notice—yet another gloss to the setting of a Klopstock ode—that appeared in the Leipzig *Allgemeine Musikalische Zeitung* for 1799. The composer was Christian F. G. Schwenke, successor to Emanuel Bach as music director in Hamburg. Like Bach, he knew Klopstock well, and the collaboration between them concerns the investment of the poet in the setting of his poetry to music: "Before Hr. Schwenke began to compose, the poet read him his ode several times. Then the composer read it to the poet. As soon as the composer completed a passage, it was performed for the poet. If the poet proposed some emendation with regard to the declamation, the expression, and so forth, the passage was revised and improved until Klopstock was entirely satisfied with it."[11]

Now it is unlikely that the poets with whom Schubert was intimate would have engaged in a similarly painstaking exercise in diction and declamation—although indeed the "Leseabenden" in which Schubert participated would have served the same practical function, even if the aesthetic mission was of a different order.[12] I do mean to suggest that Schubert was a "reader" in this deeper sense: that the poem, in all its peculiarities—formal, declamatory, grammatical, and, surely, semantically and in its powers of metaphor—will have held out its imperatives to him no less urgently.

When Schubert returned to Schiller's *Jüngling* in 1815, the poem suggested a very different manner of setting. In the composition of the roughly sixty songs between the two, something of those prerequisites of diction that so concerned Forkel and Reichardt seems to have been worked through in a

10. "Meine Melodien entstehen jederzeit aus wiederholtem Lesen des Gedichts von selbst, ohne daß ich darnach suche, und alles was ich weiter daran thue, ist dieses, daß ich sie so lang mit kleinen Abänderungen wiederhole, und sie nicht eh' aufschreibe, als bis ich fühle und erkenne, daß der grammatische, logische, pathetische und musikalische Akzent so gut mit einander verbunden sind, daß die Melodie richtig spricht und angenehm singt, und das nicht für Eine [*sic*] Strophe, sondern für alle. Soll man das nun aber so gut im Vortrage fühlen und erkennen, so muß der Sänger vorher die Worte ganz lesen, und so lange lesen, bis er fühlt, daß er sie mit wahrem Ausdruck liest, und dann erst sie singen" (Johann Friederich Reichardt, *Oden und Lieder von Göthe, Bürger, Sprickmann, Voß und Thomsen, mit Melodieen beym Klavier zu singen*, pt. 2 [Berlin, 1780], from "Auch ein guter Rath statt der Vorrede" [some good advice in place of a preface]).

11. "Ehe Hr. Schwenke die Komposition begann, las ihm der Dichter seine Oden mehreremale vor; dann las sie der Komponist dem Dichter. . . . So wie der Komponist eine Stelle nach der andern verfertigt hatte, wurde sie dem Dichter vorgespielt. Machte dieser einige berichtigende Bemerkungen in Hinsicht der Deklamation, des Ausdrucks u. d. gl., so wurde an der Stelle so lange geändert und gebessert, bis Klopstock vollkommen damit zufrieden war" (*Allgemeine Musikalische Zeitung* 1 [1798–99]: 784, together with Schwenke's setting of *Der Frohsinn*, published as "Beylage XVI").

12. See, e.g., Herbert Zeman, "Franz Schuberts Teilhabe an der österreichischen literarischen Kultur seiner Zeit," in *Schubert-Kongreß Wien 1978*, 285–304.

curriculum encompassing every manner of poem and a spectrum of genres. The setting of Goethe's *Nähe des Geliebten*, composed some months earlier, commands a view of strophic song that at once subsumes its antecedents and transcends in a few luminous phrases the abstract notion of unified "melody" toward which Reichardt seemed to have been groping.[13]

This notion of the strophic Lied is exercised—or perhaps subverted—in the new setting of *Der Jüngling am Bache*. More ballad than lyric, more narrative than reflective, it is not a poem to elicit the kinds of ambiguities and parallelisms immanent in *Nähe des Geliebten*, for it is all too plain that the music is more appropriate to certain strophes than to others. And it is not the first strophe that dictates the mode.[14]

Example 2.1 *Der Jüngling am Bache* (D. 192), mm. 7–14

The phrase that stops us is the one that veers off to the relative major (see ex. 2.1). All of a sudden, the music gesticulates—acts out in pantomime. The accents, the articulations in the bass, the new harmonic rhythm, the repeated chords in the piano right hand, and the pointed punctuation at the end of the line all contribute to a sense of interruption. The effect is reinforced in the quality of the phrase that follows on it, reengaging the discourse as it went be-

13. For a valuable discussion of just this strophic aspect of the song, see Frisch, "Schubert's *Nähe des Geliebten*," esp. 194–97.

14. Alfred Heuß was surely among the first to have argued that, even in Schubert's earliest strophic Lieder, the music may well have been conceived with some strophe other than the first in mind (see his "Ein trunkenes Jünglingslied," 622).

fore the interruption. How, precisely, are we to understand the caesura at the end of the first quatrain—a caesura marked by this mock cadence in A♭? Here the music flirts with a problem that haunted all those grammarians of the late eighteenth century. In Schiller's text, each initial quatrain is closed with a final punctuation. At the same time, the sense of distance between the two quatrains of a strophe—the relationship between the half strophes—differs in each instance.

In the first strophe, there is even ostensibly a change in voice, for, in the poem as it goes in *Der Parasit*, quotation marks set off everything that follows line 4: the *Knabe* tells his own tale. When the poem was gathered in Schiller's *Gedichte-Sammlungen* beginning in 1805, its quotation marks were left behind, and this is the text that Schubert knew. Very likely an editorial oversight, the repercussions of this omission are nevertheless profound. Now the *Knabe* is an illustration: a naive, pastoral figure made to enact the little parable that moves the poet to his complaint. In either case, the peculiar syntax of the music does not seem to serve this shift of focus very well.

The distancing between the other half strophes is less extreme. In the second strophe, there is the classic opposition—the troubled simile of awakening nature that awakens only heavy weather in the lover's breast. In the third strophe, the opposition is clearer still. "*Eine* nur ist's," the poet sings, "nah und ewig weit" (There is only one . . . near yet eternally distant). The punctuation between the half strophes here is less semantic breach than grammatical formality, a formal interruption to be sung through, elided. Now the music sets in. The mock cadence translates that sense of the punctuation: a period on the page, but not in his heart. The unexpected Db at "sie," even the harmony itself—the first personification of the "Eine"—are strikingly apropos. (A premonition of the gesture is what sets off the piano at the very beginning of the song.) The urgency of the repeated chords has an erotic tinge. And, if those very chords may be heard to suggest the little "Wellen Tanz" in the first strophe, the coming to life of a rejuvenated seasonal cycle in the second, and the literal strewing of flowers at the end, it is only in the third strophe that the real, the inner message of these palpitations breaks through.

Finally, the reprise of F minor in the following phrase is made poignant in the third strophe. It is not a phrase that sings easily those evocative lines that will come round beneath it in the fourth strophe: "Horch, der Hain erschallt von Liedern." No songs can be heard to reverberate in this wood. The very short shrift given to "Horch" suggests even an unwillingness to listen for them. The final quatrain takes on a sardonic aspect. So much for Madame Belmont's drawing room.

The setting of 1815 may not stand very high in anyone's repertory of favorite Schubert—even from the spring of 1815. But in its way, this modest song manipulates the strophic canon to its own impressive ends. The axioms on which one might reconstruct a theory of eighteenth-century song are not so much violated as turned on themselves. Reichardt's exhortation—to find a single melody whose grammatical, logical, pathetic, and musical accents are bound together so well that the melody sings agreeably for all strophes—is honored in the breach. We accept the setting as marginally appropriate for all four strophes, marginally correct. But in the third strophe, the truer meaning of the music comes clear.

A setting such as this raises fundamental questions about the efficacy of strophic procedure. Think once again of the music to the lines "Horch, der Hain erschallt von Liedern." If these lines summon forth an appropriate music in 1812, nothing of the sort happens here. And that is much to the point. The singer cannot bring himself to hear the songs, to see the brook. The singer becomes a reader in some deeper sense. More precisely, the singer is made to tell Schubert's tale, not Schiller's. The naive face of the poem has been violated. The new, sophisticated irony that Schubert brings to it is at once a function of the strophic rule and a transgression of it. Schubert does not *become* Schiller in the way that Schwenke *becomes* Klopstock. Rather, Schiller's poem is appropriated, is made Schubert's.

In one other telling detail the music seems to signal its allegiance to the syntax of the third strophe. This has to do with a chromatic inflection: the B♮ on the third beat of m. 18. Innocent on the page, it in fact mirrors a syntactic gesture in the poem. The B♮ signals a change in harmony and stands as a kind of semaphor to the singer: "*Inflect* this," it says; "the syntax hinges on it." The "und" to which it is sung in the third strophe is precisely what this inflection summons up. Not simply "and," the meaning is roughly: "Lovingly, I stretch out my arms to the beloved silhouette. Alas, I cannot reach it. *Consequently*, my heart remains *ungestillt*." Another duplicitous cognate, *ungestillt* really means "unstanched" (in the sense of the bleeding heart) and "unsatisfied" (in the sexual sense). The B♮ pierces to the heart. If it is not syntactically wrong in the other strophes, it actually stings only here.

But it is the setting of 1819 that Schubert wanted to make public. It should not take much argument to buttress the claim that here again it is the third strophe that seems to draw all the music to it. Consider the setting of the second couplet: "Eine nur ist's, die ich suche, / Sie ist nah und ewig weit." The paradox "nah und ewig weit," an eternal one in early Romantic song, is expressed in the eternal musical symbol of such double entendre, the so-called German augmented sixth that emerges through an enharmonic reinterpretation of the dominant seventh. At "Eine nur ist's, die ich suche," the music leans back toward D minor, then ahead toward the expected close in the relative major. But that, too, is frustrated. In the painful irony of "Sie ist nah," the music veers off to a cadence in E minor. Close enough to F major measured in millimeters at the keyboard, the modulation is remote in harmonic measure.

These harmonic maneuvers seem misconceived—more posture than genuinely felt—when positioned against the lines of the other strophes. Similarly, the broad new piano figuration at mid-strophe is very nearly a physical stretching in sympathy with those outstretched arms, yearning for the embrace. The expressive gaps in the voice at "kann es nicht erreichen" give a reaching of another sort. Finally, the chilling octave, up to the high A, at "das Herz bleibt ungestillt" delivers up a cry from the heart itself.

As expressive gloss, the music does not so much illuminate the other three strophes as it cloaks them in irony. In the first two strophes, the music seems about some self-fulfilling prophecy, hinting at the revelatory appeal of the third strophe. Similarly, the fourth strophe has a retrospective quality to it. The naive message is tinged with a heavy melancholy that we must now associate with the third strophe.

This new concept of strophic song—weighting it down with psychological riddles—would not have pleased Goethe and the composers close to him, for whom it was first of all a device for the declamation of the poem, a fixing of its diction, an illumination of its form. Something of what I mean comes out in an exchange on this topic between Johann Abraham Peter Schulz and the poet Johann Heinrich Voß. In a letter of 25 August 1789, Schulz writes:

> In future, avoid such iambics for my music (are they not called iambics?):
> Tănzt, Pāār uňd Paar
> Săcht, sprach ich. . . .
> Short syllables such as these that carry so much weight always trouble me, for most times I cannot give them any musical weight because of the other strophes. I become quite terrified about such things.[15]

Voß gives the poet's answer:

> I did not think that you'd have wracked your brains over *Săcht, sprāch/ĭch.* Before I wrote it down, I sought alternatives. But I found none that did not weaken the place. For in noble poesie it is always that now the natural, the sequence of ideas, now the expression, now the rhythm [*der Bewegung*], now the sound of the consonants and vowels, must be offered up. And so I think that the composer on his part must be magnanimous enough to put up with a difficulty whose reason is not to be found in the poet's negligence. Refuse him the liberty to exchange a long syllable at the anacrusis, and you rob him of a diversity in the otherwise so monotonous iambics, and, what is more important, of the kernel of expression itself, often enough. The *Misklang* in the music is not as bad as would be the far worse expression of the idea—as in, for example, *Da sprach ich: Gute Mutter, sacht!*[16]

15. "Vermeiden Sie doch künftig für meine Melodien solche Jamben (heißen sie nicht Jamben?). . . . Solche kurze Silben von so viel Gewicht scheren mich allzeit, und die mehrste Zeit darf ich der übrigen Strophen wegen gar kein musikalisches Gewicht darauf legen. Dabey kann mir denn ganz angst und bange werden" (*Briefwechsel zwischen Johann Abraham Peter Schulz und Johann Heinrich Voss*, ed. Heinz Gottwaldt and Gerhard Hahne [Kassel and Basel, 1960], 77).

16. "Habe ichs nicht gedacht, bei: *Săcht, sprāch/ĭch*—würden Sie den Kopf schütteln. Ehe ichs noch hinschrieb, suchte ich Aenderungen; aber ich fand keine, die nicht die Stelle schwächte. Da denn in der edlen Poesie alles von der Art ist, daß man bald dem Natürlichen, der Gedankenfolge, bald des Ausdrucks, bald der Bewegung, bald dem Klange der Konsonanten u

The composer as grammarian sets himself beneath the poet, Voß seems to say. Whether he means to or not, Voß argues here for a poetry in the music that responds to all those tensions between the conventions of form and the rush of idea that give poetry its vigor.

The exchange between Voß and Schulz is symptomatic of some eternal dialectic that is always in play when poem and music are put to one another. It is played out as well in these various settings of Schiller's *Jüngling am Bache*, but now the poem sets loose a rapture of composition in the singer. Had these been settings of his poem, would Voß have summoned that magnanimous posture that he exhorted of the singer in the name of poetry?

II

When, eight years later, *Der Jüngling am Bache* appeared in print, it was in company with two exceptionally moving songs: *Der Unglückliche*, to a poem by Caroline Pichler, and a second setting of Schiller's *Hoffnung* ("Es reden und träumen die Menschen viel"), whose terse concentration, expressed at once in its opening measures, counters the expansive breadth of *Der Unglückliche*, similarly captured in its opening measures. Further, *Der Jüngling am Bache* is a revision of the setting from 1819, transposed now to C minor.[17]

Instinctively, we reach for some lexicon to guide us in all the ways that the revision supersedes the setting of 1819. But that is a learned instinct. The transposition to C minor carries with it a transposition in a deeper sense as well, one in which the intensity of the original idea is compromised. Even the piano accompaniment now takes on a conventional aspect—not that it is easier to play, but rather that it participates less in the song, withdraws from it, "accompanies" it. The telling, even poetic distinction in the figuration at mid-strophe is given away. The moments of silence at the ends of some lines are now paved over. But, at the telling interstice between the strophes, the sense of continuity established in the version of 1819 is now disturbed. The intuitive, palpable way in which the final notes of the one strophe were made to lead back to the opening motive of the next is a casualty of the revision (see ex. 2.2). A small point on paper, perhaps, the detail will not be lost on the pianist, who must guide the music (and the singer) into the next strophe. And

Vokale etwas aufopfern muß; so denke ich, muß der Tonkünstler so edelmütig sein, auch seinerseits eine Schwierigkeit, die ihren Grund nicht in der Trägheit des Dichters hat, vorlieb zu nehmen. Versagen Sie ihm die Erlaubnis im Aufschwung mit einer langen Silbe zu wechseln; so rauben Sie ihm eine Mannigfaltigkeit des an sich so einförmigen Jambus, u, was noch wichtiger ist, oft das Körnichte des Ausdrucks. Der Misklang in der Musik ist nicht so viel, als der schlechtere Ausdruck des Gedankens sein würde, z. E. hier: *Da sprach ich: Gute Mutter, sacht!*" (ibid., 78–79).

17. The publication of op. 84 (later altered to 87) by A. Pennauer in Vienna was announced on 6 August 1827 (see Deutsch, *Thematisches Verzeichnis*, 369).

the decision, finally, to call back the little preamble as an epilogue at the end of the song is again a decision in favor of the conventional. There is something stark and pointed in the decisive D-minor triads that cut off the narrative. Much of the meaning in the setting seems lodged in the sheer physical act of those three chords. In its place, the new epilogue equivocates. Is the story over? We cannot know until the pianist stops playing.

Example 2.2 *Der Jüngling am Bache* (D. 638, "1. Fassung"), the reprise

But the most vexing revision affects that chilling octave leap to the high A—the *Geschrei* in which the heart pours out its complaint. The effect would in any case have been tempered in the transposition, but it is further muted in favor of a phrase that more reasonably sustains the motivic thrust of the song. One may even reconstruct the stages in the process of revision (see ex. 2.3): covered octaves in the outer voices point up a weakness in the bass; the new bass avoids a redundancy in the move between A and B♭ and firms up the cadence, but the part writing in the outer voices approaching the new G♯ in the bass is now faulty; the octave leap falls away, sacrificed in the service of a textbook contrary motion in the outer voices. It would be niggardly to hold that the revision did not gain in polish and elegance. At the same time, something innate to the expression of the passage has been effaced.

Example 2.3 *Der Jüngling am Bache* (D. 638), mm. 22–26, earlier version and revision

The editorial policy of the *Neue Ausgabe* claims the authority of the print, so it is the C minor version of *Der Jüngling am Bache*, taking privilege as a member of op. 87, that appears in the principal volume; the other versions are found side by side in the companion volume of "alternate versions," so many preliminaries to a main event.[18] The favoring of a published version on the sole ground that it appeared in print—was sold in a marketplace with the author's sanction—is an editorial bias with aesthetic implications, a repudiation of criticism itself. The matter has been addressed with great insight in a recent essay by Charles Rosen, who attacks as a fetish "the belief that the author's final version had the greatest authority and is therefore privileged":

> Here aesthetics has become oddly confused with law, and critical evaluation becomes an affirmation of property rights. In most cases, this fetish does no harm, as authors are often no worse than any one else at correcting their works. There are, however, cases in which successive versions do not produce greater polish or enrichment, but tend to weaken and even to betray the original conception. That so many examples of this progressive deterioration are found in the early nineteenth century suggests that we are not dealing with the psychological difficulties of individual authors but with a problem of style.[19]

When Beethoven revises, we have the sense less of an editorial task than of some profound reengagement with the act of composition. The music is conceived again, not simply tinkered with.[20] Often enough, Schubert engages in this deeper process of rehearing. Nothing deteriorates. Such a concept, admittedly beyond the commonly held notion of "revision," begins to get at how one might understand the differences between the versions of *Der Jüngling am Bache* from 1812, 1815, and 1819—for all that the process is decidedly un-Beethovenian. When Schubert thinks to begin the setting of 1815 with a phrase cribbed from the opening of the earlier setting, he means neither to quote himself nor to establish a supersedure in which the earlier song would be replaced. The new phrase is not meant to signify something about its origins. The similarity between them is of no more value to an analysis than is the dissimilarity between others. Reminiscence is at play here—of something recollected in no clear, rational, conscious way. Lord's *Singer of Tales* springs to mind: Schubert beginning with a phrase associated in memory with the way the narrative begins. But by 1815, the poem, in its deeper erotic strain, would have touched something quite new in him. This is the aspect that, in the resinging, subsumes everything else. The literal plotting out of the poem in all

18. *NGA*, ser. 4, vol. 4b, 218–29.

19. Charles Rosen, "Romantic Originals," *New York Review of Books*, 17 December 1987, 26.

20. The famous complaint to Treitschke during the revision of *Fidelio* is poignant testimony to this: "I could compose something new far more quickly than patch up the old with something new, as I am now doing. For my custom when I am composing even instrumental music is always to keep the whole in view—But in this case the whole of my work is—to a certain extent—scattered in all directions; and I have to think out the entire work again" (*The Letters of Beethoven*, ed. and trans. Emily Anderson, 3 vols. [London and New York, 1961], 1:454).

its pictorial variety—the nostalgic echoing of songs sung in the wood, no less than the ponderous grief felt in those thousand voices of awakening nature—is given up, so many excesses to the central complaint.

But in the transposition of the 1819 setting in preparation for publication, a discernably different process is engaged. Here one might properly speak of revision in its conventional sense. An original concept is retained, and, in that difficult confrontation in which an author excoriates his earlier self in the name of improvement, a spontaneity true to the original is now tempered. It would be demonstrably false to claim that revision in this sense did not bring a good measure of improvement, not only in the surface polish of the work, but in its deeper structure as well. Still, these improvements come at a price, for what is lost often enough is an intangible, improvisatory quality that we most prize in Schubert.

"Perhaps they were wiser than we, because one cannot write song."[21] Seeking to explain the reluctance on the part of the ancient epic singers to commit themselves to the writing down of that which is conveyed in speech and song, Lord unwittingly illuminates something essential of this distinction in Schubert between the conceiving of song and the reflective act whereby the spontaneity of the singing is "perfected" for publication. For Schubert, publication represents what writing down must have represented for the ancient Greeks: at once a vehicle for the wider dissemination of his works, an emblem of respectability, of status in the bourgeois sense, and at the same time a fixing of text with a specificity that seems to mark it for eternity. That this notion of a capturing of text had its pernicious aspect for Schubert is evident in the strikingly self-conscious *Reinschriften* that he was preparing for publication in the early 1820s.[22] Schubert's hand betrays him: it is a copyist's hand—even practiced scholars must seek out the clues to its authenticity—where the writing sets itself at some distance from the music behind the notation.

III

When did Schubert revise the 1819 version? And is it certain that he did so for the sake of publication? The autograph containing the revision in C minor has not survived, nor has a *Stichvorlage*. The evidence for a dating of the revision

21. Lord, *The Singer of Tales*, 124.

22. Walther Vetter perceives the psychological implications of this "publication" hand: "Die Reinschriften sind nicht selten bezeichnend im Negativen. Schubert stellte zwar, wie es seinem Wesen entsprach, saubere Reinschriften seiner Kompositionen her, aber er war kein Mann der Kalligraphie, und so kommt es, daß ihm, wenn er einmal eine Schönschrift liefert, zuweilen Versehen unterlaufen, die man in seinen ersten Niederschriften vergeblich suchen würde" (The clean copies are not infrequently characteristic in a negative sense. As was his nature, Schubert admittedly prepared fine clean copies of his compositions. But he was no calligrapher, and so it happens that even when he delivers a fair copy, mistakes creep in that, in the earliest drafts [*ersten Niederschriften*], one would seek out in vain) (*Der Klassiker Schubert*, 2 vols. [Leipzig, 1953], 1:377).

is entirely circumstantial, and that is the case for *Hoffnung* (D. 637), whose autograph is similarly among the missing. Both the *Hoffnung* and the *Jüngling am Bache* in op. 87 are later settings of Schiller poems earlier set in 1815; probably it is this coincidence that led Deutsch to infer a propinquity in the dates of the later settings: *Hoffnung* is assigned, without much conviction, to "ca. 1819 (?)."[23]

Apart from its publication in op. 87, *Hoffnung* otherwise survives only in a manuscript prepared for the shadowy Count Haugwitz, who seems to have had access both to autographs and to the highly valued copies made by Albert Stadler.[24] Curiously, the song appears here in B major. This we must take as evidence prima facie of an original conception, for to hold to the converse—that a copyist would transpose *to* B major *from* an original in B♭—is to postulate the implausible. The vocal range of *Hoffnung* is undemanding in either key. Why, on the other hand, a copyist might have been asked to transpose away from a daunting B major, given the extreme enharmonies that tax the opening measures of the song, should need no burdensome explanation.

In the culling of its songs, the contents of the Haugwitz manuscript may seem at a glance to be rather haphazard and miscellaneous. But the placement of *Hoffnung* among a smaller group suggests a collector's cast of mind, given to taxonomies. The songs are these:

fol. 7r–8r: *Nacht und Traüme*, D. 827 (by June 1823), B major;
fol. 8v–11r: *Greisen Gesang*, D. 778 (by June 1823), B major;
fol. 11v–15v: *Sehnsucht*, D. 636 (ca. 1821), B minor;
fol. 16r–21v: *Der Unglückliche*, D. 713 (Jan. 1821), B minor;
fol. 22r–23r: *Die Hoffnung*, D. 637 (date?), B major.

This preponderance of B (major and minor) is striking precisely because it is gained not through some imposed transposition. It is the original keys that are recorded here. And this is true of all twenty songs in the manuscript, which must have been compiled sometime after 1825, for the songs published in that year are given here in their published keys, where those differ from the original. The one exception is *Des Baches Wiegenlied*, here in D major, but published (with *Die schöne Müllerin*) in 1824 in E major.

Does the music of *Hoffnung* signal anything of its *Entstehungszeit*?

23. "Vielleicht ist es in zeitlicher Nähe zu *638* [*Der Jüngling am Bache*], dem anderen Lied nach einem Text von Schiller in op. 87, entstanden (April 1819)" (Perhaps it was composed in chronological proximity to [D.] 638 [*Der Jüngling am Bache*] (April 1819), the other song in op. 87 after a text by Schiller) (Deutsch, *Thematisches Verzeichnis*, 369). Walther Dürr, editing op. 87 for the *NGA*, is more circumspect: "Es ist denkbar daß Schubert es—wie die in op. 87 folgende dritte Bearbeitung von *Der Jüngling am Bache*—im Jahre 1819 geschrieben hat, doch hat Schubert nur selten gleichzeitig entstandene Lieder zu einem opus vereinigt" (It is conceivable that Schubert wrote it in 1819—like the third setting of *Der Jüngling am Bache*, which follows it in op. 87—and yet Schubert only rarely coupled songs that were composed at the same time in one and the same opus) (*NGA*, ser. 4, vol. 4a, p. xix).

24. On the Haugwitz manuscripts, see Walther Dürr, *Franz Schuberts Werke in Abschriften: Liederalben und Sammlungen* (Kassel, 1975), 140–52. The manuscript in question is A 15932.

Example 2.4 *Hoffnung* (D. 637), mm. 1–4, 11–14

Example 2.5 *Hoffnung*, mm. 13–14, with ellipsis filled in

Inexplicably, the song has been undervalued in the literature.[25] Its lithe harmonies speak the poem so naturally as to fuse with it. The opening measures have a mystery about them. This is not the audacious, learned, chromaticism of affect, but a phrase that touches some deeper thought, releasing an elliptic cadence at the end of the second couplet (see ex. 2.4). The ellipsis is in the omission of a harmony that would negotiate between adjacent root-position triads (shown in ex. 2.5). The supple diction of the final couplet masks an ob-

25. "A racy little song," Richard Capell thought. "It makes the effect of the wilder kind of drinking song" (*Schubert's Songs*, 2d ed. [New York, 1957], 157–58). Walther Vetter suggested that Schubert took Reichardt's setting as a measure, if not a model. Tellingly, he thought that Mandyczewski's "1819" put the song too late (see *Der Klassiker Schubert*, 2:344, n. 243). Dietrich Fischer-Dieskau (*Schubert: A Biographical Study of His Songs*, trans. and ed. Kenneth S. Whitton [London, 1976]), who has something to say about nearly every Schubert song, is altogether silent on this one.

session with that very passage, the ellipsis now explained in a double approach to the final cadence, where the G missing earlier in the bass is now positioned each time at a point of rhythmic elision (ex. 2.6). The subtlety and control of harmonic imagination is exemplary. Lodged in its midst is evidently a clue to Schubert's reading of the poem. In the superb declamation of the final lines in the third strophe—

> Und was die innere Stimme spricht,
> das täuscht die hoffende Seele nicht.
>
> (And what the inner voice speaks does not deceive the happy soul.)

—the "nicht" falls tellingly on the one *inganno* in the song: a deceptive cadence, a *Täuschung* that, whatever the intention behind it, mocks Schiller's sentiment. The inner voice, Schubert seems to say, does indeed deceive the trusting soul.[26]

Example 2.6 *Hoffnung*, mm. 17–23

Among the output of 1819, the song is a sport. Its sophistication, a deep complexity masked by an almost casual diction, is characteristic of songs composed some years later. *Gondelfahrer* (D. 808), composed in March 1824,

26. Even here, the text deceives. The print shows a six chord on the first beat of m. 21, a harmony that of itself makes no sense, unless the E♭ is understood as an unresolved dissonance. Under no circumstances can the ear tolerate E♭ as a true root here. Mandyczewski assumed it to be a misprint and printed a D in its place; the *NGA* is true to the text of the first edition and reports no variance here in the Haugwitz copy (which I have not been able to consult).

strikes a similar tone and in its formal conception seems very close to the accents of *Hoffnung*. *Dithyrambe* (D. 801), another Schiller setting, comes to mind as well. Published by Cappi and Czerny in 1826 as op. 60, no. 2, it survives in an undated *Reinschrift* that Robert Winter proposes to date 1826. A *Reinschrift* of a setting of Rückert's *Greisengesang* (D. 778), the other number in op. 60, is on the same kind of paper, but the *erste Niederschrift* is on a paper that Winter dates between January and May 1823.[27]

If, on stylistic grounds (a vulnerable criterion, admittedly), *Hoffnung* sits more comfortably among songs composed in 1823–24, another bit of circumstantial evidence invites us to consider whether the song might not have been conceived as a patch in a more extensive Schiller quilt. A manuscript dated "Mai 1823," and surviving only as a fragment, contains settings of Schiller's *Das Geheimnis* (D. 793) and *Der Pilgrim* (D. 794). Both songs are written in the hand of an "erste Niederschrift." The manuscript breaks off on the last side of a bifolio. The missing leaves would contain the closing bars (mm. 86–106) of *Der Pilgrim*. Perhaps they were cut away and lost because they contained as well some other song whose text was needed for separate transmission, at a time when the text of *Der Pilgrim* (announced for publication in February 1825) had been established in some other form. If the manuscript did once contain another song as well, no testimony to it has survived.[28]

Whatever the circumstances surrounding the loss of those leaves, the temptation to consider *Hoffnung* as a player in these circumstances is compelling. Its opening measures—in *B major*, recalling the Haugwitz copy as the closest witness to the missing autograph—spring naturally from the moving lament, in its chilling equivocation between C♯ minor and C♯ major, with which *Der Pilgrim* closes (see ex. 2.7). And perhaps it is not beside the point to recall that, on 7 August 1815, Schubert composed settings of *Das Geheimnis* (D. 250) and *Hoffnung* (D. 251) in a single manuscript. That the two might again have shared a single manuscript in 1823, along with *Der Pilgrim*, is at the very least plausible.

Schiller's pilgrim recounts his tale—eight strophes of it—in the past tense: "Noch in meines Lebens Lenze war ich" (I was still in the springtime of my life), the poem begins. "Näher bin ich nicht dem Ziel" (I am no closer to my

27. See Robert Winter, "Paper Studies and the Future of Schubert Research," in *Schubert Studies: Problems of Style and Chronology*, ed. Eva Badura-Skoda and Peter Branscombe (Cambridge, 1982), 226–27.

28. The manuscript was in this state when Mandyczewski examined it in preparing the old *Gesamtausgabe* (see *Franz Schuberts Werke: Revisionsbericht* [hereafter *Revisionsbericht*], ed. Eusebius Mandyczewski, ser. 20 [Leipzig: Breitkopf & Härtel, 1897], p. 94 [reprinted as *Editors' Commentary on the Critical Edition*, vol. 19 of *Franz Schubert: Complete Works* (New York: Dover Publications, 1969), p. 330]). It is entirely possible that the closing music underwent fundamental revision, even that the final version replaced something entirely different. Mandyczewski noted that the autograph of *Das Geheimnis* "weist gegen das Ende hin immer flüchtigere Schriftzüge auf" (exhibits increasingly hasty writing toward the end), a condition that applies equally to *Der Pilgrim*.

Example 2.7 *a*, *Der Pilgrim* (D. 794), closing measures. *b*, *Hoffnung*, opening measures, transposed

destination), he concludes in the penultimate strophe, facing the infinite expanse of ocean at journey's end. The shift to triple meter at the "Sehr langsam" underscores the shift in tense in the final strophe.

Limned in Romantic nimbus, the intrepid quest is choreographed in a stylized chorale in E major. At the fifth strophe, the music begins to mirror the loss of innocence, the corrosion of faith, through a modulatory figure of labyrinthine complexity that nevertheless masks a chromatic sequence in and about B minor. Never firmly established, the key surrenders to a cadence in G major. The hymn tune returns, elegantly varied. The aura of transfiguration is only enhanced by the modulation. The new key is liquidated soon enough, and the music takes its sinister turn to the dominant of C♯ minor.

What, precisely, is lamented in Schiller's final quatrain?

Ach kein Steg will dahin führen,
Ach der Himmel über mir
Will die Erde nie berühren,
Und das Dort ist niemals hier!

Alas, no path leads thither,
Alas, the heavens above me
will never touch the earth,
And the There is never here!

There is a resignation in these lines, but also a recognition of some cold truth about the human condition. The pointed rhythms in Schubert's music, and even the two modal forms (minor and major) in which the final line is recited, seem to hold this philosophical opposition in a state of fixed suspension.

In its paradoxical message, Schiller's *Hoffnung* seems to gloss the allegorical *Pilgrim*. In its final couplet, one might hear some consolation for the world-weary wanderer: what the *inner* voice speaks does not deceive. Surely the sentiments of *Hoffnung* follow convincingly from *Der Pilgrim*. Hope and faith are after all coupled instincts, and, in these poems, both are held up to philosophical scrutiny, even if Schiller had no such pairing in mind. The point, rather, is whether Schubert, casting about for a Schiller group, might not have perceived a linkage in the poetry susceptible to musical bonding. The quirky opening strain of *Hoffnung* speaks to such bonding, for its underlying harmonic motion, a mysterious undertow that drags at the tonic, seems almost to echo those tortuous phrases that burden the pilgrim at mid-journey, even to release the pent-up tensions generated in the earlier passage (see ex. 2.8).

Example 2.8 *a*, *Der Pilgrim*, mm. 56–64, harmonic abstraction. *b*, *Hoffnung*, mm. 1–3, harmonic abstraction

The epilogue in C♯ minor at the end of *Der Pilgrim* calls for some reflection. Final strophes that close away from the tonic are common enough in Schubert, nor is this one in any sense unconvincing. Still, the ambivalence of mode in its final measures, for all that it may be said to play on a philosophical opposition, nevertheless encourages a musical response, invites resolution. In itself, the movement to C♯ minor at the end of *Der Pilgrim* is suggestive of larger strategies of musical narrative. In retrospect, we may understand it to negotiate between an initial tonic, E major, and the dominant of B major. Further, the powerfully ambivalent inner voice at the end of *Der Pilgrim*—F♯-E♯-E♮—becomes a central aspect of the opening thematics in *Hoffnung*.

An argument from evidence of this kind can never prove, in any legal sense, the inviolability of the pairing of *Der Pilgrim* and *Hoffnung*. If it is right to believe that these two songs, together with *Das Geheimnis*, were conceived in a matrix of their own, Schubert was very quick to repudiate their kinship. *Der Pilgrim*, transposed to D major, was published less than two years later as op. 37, no. 1—its publication was announced in February 1825—paired with a setting of Schiller's *Der Alpenjäger* (D. 588), a song composed in 1817 and later revised and transposed for publication. If the music of *Der Pilgrim* is in some measure illuminated and deepened in the context of *Das Geheimnis* and *Hoffnung*, the juxtaposition with *Der Alpenjäger* recasts it in stark isolation. The decision to publish the two as op. 37 is only slightly less mystifying than the decision to dismantle what should have survived as a cogent and vigorous engagement with three Schiller poems whose sentiments encourage such consanguinity. The case for the authenticity of that original conception must be reconstructed from the persuasive, irrepressible accents of the music itself.

In the end, *Hoffnung* (now transposed to B♭) was published as a sequel to *Der Unglückliche* (B minor) and followed by *Der Jüngling am Bache*, now in C minor. Much like *Der Pilgrim*, *Der Unglückliche* sets its epilogue off from the main body of the song, a final reflection cast in a new tempo, a new meter, and pointed rhythms. Perhaps more than coincidence was at play in the decision to couple it with *Hoffnung*.[29]

No doubt the new groupings established in op. 37 and op. 87 can be defended, whether on poetic or musical grounds or behind some argument that touches the commerce of Lied publication in the 1820s.[30] The fact remains

29. *Der Unglückliche*, the expansiveness of which was admired a moment ago, suffered as well in the move to a published version. Printed in 6/8 meter, its autograph gives the song in 12/8, a notation that hints at affinities with the first movement of the great Sonata in G Major, op. 78 (1826). The meter itself is something of a topos, a formula for the broad, grand, solemn utterance. *Schwestergruß* (D. 762), from November 1822 (in F♯ minor), and the opening Andante of the overture to *Alfonso und Estrella*, from February 1822, come to mind. To anyone who knows *Der Unglückliche* in its 12/8 mode, the notation in the print is an impediment to a proper reading of its phrases, a deflation of their breadth. This can only have been a concession to a publisher anticipating that these expanses of eighth notes between the bars would disorient his myopic clients.

30. For one such defense, see Walther Dürr, "Die Lieder-Serie der Neuen Schubert-Ausgabe: Zu Schuberts Ordnung eigener Lieder," *Musica* 40, no. 1 (January/February 1986): 28–30.

that we know little about the motivation behind such regroupings, but even if we knew more and could assert with some confidence that Schubert's own wishes were realized in them, harder questions remain. They were asked earlier, in chapter 1, and they persist in the chapters that follow.

Perhaps the Schubert canon is well served to have this *Jüngling am Bache*, in its final redaction, coupled definitively with *Hoffnung*. That owes surely to Schubert's authorization to publish the two together, in turn the impetus behind Deutsch's placement of the two side by side in his *Verzeichnis*, a placement more than suggestive of a common *Entstehung*. It is explicit, too, in the publication of the two together in the *Neue Ausgabe*.

To believe so is to be deceived by the assumed infallibility of printed texts. It remains an abiding mystery how it is that Schubert time and again came to repudiate the fine, impalpable lines of internal coherence, the matrices of thought and feeling that issue in the fragile gatherings of songs preserved in the autographs. The history of Schubert's engagement with Schiller's naive *Jüngling* is rich in such gatherings. To accept op. 87 as some definitive statement, even if it is Schubert's own, is to deprive ourselves of that richness.

3

The Aesthetics of Revision

However we think to represent the complex interrelationships of thought behind the three original settings of Schiller's *Der Jüngling am Bache*, some other construct is needed to convey how the published version of 1827 is rather a *variant* in respect to the setting of 1819. As text, it is of that class of variant narrowly defined as a revision: it means to supersede the prototype, which is consequently understood to fall away, no longer a text in its own right, but a preliminary phase of no textual authority.

This explanation might satisfy the composer, whose authority in such matters is in the legal sense beyond dispute. But it cannot please the critic, for whom the privileges of authorship are rather impediments to true critical inquiry. The motives behind the revision are what need to be understood. Charles Rosen, pondering the question, reflects on variant readings in early Romantic literature and the arts: "With Romantic artists, we reach a generation often disconcerted by the implications or intentions of their own works. When this happens, the revisions become a betrayal of the work when they are not a form of tinkering. We might say that the writer has ceased being an author and has turned into an interfering editor of his own work."[1] It is Schumann's propensity to rub out the eccentricities of an original conception that is Rosen's target, and it is primarily to the generation of the 1830s (as Rosen likes to call it) that his ideas apply. Can they be extended to apply to Schubert as well? The question is a difficult one, for, in spite of what has been pieced together of Schubert as a composer about his business, the evidence that might encourage an inquiry into the question is elusive and very often misleading. It suggests in any case a rather more complex enterprise than what Rosen has proposed for Schumann.

I

At the close of a brief study that appeared some thirty years ago, Walter Gerstenberg hinted at the question in his discussion of a newly discovered autograph for an earlier version of *Greisengesang*, one of a number of settings of poems from Rückert's *Oestlichen Rosen* that seem to date from 1823.[2] In this

1. Rosen, "Romantic Originals," 31.

2. Walter Gerstenberg, "*Schubertiade*: Anmerkungen zu einigen Liedern," in *Festschrift Otto Erich Deutsch zum 80. Geburtstag*, ed. Walter Gerstenberg, Jan LaRue, and Wolfgang Rehm (Kassel, 1963), 238–39 (and facsimile between 232 and 233).

earlier version, the serpentine diminutions that embellish the closing strains in the published version are missing. (The two versions are shown in ex. 3.1.) In his notes to the old Breitkopf *Gesamtausgabe*, Mandyczewski, sensitive to "the rough treatment of the weak syllables at the end of both strophes," allowed himself to question the authority of the original edition, published by Cappi and Czerny as op. 60 in 1826.[3] His doubts concerning the fidelity of the print were fed when the text of *Dithyrambe*, the other song published in op. 60, was compared with its autograph. In the print, the five measures with which the piano introduces each strophe are repeated literally at the end as a postlude. In the undated autograph, the postlude is a terse affirmation of the tonic, and nothing more. As with those D-minor chords at the close of *Der Jüngling am Bache* in the setting from 1819, the tactic is to block any further sense of *da capo*. The authority of the autograph is what Mandyczewski valued in this instance.

Example 3.1 *Greisengesang* (D. 778), mm. 89–95 (voice alone), in two versions

Mandyczewski did not know the autograph of *Greisengesang* that Gerstenberg had before him (it is now at the Staatsbibliothek der Stiftung Preußischer Kulturbesitz in Berlin), so the appeal of this coincidence between Mandyczewski's intuition and what might now be taken as corroborative support in the form of that most persuasive of documents, the composer's autograph, was irresistible. For Gerstenberg, the fioriture "seem stranger and stranger as one grows familiar with the original melody."[4]

But there are *two* autographs that preserve the *Greisengesang*. The fair copy in the Vienna Stadtbibliothek is very much closer to the version that Cappi and Diabelli published.[5] And this led Gerstenberg to wonder whether the mo-

3. *Revisionsbericht*, ser. 20, p. 97 (Dover reprint ed., 19:333).

4. "Wie mag es zu den Fiorituren gekommen sein, die mehr und mehr befremden, sobald man sich in die ursprüngliche Weise eingelebt hat? Vor allem aber: Hat Schubert sie tatsächlich gebilligt, oder sind sie Konzession an Sänger und Publikum?" (Gerstenberg, "*Schubertiade*," 239).

5. The dating of the two autographs—neither of which bears a date in Schubert's hand—and the relationship between the Vienna Stadtbibliothek MH 1862/c and the Cappi print are con-

tivation to compose these fioriture should be construed as a genuine act or rather as a "Konzession an Sänger und Publikum."

This second autograph, the fair copy in Vienna, is an intriguing document. It seems to have been written out in 1826, in a "Konvolut" of two gatherings containing similarly clean copies of *Der Wanderer* (D. 649) and *Du liebst mich nicht* (D. 756) and on paper of a rare sort, imprinted "C. Hennigsches Notenpapier No. 2. Prag, bei Halla & Comp."[6] *Dithyrambe* (D. 801), the song finally published with *Greisengesang*, was written out on this kind of paper as well but has survived as a single leaf, not part of the "Konvolut" (Deutsch describes it as a "Reinschrift" and Walter Dürr, distinguishing it from the *Reinschriften* in the *Konvolut*, as an "erste Niederschrift"}.[7] What is of interest here is that, while the Cappi and Czerny print was announced for publication on 10 June 1826, a date that squares well with Winter's dating of the watermark of this "Hennigsches Notenpapier," and while the Vienna *Konvolut* gives every impression of a collection assembled, and written cleanly, in preparation for the engraver's work, the texts of the print and the *Reinschrift* differ from one another in more than the details that might be attributed to a copyist's negligence.

In one or two instances, variants found in the Vienna manuscript of *Greisengesang* come perilously close to the kinds of embellishments claimed to have been added in performance by Johann Michael Vogl. Two such passages are shown in example 3.2, alongside two characteristic passages from *Antigone und Oedip*, perhaps the best known, if most extreme, of Vogl's embellished versions.

Vogl's collaborations with Schubert, beginning in 1817, are well known both through anecdotal report and in documentary evidence, the most important of which is to be found in Vogl's *Singbücher*, once in Max Friedlaender's possession, surviving now only in copy.[8] How Vogl's embellishments might be factored into a concept of text—even whether they ought to be—is a much vexed question that extends beyond the pale of pure text to the broader issue of performance as an aspect of text. That is in part because we can only guess at the accuracy with which such written embellishments reflect what Vogl might have sung in this or that performance. We might even ask how it is that Vogl thought it appropriate to freeze an embellished version in writing, as though it were the authentic text itself, for, even if Vogl meant only to serve himself with a kind of *aide mémoire*, the transmission of "his" Schubert

---

tested matters. On the basis of its watermark, Robert Winter ("Paper Studies," 226) argues that the Vienna manuscript dates from 1826, not, as Hilmar maintains, 1822 (see Ernst Hilmar, *Verzeichnis der Schubert-Handschriften in der Musiksammlung der Wiener Stadt- und Landesbibliothek* [Vienna, 1978]). Winter would date the Berlin manuscript to within the months January–May 1823, again on the basis of its watermark.

6. Hilmar, *Verzeichnis*, 73–74.

7. Deutsch, *Thematisches Verzeichnis*, 501; Dürr, *NGA*, ser. 4, vol. 3b, pp. 283–84.

8. See Walter Dürr, "Schubert and Johann Michael Vogl: A Reappraisal," *19th Century Music* 3, no. 2 (November 1979): 126–40 and, on the *Singbücher*, 130.

Example 3.2 *a*, *Greisengesang*, mm. 8–11, 41–47, the ornamented version shown in the Vienna MS. *b*, *Antigone und Oedip* (D. 542), mm. 3–4, 16–18, the version with Vogl's ornamentation shown above the version in the first published edition

quickly assumed status as something more. The ephemeral quality that is inherent in such embellishment is hardened into something enduring and thus becomes a part of the text in a way that cannot have been intended.

Dürr's argument for printing Vogl's embellishments, where they exist, as appendices in the Lieder volumes of the *Neue Ausgabe* is in the service of "an edition which interprets the performance guidelines of Schubert's time, thereby aiding the performer in his search for an interpretation suitable to the work." For Dürr, Vogl's embellishments "were characteristic for Schubert's time, and Schubert surely accepted his songs as embellished by Vogl just as readily as his friends did. But it is also true that Vogl's embellishments were improvised, non-essential alterations, and as such would never have been written out by Schubert, much less published."[9]

9. Ibid., 140.

We may think that the categorical distinction between essential and "non-essential" alteration is a simple matter of definition. It is not. Each piece—certainly, each Schubert song—encodes its own limits, dictates in its style to what degree even the most trivial of ornaments might be permitted without violation of the *text* of the work. But there is a deeper issue here. "The musical impulse behind Vogl's embellished versions would be lost entirely were today's singers to reproduce them literally, as if they were authentic versions of Schubert's song," Dürr warns. "Contemporary examples can convey the type and manner of embellishment appropriate to Schubert's Lieder, clarifying the principles involved. Simply repeating the ornaments found in contemporary copies would unwittingly raise these alterations to the status of composed ones, and hence would become part of the work itself."[10] But surely the instance of performance is, by some understanding, an expression of the text of the work—is the work itself. The variables of performance—and here I wish to isolate the kinds of embellishments that seem to have characterized Vogl's performances—may either reinforce what we take, by definition, to constitute the text of the work or contradict and subvert the text. Just how to discriminate the one from the other is not always self-evident, and that is because performance is by its nature subject to the shifting ephemera of taste and style.

Vogl, nearly thirty years older than Schubert and much the more celebrated of the two, having been engaged at the Vienna Court Opera as early as 1794, may have had other motives in situating himself in the substance of Schubert's music. Perhaps Schober's wicked caricature—the inflated Vogl walking several paces ahead of a dwarfed, diffident Schubert—tells us something about the dynamics of their musical partnership as well.[11] Nor has it been suggested that these habits of performance might belong to another age—even in the 1790s they were probably antiquated—and to a genre (opera) where such embellishment was once obligatory. Do Vogl's alterations speak to a concept of performance in tune with Schubert's Lieder, even as early as 1817? Or is there a discrepancy here that the dynamics of performance in the Schubert circle served only to exacerbate?

Even if the variants in *Greisengesang* were, like the Vogl embellishments, conceived as an indulgence for the performer, they are now irretrievably "in the text." Schubert, we may suspect, tolerated Vogl's idiosyncrasies in performance because to do otherwise would have been to jeopardize what was on balance a fruitful collaboration that served in the public aspect of his career—an aspect that he himself seemed capable only of undermining.

The Vogl embellishments are surely worth something as evidence of how the Schubert circle, for better or worse, encountered the songs in performance. But to take these embellishments as prescriptions for a more general

10. Ibid.

11. The drawing, often reproduced, can be seen in *Franz Schubert: Ausstellung der Wiener Stadt- und Landesbibliothek zum 150. Todestag des Komponisten*, ed. Ernst Hilmar and Otto Brusatti (Vienna, 1978), 164. An earlier sketch for it was published in *Franz Schuberts Briefe und Schriften*, ed. Otto Erich Deutsch (Munich, 1919), following p. 74.

theory of performance is to mistake the idiosyncrasies of an aging and by some accounts eccentric singer—with all respect for his widely acclaimed powers of dramatic expression—for the principles of style.

This is not the place to tease out all the evidence behind a determination of some textually definitive version of the two songs finally published in op. 60.[12] Yet these deviant variants address, if obliquely, the very issue that concerns Rosen. Even if we had the evidence to demonstrate that the Cappi and Czerny texts are Schubert's texts through and through, the question remains: Are the emendations toward a public, published text to be understood as authorized in any but the most routine sense? I am not of course suggesting that the text of *Greisengesang* in op. 60 be repudiated. Indeed, its credentials are enhanced in the company of the Vienna autograph. As an instance of revision, the florid surface of the song seems more an effort to preempt those kinds of embellishments that singers like Vogl would otherwise have applied in blithe self-indulgence. I mean only to suggest that, in fixing such embellishments in the print, Schubert guarantees an integrity between surface and structure, between performance and text, that is otherwise vulnerable to the vagaries of the singer. The variants finally published in *Greisengesang* may owe something to embellishments once sung by Vogl, filtered now through the composer's ear. Even if the evidence were at hand to prove the point, the questions raised by Mandyczewski and Gerstenberg will not go away. To establish the credentials of the text, its authority, and even its priority in a stemma of sources—to engage in textual criticism, that is—is only to construct a base of evidence. The critic begins not here but rather (Mandyczewski-like) with his intuition. Where the textual evidence seems tightest, it is more likely to conceal a truth, and that is why the critic must begin as though nothing had been proved.

If these variants in *Greisengesang* bother us, we may seek comfort in the thought that, acquiescing to external pressure, Schubert vitiates something striking and elemental in the original conception. But of course we do not know in this instance whether the revision was in fact prompted by a concession to public taste and the exigencies of local performance habits or whether such revision only appears to have been so—whether, that is, our own critical sensibilities prefer to understand a revision as rooted in some cause that might relieve Schubert of any genuine engagement in the process. But even if the question of motivation could be answered, Schubert cannot be absolved of responsibility. The song, in all its three versions, remains his, even when the composer and the editor in him are at odds.

II

The revisions superimposed in pencil on the autograph of *Die Götter Griechenlands* (D. 677) raise the stakes to a higher level. Less to do with the

12. The evidence—or, at any rate, a listing of variants—is to be found in the *NGA*, ser. 4, vol. 3b, pp. 281–84.

superficial aspect of performance, these revisions cut to the essential substance of the piece.[13] The song was evidently not submitted for publication. Still, the prospect of publication—the intention to prepare a song for public circulation—here, as elsewhere, seems to have motivated the revision. Again, it is in the final measures of the song that the concept of revision is most keenly tested (see ex. 3.3). The backing off from the irresolute, fundamentally dissonant $^6_4$ with which Schiller's "Schöne Welt, wo bist du?" (Fair world, where are you) is made to echo into eternity is cause for regret. The emendation is made consistently throughout the song. One must wonder whether Schubert, anticipating the bad press, finally thought better of an audacity that might well have drawn the critic's ear to the exclusion of all else, as often happens.[14]

Example 3.3 *Die Götter Griechenlands* (D. 677), the two versions, final measures

More than that, the decision to "close" the song with at least the trace of an affirmative cadence contradicts Schiller's punctuation: the point of interro-

13. The autograph is at the Vienna Stadtbibliothek, MH 2064. For a description, see Hilmar, *Verzeichnis*, 70. Schubert's title is "Strophe von Schiller"; his text is the twelfth strophe of Schiller's *Die Götter Griechenlands*, in the version revised for publication in 1800. In the more vivid language and more vigorously held views of the version published in 1788, the poem generated considerable echo. For an appreciation of it, see Benno von Wiese, "Friedrich von Schiller: Die Götter Griechenlandes," in *Die deutsche Lyrik: Form und Geschichte*, 2 vols., ed. Benno von Wiese (Düsseldorf, 1956), 1:318–35.

14. A passage from the cranky review in the conservative, widely read *Allgemeine Musikalische Zeitung* (24 June 1824, cols. 425–28) on the publication of Schubert's opp. 21–24 is a specimen of what he might have expected: "Whether in Op. 23 No. 1 [*Die Liebe hat gelogen*] the progres-

Example 3.4 *Die Götter Griechenlands*, the two versions, mm. 19–28 (19–27)

gation is now grounded in the tonic. Concomitantly, the revision defeats the strategy in repeating the opening couplet and the plaintive question, repeated a final time, with which the strophe begins, for the repetition at once suspends the strophe, separating it out from the greater context of Schiller's poem and furnishes it with a "self-contained" form. In closing with its opening, the music dwells on Schiller's evocative question, made to reverberate in a cosmic, timeless infinity. In the revision, the effect is traduced.

Less profound, perhaps, but no less challenging, are the emendations that infiltrate into the thematics of the piano part beginning at m. 18, evidently in response to an interstice between the repetition of lines 3 and 4 (see ex. 3.4). There is something pure, uncluttered, and immediate in the retaking of F♯ minor at the beginning of the repetition, and it is a question whether the new phrase in the piano diminishes the appeal of the moment. The phrase generates its own repercussions: to maintain the parallelism, it must be repeated, now in A major, replacing the little phrase that originally punctuated the first quatrain.

That little phrase, for all its modesty, had some issue in the song, seeming to flare up again in the very similar, rhythmically cognate phrase with which the piano negotiates between the repetition of lines 5 and 6. An intangible sense of intimacy between these two phrases is sacrificed. But something is gained in the process, for the new echos at mm. 18 and 22–23 now gently evoke the romance of Schiller's nostalgic "Ach, nur in dem Feenland der Lieder. . . ." Further, the "tail" of the echo in m. 23 discourages closure—indeed, leads the singer to the next thought. Suggesting, as it does, an expansion of the opening phrase ("Schöne Welt, wo bist du?"), the two halves of the song, perhaps too clearly articulated in the original version, are now elegantly fused (see ex. 3.5)

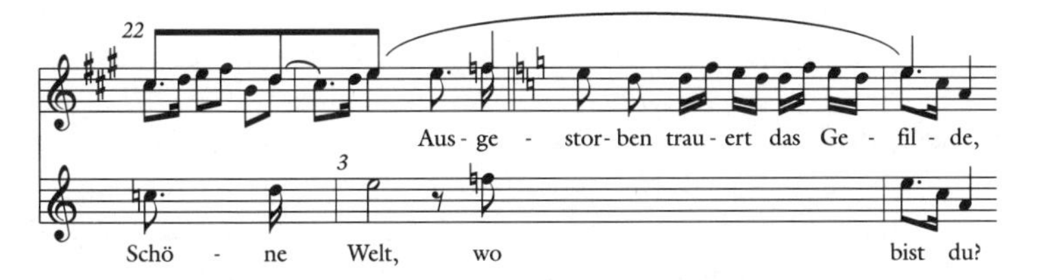

Example 3.5 *Die Götter Griechenlands*, mm. 22–25, shown against the opening phrase

Still, the process of revision seems to tug in two directions. For all that is gained in polish and in the more studied interaction between voice and piano,

sions in the third bar from the end were intentionally written as being truly new and original, although sufficiently hideous, or whether they are misprints, the reviewer dare not venture to decide, for all that he has some reasons to believe the former" (see Otto Erich Deutsch, *The Schubert Reader: The Life of Franz Schubert in Letters and Documents*, trans. Eric Blom [New York, 1947], 479; the German original can be found in Deutsch, *Dokumente*, 244).

something essential in the original inspiration—most of all, the daring of its final harmony—is sacrificed.

Can we date the revision? This is not an idle question, for the Schiller setting of November 1819 is one of a number of exceptionally moving songs from roughly the period 1818–20 where the audacity of the conception, bound in with an intimacy that perhaps touched some deeply personal chord, seems to have discouraged Schubert from seeking publication: the third of the Petrarch Sonnets, "Nunmehr, da Himmel, Erde schweigt" (D. 630, December 1818), *Die Gebüsche* (Friedrich Schlegel; D. 646, January 1819), *Berthas Lied in der Nacht* (Grillparzer; D. 653, February 1819), and *Nachthymne* (Novalis; D. 687, January 1820) come to mind.

The autograph of *Die Götter Griechenlands* is an ambivalent document. Itself a *Reinschrift*, it presupposes some preliminary work—an "erste Niederschrift" that has not survived. And this would encourage the view that these penciled revisions came somewhat later, perhaps years later during one of those periodic harvestings of earlier songs for publication. For Schubert, the sketching in pencil of ideas toward a revision is itself a rare and tentative sign. As it stands, the emended text is not easy to read, and it is even unclear whether Schubert meant for it to be read.

The fact is that these ideas toward a revision did not issue in a second *Reinschrift*. That, too, is atypical. And so one must question whether the version published by Diabelli and consequently taken as the preferred text is in effect a distortion of the evidence—a well-meaning one, but a distortion nonetheless.[15] Surely, this draft toward a revised version has much to commend it. But it remained a draft, and, while we cannot know why it remained so, the circumstances invite us to contemplate Schubert "in irons," stopped by a conflict in judgment. The bold spontaneity of an original conception is tempered in a retreat to the orthodox.

More vexing are those cases where transposition permeates into the infrastructure of the song. In revising a setting of Schiller's *Der Alpenjäger* (D. 588) for publication, Schubert transposed the song from E♭ to C, seemingly to bring low those B♭s that the impatient hunter sings in response to the

15. It is tempting to speculate whether these emendations might stem not from Schubert at all but from Diabelli, who had presumably acquired the autograph with the lot of manuscripts purchased from the estate shortly after Schubert's death. (On the acquisition of the *Nachlaß*, see Deutsch, *Reader*, 901–06.) But Diabelli's scruples as an editor, long under attack, have been defended by Maurice J. E. Brown (see "The Posthumous Publication of the Songs," 275–77). Of the other autographs known to have passed under Diabelli's scrutiny, none bears evidence of editorial emendation of this kind. But *Die Götter Griechenlands* is an exception. The new disposition of the voicing in the opening and closing strains in the piano, the kind of simplification that editors seek out, is not among the penciled emendations, and this is at once evidence that Diabelli did indeed tinker with Schubert's text, that his engraver very likely worked from a specially made *Stichvorlage*, but that the revisions in pencil are Schubert's, not Diabelli's. Revisions in pencil are altogether rare among Schubert's manuscripts. Another exceptional case, both the "erste Neiderschrift" and the "Reinschrift" of *Der zürnenden Diana*, both dated December 1820, show penciled emendations (see *NGA*, ser. 4, vol. 2b, pp. 312–14; and Hilmar, *Verzeichnis*, 71).

mother's complaint.[16] In the second of its three grand scenes, the hunter pursues the gazelle in its trek across the mountain to a rocky precipice, an action narrated in four vivid strophes and set to an entirely new music in B major. The appearance of a hoary mountain sage is sudden and unexpected:

Plötzlich aus der Felsenspalte
Tritt der Geist, der Bergesalte.

(Suddenly, from the cleft in the rocks steps the ancient mountain spirit.)

At the point of interruption, the music has enacted a transient cadence in A major, heard locally as an elaboration around ♭VI in C♯ minor, which, in earlier strophes, is logically absorbed in the return to B major. But here, at the edge of the supernatural, the music breaks off altogether.

The narrative, now in bardic, declamatory accents, announces the apparition. Its tonal deployment is bold, disruptive, yet coherent (see ex. 3.6a). The precarious cadence around A major—the bow drawn taut—is deflected. The effect is not that the arrow has misfired but that some firm hand now guides it.

When the song was transposed down a minor third for publication (as op. 37, no. 2) in 1825, the closing section, beginning with the declamatory music at "Plötzlich aus der Felsenspalte," was set a perfect fourth *higher* and without any intermediary music to renegotiate the breach from that wayward, hanging cadence, which now sounds in G♭ major (see ex. 3.6b). In explanation, it has been claimed that Schubert had originally two singers in mind: a low voice for "der Bergesalte," a high one for the other parts.[17] The internal transposition in the published version, bringing the "Bergesalte" up into a tessitura that lies more comfortably with the music of the earlier strophes of the song, is taken as evidence that Schubert now thought better of a division of labor between two different singers—something that indeed might limit the publisher's market for the song.

The "two singer" hypothesis is an interesting one, and yet troubling in that the evidence for it is contrived in speculation. Schubert's notation simply does not specify a change of voice. This is not as trivial a complaint as it might seem, for to accept the view that a shift in register, aligned with a shift in poetic voice, is a coded signal for the entry of a second singer is to accept as well

16. On the complicated reconstruction of sources for the two versions, see *NGA*, ser. 4, vol. 2b, pp. 317–18. Pertinent here is that the autograph containing the first version is incomplete, breaking off at m. 34, *before* the contested passage at mm. 72–73, and that a fragmentary copy from the *Nachlaß* of Heinrich Kreißle von Hellborn, based on a manuscript of "Fragmenten aus Franz Schuberts eigenhändig geschriebenem Nachlasse" (now missing), contains the earlier version, but breaks off at m. 60. The original version must be deduced from a handwritten leaf attached to a copy of the original edition contained in the collection Witteczek-Spaun and from a copy in the Sammlung Spaun-Cornaro, which must have been based on the revised autograph but which preserves the key relationships attributed to the original version.

17. The notion was first expressed by Mandyczewski in the *Revisionsbericht* (1897) to the old *Gesamtausgabe* (ser. 20, p. 69 [Dover reprint ed., 19:305]).

Example 3.6 *Der Alpenjäger* (D. 588). *a*, Earlier version, mm. 43–51. *b*, Published version, mm. 68–76

that Schubert intended such a division in a good many other songs even though nothing in his notation confirms that intention. In the case of *Alpenjäger*, the matter is further confounded. To imply, as Mandyczewski surely does, that the second voice would take up at the lines "Plötzlich aus der

Felsenspalte"—that is, at the point where the transposition is cued in—is to violate the integrity of the narrator's role. More than that, the personification of the "Bergesalte" in the new singer abrogates the very convention, inherent in Lied, whereby one and the same singer must personify all the speaking roles. Multiple role playing of this kind—*Erlkönig* is the locus classicus—is innate in the genre.

The issue was smartly addressed by Thrasybulos Georgiades, who makes a fundamental distinction between the "singer" resident in the poem and the competent musician who actually sings the song ("zwischen dem 'Sänger' der Dichtung und dem zünftigen Musiker-Sänger").[18] The singer *in* the poem steps in and out of the personae who figure in the tale; he personifies them. That is the privileged role of the ballad singer, and it obtains even in those poems in which the narrator's explanatory text falls away. This is the case in the Claudius poem *Der Tod und das Mädchen*, which Georgiades understands as "eine Art epigrammatischer Extrakt einer balladeske Erzählung."[19]

To attack the *idea* that role taking in the poem is a signal for performance by more than one singer is to criticize a breach in aesthetics. This is quite distinct from an argument directed at the evidence as to whether Schubert might have had such a device in mind. In fact, the argument for two voices in *Alpenjäger* derives from a coincidental similarity in the circumstances involving the revision of *Der Jüngling und der Tod* (D. 545), composed seven months earlier, in March 1817.[20] Spaun's poem, like *Der Tod und das Mädchen*, which it parodies, is a literal dialogue. Here again, while Schubert's notation does not rule out a performance by two singers, it does not encourage it either. And, here too, a substantial revision by the composer—again, an internal transposition in essence—obliterates the spacing by tessitura of a dramatic opposition.

Considerably more is at stake than a problem in the performance of the song—whether, that is, the song should be sung by one singer or two—for, in both cases, the revision plays havoc with the structure of the song and even with the immediate conduct of its harmonies at a juncture where such conduct is of signal importance.

The two versions of *Der Jüngling und der Tod* have sparked considerable interest, for, in the revised music for its closing section, Schubert now clinches in musical quotation the indebtedness of Spaun's poem to its antecedent—an antecedent that everyone around Schubert would have had in mind from the outset. *Der Tod und das Mädchen* was composed only a month earlier, and it

18. Thrasybulos G. Georgiades, *Schubert: Musik und Lyrik* (Göttingen, 1967), 208.

19. "A kind of epigrammatic extract from a ballad-like tale" (ibid., 208).

20. It was Mandyczewski who drew attention to the parallel between the two songs (see *Revisionsbericht*, ser. 20, p. 61 [Dover reprint ed., 19:297]). The revision, Mandyczewski claimed, was made for practical reasons, "damit das Lied auch von *einer* Stimme gut ausführbar sei. Denn wie es ursprünglich niedergeschrieben wurde, war das Stück für eine hohe und eine tiefe Stimme gedacht" (so that the song could be performed equally well by a *single* voice. For the piece, as it was originally written down, was conceived for a high and a low voice).

seems perfectly reasonable to assume that a performance of it was the inspiration for Spaun's poem. In the new music for the revised close, Schubert introduces the telltale dactyls that evoke the opening bars of *Der Tod und das Mädchen*, leading Christoph Wolff to venture that Schubert had "first tried to avoid too close references" to the earlier song.[21] A curious notion. The two songs are blatantly different in every respect. Still, it is difficult to imagine Schubert motivated in the conceiving of song by some negative constraint of this sort. The bolder question is whether, even in its provocative allusion to another song, the revision can be taken altogether as an improvement.

Here it would be good to recall that *Der Jüngling und der Tod* is one of a number of songs, mostly from the years 1815–17, that begin and end in different keys. In some of the longer ones, the sheer expanse of the tonal landscape discourages any rational exegesis that might tell how the end is forecast in the beginning or the beginning justified in the end.[22] But *Der Jüngling und der Tod* is very different in this regard, and of such intense focus that the few measures after the fermata at m. 23, and the emphatic diminished seventh chord at the second half of m. 25 especially, will be heard as transformational, playing on a construct that guides the harmonic track of the song from its opening bars (see ex. 3.7). Taken in fullest context, the diminished seventh at m. 25 suggests itself as an inflection of the dominant ninths in both C♯ minor and E major/minor, the tonal dichotomy from which the song springs. In the eloquence of m. 26, D♯ is transformed to E♭, clinching finally the move to G minor implicit in the music just prior to the fermata.

Indeed, this new deflection away to G minor responds (as "Der Jüngling" perhaps hoped it would not) to the thrice-asked dominant at mm. 22–24. The A with which the "Jüngling" breaks off at "o komm!"—a pitch that is virtually sustained and intensified over the following interlude—is led finally to the G with which "Der Tod" announces itself. For the singer—singers, if one must have two of them—this physical connection is powerful. The breach between *Jüngling* and *Tod* is illusory. The one is the ineffable sequel to the other. The paradox of death as an aspect of life is somehow captured in the logical deceptions of the harmonies here.

All this is lost in the revision (shown in ex. 3.8). To sing the entrance of "Der Tod" directly after the cadence at "o komm" is to feel the difference between the two versions, the breach of harmonic syntax, with painful clarity.

21. Christoph Wolff, "Schubert's 'Der Tod und das Mädchen': Analytical and Explanatory Notes on the Song D 531 and the Quartet D 810," in *Schubert Studies: Problems of Style and Chronology*, 154.

22. The extreme case actually dates from 1818. The setting of Mayrhofer's *Einsamkeit*, a song that Schubert, in a letter dated 3 August 1818, called "mein Bestes, was ich gemacht habe" (the finest that I have written), deploys its cantata-like scenario across the full tonal spectrum, matching the panoramic views of Mayrhofer's epic romance. Paul Mies (*Schubert: Der Meister des Liedes: Die Entwicklung von Form und Inhalt im Schubertschen Lied* [Berlin, 1928], 200) understands Schubert's high estimation of the song as a sign that it represented the culmination of certain dramatic tendencies toward which Schubert strives in a good many songs from 1817.

Example 3.7 *Der Jüngling und der Tod* (D. 545), early version, mm. 1–9, 23–33

Example 3.8 *Der Jüngling und der Tod*, later version, mm. 23–34

Yet one gives up the exquisite new postlude (the final measures in the piano) reluctantly. The interstice between "Der Jüngling" and "Der Tod" is of inspiring beauty—provided that we do not think too hard about the lapse in coherence between "o komm!" and "Es ruht sich kühl."

It may well be that Schubert was led to transpose the music of "Der Tod" in response to a criticism directed at the difficult ambitus for the voice and—bound up in the same issue—on recognizing that the song was better served by one singer than by two.[23] And perhaps it was Spaun himself who wondered aloud whether some reference to the dactyls in *Der Tod und das Mädchen* might not heighten the effect. All the same, there is a perceptible loss in con-

23. The setting of Mayrhofer's *Antigone und Oedip* (D. 542, 1817) throws the issue into relief. In Schubert's autograph and in Hüttenbrenner's contemporary copy, the music of the two protagonists is notated in different clefs. In this instance, the poem is an operatic *scena*, and that is how Schubert imagined it. But in Vogl's copy, richly ornamented for performance (see ex. 3.2b above), the song is recast in a single clef, and this was how Cappi and Diabelli published the song in 1821. Opus 6 was in fact dedicated to Vogl.

centration here, to the point where the revision may be said to have severed an essential thread of continuity that runs through the original concept.

The revision in *Der Alpenjäger*—a mechanical transposition—is yet more extreme. The finely tuned hearing that governs the interruption at "Plötzlich" is obliterated. Indeed, the very attack at m. 48 is a symptom of the fundamental difference that is at stake here (see ex. 3.6 above). Again, as in the analogous passage in *Der Jüngling und der Tod*, the tone left hanging at the end of the first section is sustained and embellished, a kind of recitation tone, and resolved, finally, at the onset of the new music at m. 52. The harmony at m. 48 will be heard for the moment as yet another ♭VI, echoing the cardinal relationships in the song (for the B major of the middle strophes is approached from the dominant in E♭ as though it were C♭, as a temporary ♭VI). Even the grave intonations of the mountain spirit—"Mußt du Tod und Jammer senden . . . bis herauf zu mir?" (Must you send death and misery up here to me?)—dwell on F♯ as a dominant, giving ironic echo to the overriding B major of the middle strophes.

When the song was revised for publication, the rift at "Plötzlich" was made considerably more extreme—at the expense of all coherence. No singer will welcome the sacrifice of a continuity ensured by the common tone that prepares "Plötzlich"; the identity of pitch only heightens the shift in scene here. Indeed, as a consequence of the transposition of the song to C major, to have retained the common tone would have meant generating an uncomfortable enharmonic identity: the G♭ must become F♯. A relationship perfectly normal in an original conception is rendered bizarre in transposition.

In the revision, the thread snaps. The voicing of the two contiguous harmonies, root-position triads on G♭ and G, delivers up the kind of parallelism that assaults any sense of logical connection. The B♮ cannot be heard to follow from its antecedents. Nor can the cadence at "Bergesalte" be understood to reinterpret the hanging cadence at "legt er schon den Bogen an."

There is some evidence that the decision to transpose the closing music in the version that was published by Cappi in 1825 was in fact contested—if not by Schubert, then by his colleagues. In the collection of early editions and handwritten copies known as Witteczek-Spaun, the first edition of op. 37 contains with it a handwritten leaf of the closing music beginning at the "Langsam," agreeing in all detail with the published version, but transposed to begin on D—preserving, that is, the relationships that obtain in the earlier version. Mandyczewski, who discovered the leaf—but was entirely unaware of the original version for the closing music—was nevertheless struck by the logic of the handwritten alternative. "Es ist nicht unmöglich," he writes, "daß das ein früherer Versuch Schubert's war, das Erscheinen und die Stimme des Bergesalten zu charakterisiren. Jedenfalls schließ sich diese Partie auf diese Weise dem Vorhergehenden harmonisch besser an."[24]

24. "It is not impossible that this was an earlier attempt by Schubert to characterize the apparition and the voice of the 'Bergesalter.' In any case, in this fashion the section makes a better

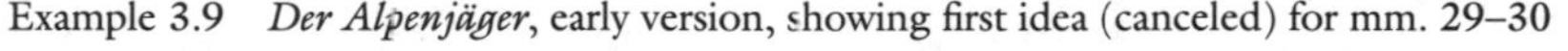
Example 3.9 *Der Alpenjäger*, early version, showing first idea (canceled) for mm. 29–30

Example 3.10 *Der Alpenjäger*, hypothetical extension in the earlier version

In his description of the earlier fragment, Mandyczewski called attention to a striking revision at a critical juncture in the song (see ex. 3.9).[25] The original thought, deleted in the manuscript, sets off waves of speculation as to how Schubert might have envisioned the music that would follow when this passage was to come round again at "legt er schon den Bogen an" (see ex. 3.10). The chain of relationships generated in the shifting of the closing music up a semitone is at once evocative and convincing, and it is very difficult to say whether the decision to tame the passage at mm. 29–31, restraining it within the sphere of the subdominant once removed, serves the larger design as well as what is implied in the original conception. Perhaps the brightening suggested in this motion *up* a semitone was perceived to violate the sense of the text in each of these three strophes:

harmonic connection with its antecedent" (*Revisionsbericht*, ser. 20, p. 69 [Dover reprint ed., 19:305]).

25. Ibid.

Strophe
4 . . . an des Berges finstern Ort,
5 . . . trägt sie der gewagte Sprung,
6 . . . und verschwunden ist der Pfad.

(4: . . . to the dark place of the mountain; 5: . . . her bold spring carries her; 6: . . . and the path vanishes.)

One might regret that at the analogous line in the seventh strophe—"legt er schon den Bogen an"—Schubert did not seize the opportunity to crank up the tension a notch, calling forth the original inflection repressed at mm. 29–31. But to have taken that option here would have constituted a transgression of another kind, a violation of the strophic rule. Complying with the rule has its deeper ramifications, for the ambiguities around mm. 29–31 are now illuminated in the new directions taken at m. 48. Finally, a return to the tonic (E♭ major) for the epilogue at "Und mit seinen Götterhänden," the inevitable consequence of this hypothetical plotting out from the rejected mm. 29–31, is hard to justify, and it may have struck Schubert all at once that any whiff of tonal reprise at this point is simply untenable.

Example 3.11 *Der Wanderer* (D. 489). *a*, Earlier version, mm. 20–23, 61–68

(Whether the epilogue was to have ended in the subdominant, as it does in the finished version, or in the tonic—this the fragmentary manuscript cannot tell us.)

It must be said that the authority for the version published by Cappi remains obscure: the autograph of the revision has never surfaced. Consequently, we cannot know beyond a doubt that the internal transposition conveyed in the Cappi print owes to a deliberate alteration on Schubert's part. At the same time, there can be little doubt that Schubert prepared an improved version of the song for publication. This is clear from all those subtle details in the voicing of the accompaniment that are lacking in the early autograph. But until this second autograph is retrieved, we cannot know whether the text of the version now accepted as the authoritative one was entirely the work of Schubert.

Internal transposition is an extreme response to the conflict between an original conception and a tendency to rein in the voice to an ambitus that singer and publisher would find comfortable. Less extreme, the revisions imposed on the original version of *Der Wanderer* (D. 489, 1816) are nonetheless provocative. When the song was revised for publication, two passages were slightly emended, plainly for the comfort of the singer (see ex. 3.11).

Example 3.11, cont. *b*, Later version, mm. 20–23, 61–68

(Further, the final two bars in the voice, originally notated in bass clef, are "normalized." There is no substantive change here, and Schubert's notation may even be taken as evidence that a breaking of the part into two clefs does not necessarily signal performance by two singers.) In effect, very much more is at stake here than a singer's discomfort. The striking embellishment at m. 22 is worth a moment's reflection. Especially piquant when the voice is a tenor (and not a soprano), the cross-relation between the F♯ in the voice and the F𝄪 in the piano is a dissonance with firm theoretical support, pointing up the ambivalence of the so-called French and German augmented sixths and at the same time developing a fine motivic play within the cadence (see ex. 3.12). When the F♯ is expunged in the revision, the repetition of the augmented sixth loses all nuance. The passage is flat. Indeed, the F♯ seems innate in the rhetoric of the passage, born of a concomitant liberty in the poetic text. The quatrains in Schmidt's poem comprise simple iambic tetrameters. The "immer wo," not a contiguous pair in Schmidt, is rather Schubert's conflation of the line, so the heightened dissonance is to the point.

Example 3.12 *Der Wanderer*, earlier version, mm. 20–22, abstracted

When the passage comes round again at mm. 62–63, the consequences of the revision are striking. In the original, the singer must reach down to a low G♯. The sixth that generates the phrase at "Im Geisterhauch tönt's mir zurück" plays eloquently on the same interval, pitched an octave higher, in the preceding line. The ghostly octaves clinch the connection. So it comes as something of a shock to discover that this low G♯—and, consequently, the telling interval that springs from it—is expunged in the published version. The loss is compounded because it is clear that the connection to the low G#—even the rhythmic relationship—is meant to play on the connection at the analogous fermata back at m. 22, where an isolated G♯ is anacrusis to the famous strain at "Die Sonne dünkt mich hier so kalt." There is yet another consequence of the revision, for the dissonant F♯ resolving locally to a higher-order dissonance in the augmented sixth itself is in effect played out in the great arch of melody that springs from that low G♯ (sketched out in ex. 3.13).

The bold concept is not always the earliest. Tellingly, the autograph of 1816 shows that the cross-relation at m. 21 grew from some doubts about an earlier reading that in effect agrees with the measure in the printed version: the F♯ was originally a D♯.[26] The parallel passage at m. 63 shows an emenda-

26. *NGA*, ser. 4, vol. 1, *Quellen und Lesarten*, p. 10.

Example 3.13 *Der Wanderer*, earlier version, mm. 62–68, analytic sketch

Example 3.14 *Der Wanderer*, Stadler copy, mm. 21–22, 63–64

tion that must have been made retrospectively, perhaps in conjunction with the revision for publication. The alteration, made in pencil, moves in the direction of the printed version. In the light of all this indecision—and perhaps inspired by it—the version of mm. 21–22 and 63–64 as it is preserved in Albert Stadler's copy, surely prepared from *some* autograph of 1816, speaks volumes (see ex. 3.14).[27] Is it that Stadler, confronting the ambivalence in the manuscript, chose rather a line of less resistance? Or might we imagine that Stadler's access was to an even earlier source—or to the autograph that we have, but at some earlier stage in its genesis?[28] This latter might better explain why Stadler inserted rests in the voice and hints that, in some *Urlied*, Schubert remained faithful to Schmidt's text.[29]

IV

> The first version shows the piece as it originally sprang up in Schubert's imagination, the second as he adjusted it for practical use. One might be inclined to take this for the work of the publisher, were it not the case that Schubert, in all the freedom of composing, never lost sight of the practical.[30]

27. *NGA*, ser. 4, vol. 1b, pp. 201, 203.

28. "Ich habe sie in der Regel immer gleichsam noch vom nassen Blatte kopirt" (As a rule, I always copied them directly from the wet page). This was how Stadler, in 1858, recalled his activity in the years 1814 and 1815. The volume containing *Der Wanderer* was inscribed "Stadler. 1817" on the cover; we need not take that date to apply to the copying but rather to the year in which the album was assembled (see Dürr, *Franz Schuberts Werke in Abschriften*, 25, 30; see also Siegfried Mühlhäuser, *Die Handschriften und Varia der Schubertiana-Sammlung Taussig in der Universitätsbibliothek Lund* [Wilhelmshaven, 1981], 59–62).

29. A third version of the song has survived, an undated copy in Schubert's hand, showing the song transposed down to B minor. The wisdom in the *NGA* is that it was prepared during the summer of 1818, during Schubert's sojourn in Zseliz (see *NGA*, ser. 4, vol. 1a, p. xxi, and, for the song itself, vol. 1b, pp. 204–7).

30. "Die erste Bearbeitung zeigt das Stück, wie es ursprünglich Schubert's Geiste entsproß; die zweite, wie er es für praktischen Gebrauch herrichtete. Man könnte geneigt sein, diese für eine

Mandyczewski's taste for the spontaneity of an original concept, his mistrust of the meddling editorial hand, was stimulated in this instance by the setting of Jacobi's *Lied des Orpheus, als er in die Hölle ging* (D. 474), composed in September 1816.[31] Indeed, the evidence for Schubert's hand in the revision is inferential, and the survival of the original version in all the other authenticated copies only contributes to the grounds for suspicion. Still, the revision is a complicated one, and an evaluation of its substance seems in order all the more because the circumstances under which it was prepared are unclear.

The original version demands an uncommonly agile voice, one that must sing with equal confidence in the upper and lower limits of the tenor range—from high A at the climactic moments to the A♭ two octaves and a semitone below it. In addressing these extremes of range, the revision, no simple transposition, cuts deeply into the infrastructure of the song.

The principal theater of revision begins at the fifth strophe and continues up to the massive cadence in the middle of the seventh strophe, at "bricht ein Strahl von Hoffnung" (a beam of hope breaks through), which plants the music at the threshold of a final *stretta*. (The two versions are shown in ex. 3.15.) At two locations, the process of revision is especially palpable. The less striking of the two is at the approach to the poignant line "O, ich sehe Thränen fließen" (Oh, I see tears flowing). On the face of it, there is not much to choose between the two versions. The set phrase itself is unchanged, a simple transposition to the third below. But the very fine approach to "O, ich sehe," where the descant in the piano literally guides the voice to its inevitable D♯, is replaced by a routine cadence that renders the entrance of the voice as an intrusion. The resolution of the cadence is disturbed. The *ritardando* only exacerbates the breach.

Jacobi's text seems not to justify a rhetorical *interruptio* here but wants, rather, a compassion that grows from the previous strophe. That seems to have been the point in the flow of pitches in the interlude between the strophes. In the original version, the phrase at "O, ich sehe Thränen fließen" is embraced in that flow. In the revision, the interlude is extended several measures to accommodate a shift in the ratio of transposition. But the mechanics of the modulation turn against the integrity of the passage, now badly damaged.

More striking still is the revision affecting the articulation between strophes 5 and 6. This is a critical moment in the poem, and it must be said that a textual confusion here has led to some misunderstanding in the construing of it. The two strophes in Jacobi's text go this way:

Arbeit . . . des Verlegers . . . zu halten, wenn man nicht wüßte, daß Schubert bei aller Freiheit des Componirens die Rücksicht auf das Praktische nie verlor" (*Revisionsbericht*, ser. 20, p. 52 [Dover reprint ed., 19:288]).

31. The song was first published by Diabelli in the posthumous series, the *Nachlass Lieferung*, [vol.] 19, in 1832; this is the year tentatively ascribed by Dürr to the copy in Witteczek-Spaun, on the slender argument that these albums tended to exclude works already in print (see *Franz Schuberts Werke in Abschriften*, 74–75, 92).

5 Meine Klage tönt in eure Klage;
Weit von hier geflohen ist das Glück;
Aber denkt an jene Tage,
Schaut in jene Welt zurück!

6 Wenn ihr da nur einen Leidenden umarmtet,
O, so fühlt die Wollust noch einmal,
Und der Augenblick, in dem ihr euch erbarmtet,
Lindre diese lange Qual.

7 O, ich sehe Thränen fließen! . . .

My lament sounds in yours;
Happiness has fled far from here;
But remember those days,
Look back to that world!

If you embraced there even one sufferer,
O, then once more know desire,
And may that moment in which you felt pity
Soothe this long torment.

O, I see tears flowing. . . .

In the original conception, Schubert seizes the interstice between strophes 5 and 6 as the moment of uncontrolled passion in Orpheus's song, for these lines, addressed to the long-suffering tenants of the underworld, in fact express a torment that Orpheus himself feels only too keenly: the loss of that state of sensual pleasure that comes only from the experience of deeply felt and reciprocal love.[32]

The phrase at "Wenn ihr da nur einen Leidenden umarmtet," taken emphatically *without* breath, deliberately underarticulated, soars to the high A in a swift *crescendo* from a *fortissimo.* The revision may well have been prompted by some pleading from Schubert's overly taxed singer—or by a downright failure in performance. Still, it shows new respect for the syntax of the poem. Intentionally or not, Orpheus reclaims his composure. Unquestionably, the revision gains in the polish of the keyboard writing and in the interplay between piano and voice, even while we may deplore the deflation of the phrase at the beginning of strophe 6. But, in the end, whether or not we agree that the revision is closer in mood to Jacobi's Orpheus, the original intensity that drove one phrase to the next is now cooled.

Similarly, Schubert may have been well advised to end the ecstatic music of the coda with a bang—as he does indeed in the revision—but, in the process,

32. The verbs in lines 1 and 3 are clearly in the past imperfect, not (as given, e.g., in *The Fischer-Dieskau Book of Lieder*, ed. Dietrich Fischer-Dieskau, trans. George Bird and Richard Stokes [London, 1976], 314) in the present (denoting future), in which the "da" in line 1 would refer to the underworld, not, as it must, to "jene Tage" and "jene Welt" evoked in the previous strophe.

Example 3.15 *Lied des Orpheus, als er in die Hölle ging* (D. 474). *a*, Earlier version, mm. 56–72

Example 3.15, cont. *b*, Later version, mm. 56–75

we lose a genuine *Nachhall*, both in the sense of its harmonic reflection and in what it suggests about the complex ambivalence of the figure of Orpheus in this troubling *scena*.

V

Jacobi's picture of Orpheus descending into the underworld, ministering to its tormented souls, must call to mind Schiller's *Gruppe aus dem Tartarus.* When Schubert composed the famous setting of Schiller's poem in September 1817 (D. 583), he surely had before him (in his ears, if not on paper) a setting composed some eighteen months earlier, in March 1816 (D. 396). This earlier setting is known only in a fragment that breaks off at the text "Schmerz verzerret" at the beginning of the second strophe (shown in ex. 3.16). It was entered on the verso of the final leaf of the autograph of the Violin Sonata in D (op. 137, no. 1).[33] The remaining three leaves of a gathering, which would have contained the completion of the song, have not survived.[34]

The familiar setting (D. 583) is an overpowering one, and any appraisal of the fragment is likely to fall victim to its spell. Still, this earlier setting must count as a signal contribution to the encounter with Schiller's poetry in the spring of 1816—the most audacious of the songs from those months, one might claim. Whether the promise of the surviving fourteen measures will have inspired a song that sustains the grand sweep of the opening is of course not given to us to know.

The audacity of it speaks directly in its opening measures. Schiller's hortatory "Horch" breaks in on a music already in motion, on a dissonance in mid-phrase. In no earlier song and in very few later ones does the voice manage an entry as precipitous as this one.[35]

33. The fragment is shown in facsimile in *Franz Schubert: Sonate für Klavier und Violine D-Dur Opus 137 Nr. 1, D 384: Faksimile nach dem Autograph und einer autographen Abschrift* (Munich, 1988). For a transcription, see the *NGA*, ser. 4, vol. 2b, pp. 271–72.

34. John Reed (*The Schubert Song Companion* [New York 1985], 253) proposes that, while "it is at least possible that the song was completed . . . , more likely Schubert's own poetic insight warned him that he was not yet ready to match the Rembrantesque richness of the poem in music." This is a troubling hypothesis. For one, Schubert seems never to have felt inadequate to a poem to which his aesthetic sensibilities had been drawn. For another, the signs of a concept left incomplete are generally clear enough. See, e.g., the concept for Tieck's *Abend* (D. 645), where only the first few words of text, and only an occasional entry for the piano, are entered in a draft that runs on for some 119 measures.

35. In three Claudius settings from November 1816—*Bei dem Grabe meines Vaters*, *Am Grabe Anselmos*, and *An die Nachtigall*—the voice enters somewhat tentatively in mid-phrase. In *Freiwilliges Versinken* (September 1820), the distracted interjections in Mayrhofer's opening line are set in the midst of a serpentine harmonic sequence that begins away from the tonic. Indeed, the precise opening pitches in the voice are a matter of some dispute (see Brown, "The Posthumous Publication of the Songs," 278). Other complicated and fragile beginnings in mid-phrase are *An die Entfernte* (D. 765), from December 1822, and *Daß sie hier gewesen* (D. 775), presumed to date from 1823.

Example 3.16 *Gruppe aus dem Tartarus* (D. 396), fragment of an earlier setting

Some months earlier, Schubert might have thought to treat these lines in the declamatory style characteristic of many of the settings on themes of classical antiquity. Schiller's *Die Bürgschaft* (D. 246, August 1815) and Klopstock's *Dem Unendlichen* (D. 291, September 1815) come to mind, and so too does Goethe's *Geistes-Gruß* (D. 142; the earliest version, in Stadler's copy, is dated March 1816). Schiller's *Gruppe*, inspired, one may guess, by some Attic frieze, would seem to invite a *scena* in this manner. But Schubert's tactic here is very different. The entire first strophe, complex in diction and syntax, pushes its unlikely subject, the "qualerpreßtes Ach," to the very end. And it is not until this "Ach!" that the music, finding a root-position dominant in E♭ minor, affirms a structural downbeat. The music to the entire strophe seems poured molten from its anguished source, oblivious to the decorum of orthodox root motion and voice leading, indecorous in its four consecutive perfect fifths (hearing the bourdon-like middle tones in the left hand of mm. 3–6 as "real"). We can only speculate how Schubert might have managed to sustain the impetuosity of this feverish opening rush. The one measure that remains of the second strophe hints at a process of dissipation and exhaustion.[36]

The tension of Schiller's language was evidently too much for Schubert, who, in his impatience to capture it, quite mangled the text, omitting the predicate and confusing the actual subject! Schiller's strophe:

> Horch—wie Murmeln des empörten Meeres,
> Wie durch hohler Felsen Becken weint ein Bach
> Stöhnt dort dumpfig-tief ein schweres—leeres,
> Qualerpreßtes Ach!

(Hark! Like murmuring of the rebellious sea, like the brook that cries in the hollowed rocky vortex, a heavy, empty tormented "Ach" groans there from the dank depths.)

is compressed to:

> Horch—wie Murmeln des empörten Meeres,
> wie durch hohler Felsen Becken
> weint ein Bach ein dumpfig tiefes, schweres, leeres,
> qualerpreßtes Ach!

In pushing "weint ein Bach" to the beginning of the third line, I mean to show that Schubert's setting makes a declamatory break between "Becken" and "weint," which further suggests that the syntactic confusion in Schubert's mind occurred precisely here: "weint" assumes the function of Schiller's

36. Maurice J. E. Brown ("Some Unpublished Schubert Songs and Song Fragments," *Music Review* 15 [1954]: 98) proposes that this final measure shows "that the song was 'durchkomponiert.'" But surely the poem itself, composed in three strophes of decidedly unequal measure and prosody, is evidence a priori against a strophic setting. More to the point, the precipitous sweep of the music to the first strophe, collapsing, finally, on the dominant of E♭ minor, is antithetical to strophic repetition.

"stöhnt," and the shift forces on "Bach" the role of subject; the final "Ach" is transformed to an object. The meaning of the poem is thoroughly corrupted.[37]

The error, so grievous that it must count as the principal reason for the suppression of the song, yet tells us much about the conceiving of song. It suggests, first of all, that Schubert does not always have the text before him but rather that the poem will have become a part of his thinking, absorbed and "made music" before anything is committed to paper. Perhaps this is to overidealize the process. But I do think that we must believe Schubert capable of committing the poem to memory and that—just as a performer will admit that having to read is an impediment to the *idea* of performance—learning the poem, internalizing it, getting past the paper on which it is printed, must unconsciously have played into the process of singing, of song making.

If the setting of September 1817 is conceived on a scale beyond the conceptual powers of a Schubert eighteen months younger, it is yet indebted in certain of its aspects to the earlier song. It too announces its "Horch" in midflight, deep in the unfolding of the opening music. And the modulatory design of the opening, bent on an obfuscating motion that spirals away from a tonic C minor never established, is an extreme expression of what in fact happens across the opening page of the fragment.

But in other respects, the two settings are very different. Fischer-Dieskau observed a new relationship between the voice and the surrounding music in the later version: "The raging representation of those banished to Tartarus . . . is far removed from the conventional Lied, even from Schubert's own. The voice no longer has a 'song melody', the action is depicted more by the harmonic and rhythmical audacities of the piano than by the song."[38] It is the "no longer," placing the setting in an evolutionary track, that must be challenged. For one, there are very few songs *after* this one that come close to matching the epic quality of the music. That has of course to do with Schiller's text. The poem is an impersonal one, decidedly not a Lied in the conventional sense. Even its attachment to antiquity is not of the specific kind. The poem does not conjure up a narrative from Homer or Virgil but depicts rather what seems a conflation, a situation abstracted from some collective reading in the Greek myths. And so it is not surprising that Schubert was swayed in the direction of a grand instrumental tableau whose turbulent harmonic trajectory and clangorous accompaniment do not treat the voice kindly.

Indeed, the piece even makes a certain sense when the voice is left aside altogether. That Brahms felt inclined to orchestrate the song is in itself a symp-

37. It must speak to the intensity of Schubert's setting that not one of the recent appraisers of it—neither Brown, nor Reed, nor Dürr, nor even Fischer-Dieskau—noticed the error. It goes without saying that inadvertent corruption of the text—of which this is clearly an example—needs to be distinguished from those cases in which Schubert intentionally alters the text to exaggerate a rhetorical emphasis.

38. Fischer-Dieskau, *Schubert*, 99. I have adjusted the garbled translation, which speaks of "Tartarus's banishment." For the original, see Dietrich Fischer-Dieskau, *Auf den Spuren der Schubert-Lieder*, 2d ed. (Kassel, 1976), 118.

tom of its remove from a genre in which a shared intimacy between singer and pianist, between poem and music, is of the essence. This is not in any way to denigrate the work but only to suggest that it forces a fundamental aesthetic issue. We need only recall Klopstock's angst at the thought of "losing" his poem to infelicitous diction in Schwenke's cautious setting of it. An extreme bit of pedantry, we may think. But, in fact, the incident vividly represents what was taken to be the true relationship between poem and music: music as refined diction; poem as a code for *Gesang*.

In *Gruppe aus dem Tartarus*, this tidy equation is exploded. It is not, of course, that the diction is faulty (it is not) or that the declamation of the couplet beginning "Fragen sich einander ängstlich leise" stands outside a tradition (it does not). Rather, it is that a cataract of music is unleashed the opening action of which resets the relationship between harmonic conduct and poetic diction. We no longer listen for the deft inflections that grow from a reading of the poem, where a turn in the language, a bend in the syntax, is caught in the singing. The sweep of the music hardly encourages a picture of Schubert, Schiller's *Gedichte* in hand, studying the poem for its formal inflections, even *singing* the opening lines of what the voice will be made to sing. The conceiving of the song must have followed from other imperatives.

To suggest, as Fischer-Dieskau seems to, that with this second setting of *Gruppe aus dem Tartarus* Schubert moved away from the genre as it had come to be defined is to miss a central point. Some of the earlier songs—indeed, some of the earliest—imply this resetting of balances. But later ones retrench. The return to a concept of Lied in its purer sense is swift and sustained. At the end, hardly a song in *Winterreise* or in the Rellstab and Heine cycles can be claimed to stand outside these fundamental guidelines in the way that *Gruppe aus dem Tartarus* brazenly does.

If the distance that separates the original concept of *Gruppe aus dem Tartarus* in 1816 from its sequel in 1817 articulates what is in effect a fundamental difference in how song is conceived, there is yet a sense in which the two together must be understood as a kind of discourse, a dialectic in which the one reading of the poem is impossible without the other. I do not of course mean to suggest that the one setting cannot be understood without reference to the other. But, in seeking to comprehend how the poem can have set loose two readings so radically at odds, one might wish to think that the leap to a concept of "orchestral" song—of song essentially without words—can only have happened because Schubert had put himself through the exercise of Lied in the obligatory sense, had in the earlier version dispatched that obligation with a passion unequaled in the songs of 1816. Here too I would hold that we learn much from the composite narrative embedded in these two singings of Schiller's agonized scene.

The two settings of *Gruppe aus dem Tartarus* may be said to test an extreme limit of the variant/version axis. Clearly, the music of 1817 is a fresh conception. If Schubert had set out to improve the setting of 1816, it must have struck him early on that what he had before him was quite beyond improvement, both because it would be difficult indeed to imagine a setting conceived along the same aesthetic lines that could express Schiller's strophe any more cogently and because the original conception was wedded to an imperfect transmission of the poem. In effect, the imperfection of it invalidates the reading altogether, and we must assume that it was this astonishing circumstance that forced Schubert to place the project back on his agenda.

My point is a modest one. The new setting was meant to efface the earlier one. The eclipse is total. It was the setting of 1817 that was performed in public as early as 1821 and that Schubert would publish in 1823. Yet the earlier setting will not go quietly.

III

Distant Cycles

❄

An die Entfernte

Geschwinder
ü - ber ihm die Ler - che singt: so drin - get ängst - lich hin und wie - der durch Feld und
Geschwinder
cresc.
Wie oben
Busch und Wald mein Blick; dich ru - fen al - le, al - le mei - ne Lie - der; o
Wie oben
fp
p
komm, Ge - lieb - te, mir zu - rück, o komm, Ge - lieb - te, mir zu - rück! Dich ru - fen
fp
al - le, al - le, mei - ne Lie - der; o komm, o komm, Ge - lieb - te,
fp
fp

mir zu - rück!
pp
fp
ppp

4

A Poetics of the Remote: Goethe's *Entfernte*

Few of Schubert's mature songs have suffered a neglect less deserved than the setting of Goethe's *An die Entfernte* (D. 765). Complex and introspective, rich in formal nuance, its harmonies probe Goethe's fragile lyric and overwhelm it. The poem intimates a way of return that is closely tuned to something innate in Schubert's manner:

Dich rufen alle meine Lieder:
O komm, Geliebte, mir zurück!

(All my songs call to thee; O come, beloved, back to me!)

Decidedly not triumphant and confirmatory, this return is an implicit one, more about upbeats than closure. It pulses with anxiety.

And Schubert, responding to just this twist in the poem, does indeed make a difficult return of it, for the subdominant at m. 26 accepts its identity only in retrospect. The impatient return of the opening phrase thrusts that function on it. F minor, casting its pall over all the middle section, seems finally to establish itself as a tonic. Poised for resolution upward to A♭, the high G at "Blick" is turned back. And yet for all its wayward harmonic antecedents, the reprise does not sound unexpected. That owes something to the power of the diminished triad on D♯ at "Wald," which under normal conditions would charge the C above it to resolve to B, the natural root of the harmony. The inflection is so strong as to countermand the superficial sense of the harmony at m. 26, where the E, doubled in the bass, encourages a shift in its function from leading tone to root. Here, too, the tendency of the C to resolve to B is denied. The fermata only exacerbates matters. The irresolute C, having controlled the vocal line through most of the middle section, is prolonged into the reprise.

But it is to the brooding F minor of the middle section that the ear returns: a restless and unstable F minor, disoriented in its unsuspected following on the dominant on F with which the first strophe breaks off. The very tenacity of the F in the bass—its refusal to move—contributes to its instability. The mythic lark, in Delphic song, sings the harmony right. Symbol both of the flown lover whose imprint is recorded in "ein jeder Ton" and of the eternal *Ton-Dichter* himself who calls to her through his songs, the figure is full of

Romantic wonder, illuminated in the quickening turn to A♭. The image flares for an instant, and then recedes. The cadence is central to the song, for it is an A♭ that disturbs the tonal equilibrium established at the end of the first strophe. And it is toward A♭ that the voice strains, quite in vain, before the poignant reprise.

In Romantic song, things are not always what they seem. It is the elusive "other" world of the *Entfernte*, both imaginary and real, that regulates every gesture in both poem and song. But the barren world of convention is inexorable. After much procrastination, a cadence in G—the *only* cadence in G—extinguishes the song. The song lives for A♭ and dies in G. Why A♭? The idea of two antagonistic keys as uneasy neighbors is not uncommon in music of the early nineteenth century. But the specificity of A♭ here is pointedly referential.

II

An die Entfernte was not published during Schubert's lifetime. It survives in an autograph manuscript the contents of which include three other Goethe settings.[1] The structure of the manuscript and its content are shown in table 4.1. There will be more to say of *Am Flusse* and *Willkommen und Abschied*. But it is *Der Musensohn*, and its bearing on *An die Entfernte*, that claims our attention.

TABLE 4.1
The Manuscript Structure of Mus. Ms. Autogr. Schubert 27

	Folio	Content
Gathering A (14 stave)	1	*Der Musensohn*, 1r–3r
	2	
	3	*An die Entfernte*, 3v–4v, stave 7
	4	*Am Flusse*, 4v, stave 8–5r
Gathering B (16 stave)	5	*Willkommen und Abschied*, 5v–7v
	6	
	7	
	8	8r–v blank

Source: Berlin Staatsbibliothek Preußischer Kulturbesitz.

Against the tenuous, probing harmonies of the untracked lover in *An die Entfernte*, the A♭ of *Der Musensohn* is pervasive and implacable. Nearly everything sounds in root position. Even the naive C major of the alternate strophes serves to delineate the tonic, setting it off smartly against its bright mediant. There are no complications here, only a spontaneous affirmation of creativity—of musical creativity, in the poet's language—and of love.[2] The

1. Berlin Staatsbibliothek Preußischer Kulturbesitz, Mus. ms. autogr. Schubert 27.

2. "Es spricht *der Musensohn* in Gestalt eines Musikers, was bei Goethe nicht oft vorkommt; in den Künstlergedichten der Jugendjahre waren es immer Maler" (The *Musensohn* speaks in the form of a musician, which does not often appear in Goethe; in the artist poems of his youth, it was always painters) (thus Erich Trunz, in *Goethes Werke: Hamburger Ausgabe in 14 Bänden*. vol. 1, *Gedichte und Epen* [1948] [reprint, Munich, 1981], 643).

Example 4.1 *a*, *Der Musensohn* (D. 764), mm. 40–50, with voice leading abstracted

Example 4.1 cont. *b*, *An die Entfernte* (D. 765), mm. 19–27, with voice leading abstracted

final cadencing stomps and dances and echos off to the gods. Its reverberations penetrate deep into the reclusive world of *An die Entfernte*, whose opening measures, fragile and vulnerable, evade commitment of any kind. The incessant downbeats of *Der Musensohn* continue to sound. Even the obstinate C, coaxed to resolution at "Dich rufen alle meine Lieder," may be heard to sustain what amounts to a recitation tone that guides *both* strophes of *Der Musensohn* (see. ex. 4.1).

If Goethe never intended the two poems to be read side by side, it seems manifestly clear that Schubert conceived the two settings as contextual. The autograph is the one document that stands in evidence of the conception. In choosing some years later to publish *Der Musensohn* and *Willkommen und Abschied* separately, each in its own group of three songs, the composer may be said to have vitiated the spontaneity of that conception.[3] The point will need further argument. We might simply remind ourselves of the lessons learned in chapters 2 and 3, where acts of revision were shown to undermine in much the same way something ingrained in the conception of the song.

To sing all four settings through just as the autograph prescribes is to be struck at once by the deeper continuities that unfold along the way and by the plain good stage sense with which one song follows another. *Am Flusse* and *Willkommen und Abschied*, taken as a pair, invert the oppositions of *Der Musensohn* and *An die Entfernte*. Songs sung but not heard, an idea central to *An die Entfernte*, resonate in *Am Flusse*. As in *An die Entfernte*, the meaning of the setting hinges on an enigmatic harmonic inflection. Here it is the mysterious allusion to F♯ minor, a tonicization more suggested than realized, at the phrase "zum Meere der Vergessenheit" (to the sea of oblivion) and again at "ins Wasser eingeschrieben" (engraved in water). The imponderable ambiguities of these two rhyming images in the poem are pondered in Schubert's haunting phrase.[4] The infinite flow of the river swells and deepens. The lover's songs are betrayed. In an act of sublimation, he releases them to the Sea of Oblivion. The suffering of *An die Entfernte* is dissolved.

III

The aura of timeless oblivion is rudely disturbed. *Willkommen und Abschied* is a poem of a different order, ballad-like and specific where the others are reflective and lyrical. All in the past tense, it narrates a wild ride through the night to a waiting lover.

3. *Willkommen und Abschied* was announced for publication on 14 July 1826 as op. 56 with *An die Leier* (Bruchmann, after Anacreon) and *Im Haine* (Bruchmann). On the suggestiveness of this grouping, see n. 20 below. *Der Musensohn* was published with *Auf dem See* and *Geistes-Gruß* as op. 96, announced on 11 July 1828 (see Deutsch, *Thematisches Verzeichnis*, 461–63.

4. An earlier setting of *Am Flusse* (D. 160, composed in 1815) conveys only the melancholy of the poem and nothing of its metaphysics.

Es schlug mein Herz, geschwind zu Pferde!
Es war getan fast eh' gedacht.

(My heart was beating. Quick, to horse! It was done before it was thought.)

the poem begins. But it is fourteen lines of riding before we can know what has prompted the initial act. The third strophe (lines 17–24) describes the encounter, and it is a passionate one. The climax comes at

Ganz war mein Herz an deiner Seite
und jeder Atemzug für dich.

(My heart was entirely with you, my every breath was for you.)

Passion spent, the moment is transfigured, bathed in a roseate, springlike glow:

Ein rosenfarbnes Frühlingswetter
Umgab das liebliche Gesicht,
Und Zärtlichkeit für mich. . . .

(A rosy springlike aura enveloped your lovely face, and tenderness for me. . . .)

From the outset, Schubert's settings puts us in mind of other songs and past events. The opening éclat, exploding from the very sonority with which *Am Flusse* silently closes—the pianist hardly moves a finger—signals that intention, just as its impatient opening phrase mocks the quiescent contour that closes into that sonority (see ex. 4.2). But the signal has a deeper motive. On the face of it, *Willkommen und Abschied* wants to parody the sentiments expressed in *Am Flusse*, but in fact it is the other way round, for it will gradually emerge that the narrative of *Willkommen und Abschied* speaks of those actions on which *An die Entfernte* and *Am Flusse* reflect. The tranquility of the phrase to which the poet sings "so fliesst denn auch mit ihm davon" (they flow away with [the water]) must instead be understood as a sublime recollection of the impetuous, angst-ridden phrase with which *Willkommen und Abschied* breaks forth. It is just that we hear the reflection before its image.

The gist of the poem—the end to all this riding and the unspoken middle between "Willkommen" and "Abschied"—is the love scene of the third strophe. And it is the gist of Schubert's music as well. The subdominant tinges the quivering ecstasy of the moment. Such emphasis on the subdominant is likely to threaten the priority of the tonic; as a consequence, the relationship between the two functions is confused. By convention, we take the struggle to get free of the tonic as a rule of the game in the Classical sense. But the struggle must be off to the dominant. In Schubert, that struggle very often seems to fail. Here, the early forays into F minor, G minor, and B♭ major (the subordinate areas in *An die Entfernte* as well) are all subsumed in the peremptory return to the tonic, the ecstatic phrase at "In meinen Adern welche ein Feuer" with which the second strophe closes.

The arrival at G major seems almost accidental. The rider, we imagine, comes on a clearing quite unexpectedly, for it is deep night, and the moon is

Example 4.2 *a*, *Am Flusse* (D. 766), mm. 27–33. *b*, *Willkommen und Abschied* (D. 767, "1. Fassung"), opening measures

clouded over. The subdominant region, not pointedly the goal of the action across the first two strophes, becomes it by default. Its Classical function as subdominant is usurped, and this skewing of normal syntactic dynamics undermines the Classical function of the tonic as well, for, although the piece begins and ends in D major, and in spite of the soaring phrases that clinch tonic cadences at the end of the second strophe and again at the end of the song, there is more than a faint sense in which the behavior of this D is as dominant to G. And that accords with the sense of a poem decidedly not about departure and return but rather about the arrival and withdrawal implicit in "Willkommen" and "Abschied." The outer ends, anchored by convention to the tonic, are yet made to feel remote and even, by extension, dissonant, for, while Schubert's language is set fast in a Classical syntax, the rub of a Romantic temperament against its conventions—a friction that Goethe's poetry seems only to exacerbate—is not always resolved without contradiction.

The G major at "Dich sah ich," by no means simply the subdominant, is laid over with implications that reach back to earlier songs. The climactic phrase at "und jeder Athemzug für dich," a phrase that Schubert sings twice, and yet a third time in cadential variant, is perhaps the most explicit in that regard. The eroticism of the phrase flashes back to another climax: the thwarted one at the crux of *An die Entfernte* (see ex. 4.3).

If it cannot be claimed that this phrase means to resolve the incomplete sense at "so dringet ängstlich . . . mein Blick," the two passages play on one another, intimately. The Cs suspended irresolutely above the D♯ and E in *An die Entfernte* vanish in the cognate phrase: such equivocation has no place in the rush of this passion. Again, the narrative of *Willkommen und Abschied* is retrospective, setting out earlier events that offer a context for the anguish reflected in *An die Entfernte*.[5] The ecstasy at "jeder Athemzug" must be imagined to sound before the anxiety at "dringet ängstlich." And this play with the events of memory further unsettles the sense of a Classical tonal syntax.

Syntax seems to erode altogether at what might be taken as the nub of the poem, at its luminous center:

Ein rosenfarbnes Frühlingswetter
Umgab das liebliche Gesicht,
Und Zärtlichkeit für mich—Ihr Götter!
Ich hofft' es, ich verdient' es nicht!

(A rosy spring-like aura enveloped your lovely face, and tenderness for me—ye Gods! I hoped for it, but I didn't deserve it!)

Here is the eye of the poem. Time is suspended. The language bends at its limits. For what had he hoped? What did he not deserve? Why are the gods addressed? Why is there no coordinate to differentiate "hoffen" and "verdienen"? What, finally, is the syntactic position of "Und Zärtlichkeit für mich"? What is its predicate? To answer these questions in a reasonable way—to assert that they can be so answered—is yet to miss the point, for they are questions of the kind that hint at the imponderable. The asking of the question is itself a kind of answer.

Schubert, too, seems caught in these temporal and linguistic snares: how to convey the grammar of the quatrain and at the same time probe the Goethean

5. Coincidentally, the two poems were first published together in just this ordering—*Willkomm* [*sic*] *und Abschied* (p. 115) and *An die Entfernte* (p. 117)—in vol. 8 of *Goethe's Schriften* (Leipzig, 1789). In this earlier version of *Willkommen und Abschied*, the roles are reversed in the final stanza, the lines of which run "Du gingst, ich stund und sah zur Erden / Und sah dir nach mit nassem Blick," from which the apostrophe *An die Entfernte* follows rather more logically (see Hans Gerhard Gräf, *Goethe ueber seine Dichtungen*, vol. 9, *Dritter Theil: Die lyrischen Dichtungen* [Frankfurt, 1914], 908).

Example 4.3 *Willkommen und Abschied* (D. 767, "1. Fassung"), mm. 52–70

riddle of its final lines. The music quickens at "Zärtlichkeit," breaks off into silence at "Ihr Götter!" and finds a brooding new tempo at "Ich hofft' es." The tonal strategy is no less manic: a move to the subdominant of G, underscored with a full close at "liebliche Gesicht"; a difficult diminished seventh at "Zärtlichkeit"; a no less difficult ascent to the E♭ of the gods;[6] an ambiguous piece of unaccompanied phrase at "Ich hofft' es"; and, finally, a full close in E♭. Dawn comes. The scene dissolves.

For Schubert, if not for Goethe, the crux of the passage is at "Ihr Götter!" The phrase reaches to A♭ and, when it is repeated, finds an interval that clinches an association with that other climactic phrase, at "und jeder Atemzug für dich." And it is the turning of the A♭ down to G that brings to mind all those associations that linger in the backgrounds of *Der Musensohn* and *An die Entfernte*. There, A♭ and G are tonicized. Here, they are upper tensions.

IV

When we come on these poems in the contemporary authentic publications of Goethe's collected writings, there can be no question of internal reference, for at best the poems sit in only a general propinquity with respect to one another within the greater collection of "Lieder," which, taken as a whole, makes no pretense to an integrity of narrative or of topic.[7] The four poems were composed at very different times and for different purposes. But, when they are sung as prescribed in Schubert's autograph, the effect is stunningly different. By an imposed consanguinity, the poems are made to respond to one another. The music catches moments of interior reference and, forcing its own priorities, establishes finally a structure in all its diverse complexity and singleness of design.

But structure of what kind? We have come to take a Schenkerian model as paradigmatic for certain repertories of tonal music. What such a model demonstrates, in its projection of the musical work on an axiomatic *Ursatz*, is the coherence of the piece in some elemental, even tautological way. When the relationship between levels (*Schichten*, in Schenker's language) is viewed as

6. "E-flat in the older Neapolitans was the key of dark, solemn pathos, especially at the invocation of the deities and in ghost scenes." Wolfgang Hildesheimer, tongue half in cheek, recites Hermann Abert's recounting of this rhetorical cliché (see his *Mozart*, trans. Marion Faber [New York, 1982], 201). For Abert's passage, see his *W. A. Mozart*, 2 vols. (Leipzig, 1955), 1:206. Contemporary with Schubert's revivification of the topos, Beethoven was endowing E♭ with transcendental significance both in the *Missa solemnis* and, at the setting of "über Sternen muß er wohnen," in the finale of the Ninth Symphony (see William Kinderman, "Beethoven's Symbol for the Deity in the *Missa solemnis* and the Ninth Symphony," *19th Century Music* 9 [Fall 1985]: 102–18, esp. 116).

7. Schubert's source seems to have been *Goethes sämtliche Schriften*, vol. 7, *Lyrische Gedichte* (Vienna, 1810), where the four poems appear in this order: "Der Musensohn" (p. 9), "An die Entfernte" (p. 31), "Am Flusse" (p. 32), and "Willkommen und Abschied" (p. 39); the two central poems are contiguous. For more on Schubert's source, see *NGA*, ser. 4, vol. 3b, p. 271, and vol. 5b, p. 260.

essentially synchronic, the function of things (of events, of phrases, of harmonies, and so forth) is shown to have meaning outside the temporal axis of the piece or, rather, is suspended in tension with it.[8] Schenker's ideas are deeply rooted in organicist theories about the evolution of individual form (the piece in all its idiosyncratic detail) from archetypal physiological process.[9] Organicist theory does indeed have its synchronic aspects: the evolutionary process captures the maturation of the individual at a moment of stopped action, where the process itself seems to freeze.

Whether one takes the *Ursatz* and the hierarchies that it generates as an exemplification of a transformational grammar (as latter-day structuralists would take it) or of the organicist concept of physiological process (the Goethean *Urpflanze*), it will differ from either model in one fundamental respect: the *Ursatz* signifies a motion that is strictly teleological.[10] The end is closure in the tonic, from which all those tones were generated in the first place. The power of the telos is so compelling that, as in too many of Schenker's studies, the posting of the structural tones that constitute the *Ursatz* is pushed further and further toward the end as the process unfolds to the lower, more specific generations. It is innate in the system that even the most eccentric harmonic events—those that give the piece its character and motivate its action—must be shown ultimately as subordinate to the fundamental lines of the *Ursatz*, explained away as so many interruptions toward the true goal. And when such events cannot be so explained, the piece is shown to lack the coherence axiomatic in the criteria by which the *Ursatz* is postulated in the first place.

Now it is axiomatic as well that the *Ursatz* can comprehend only self-contained works. How, for example, the second movement of the *Eroica* Symphony might bear on the first is not a question that Schenker will entertain, for the two movements, perceived as pure structure, are each complete in themselves.[11] Their coherence is perfect. The relationships that may, and invariably do, obtain between such movements, whatever their

8. As Allan Keiler expresses it, "Once the content of the structural levels comes into being, so to speak, or is actualized, present and past (i.e., potential as background, and real as foreground) exist simultaneously" ("On Some Properties of Schenker's Pitch Derivations," *Music Perception* 1, no. 2 [Winter 1983–84]: 206).

9. This aspect of Schenker's thought is the topic of Ruth Solie, "The Living Work: Organicism and Musical Analysis," *19th Century Music* 4 (Fall 1980): 147–56. Solie documents the extent to which Schenker himself conceived how the repertory of masterworks on which he theorized was the fruit of an organic process; she does not pursue the difficult issue how the synchrony of *Ursatz* and "surface" at once succeeds and fails as the enactment of a metaphoric script with organic pretenses.

10. Keiler ("On Some Properties of Schenker's Pitch Derivations," 214–28) explores the "conceptual similarities of Schenker's musical derivations with certain properties of generative tree structures in linguistics."

11. Schenker on the *Eroica* is apposite, for this is the latest of his studies to encompass the several movements of a complete work (the essay is "Beethovens Dritte Sinfonie zum erstenmal in ihrem wahren Inhalt dargestellt," in his *Das Meisterwerk in der Musik*, vol. 3 [Munich, 1930], 25–102).

claim to significance and meaning, are yet irrelevant to this central truth about their inner integrity.

But the self-containedness of songs distributed in cycles has always been challenged, ever since Beethoven's *An die ferne Geliebte* (1816) established a rigorous model, one that Schubert seemed intent on putting out of sight, if not out of mind. In its explicit continuities between songs that in themselves seem almost too frail to make their own way, *An die ferne Geliebte* explores this new notion of the work in toto as a function of all its parts in some organic whole, a concept broached as well in a number of works by Beethoven beginning around 1815 and continuing into the final quartets. The experiment was at once bold and cautious, for Jeitteles's poems, in themselves naively subordinate to the greater *Zyklus*, offers a simple modus operandi. The poetic idea of return in the sense of cyclic closure finds its echo in the music, first in the veiled reminiscence of the opening music at "Nimm Sie hin denn, diese Lieder," and finally in the literal recapitulation of the opening strophes of the cycle.[12] And the work coheres in its orthodox, diatonic tonal plan, a blowup, very nearly, of the opening phrase itself. Omit a song, and the tonal coherence is audibly shaken.

The songs that constitute the great Müller cycles are dependent on one another in nothing like the ways suggested in *An die ferne Geliebte*. The mapping of coherences in *Winterreise* is a notoriously thorny matter (see chapters 7 and 8 below). Less problematic in this sense, but similarly distant from the ethos of Beethoven's cycle, *Die schöne Müllerin* draws heavily on the conventions of *Liederspiel*. If the personae of the cycle do not actually move on the stage, they make claims to an actual stage presence: "a kind of unstaged concert *Liederkreis*" it has been called.[13] The implicit, internal narrative of the Goethe set, closer in spirit to Beethoven's cycle, is of a different order. It will find a fuller realization in the two groups of songs in the *Schwanengesang*—studied in chapters 5 and 6 below—and especially in the Heine set, whose bold concept of musical continuities depends on an overlay of ambiguous beginnings and telltale endings.

The new power of continuity in the Heine cycle is owed to a tonal plan of great originality and sophistication. Set deep in the cycle, a tonic is portrayed—more a metaphor for tonicity than the thing itself—toward which the music coalesces and from which it must recede, in sympathy with its poetic texts. Such a concept is incipient in the set of Goethe songs from 1822. If these songs do not constitute a cycle by any conventional definition of the

12. For a penetrating study of Beethoven's cycle, see Joseph Kerman, "*An die ferne Geliebte*," in *Beethoven Studies 1*, ed. Alan Tyson (New York, 1973), 123–57. At the outset, Kerman invites us to imagine a collaboration between Jeitteles and Beethoven.

13. By Susan Youens, in an illuminating study of its literary antecedents ("Behind the Scenes: *Die schöne Müllerin* before Schubert," *19th Century Music* 15 [1991]: 3–22). Antecedents, with a focus on Conradin Kreutzer's setting of Uhland's *Neun Wanderlieder*, are the topic in Barbara Turchin, "The Nineteenth-Century *Wanderlieder* Cycle," *Journal of Musicology* 5 (Fall 1987): 498–525.

genre, they yet intimate a tendency that has been described as Schubert's "zyklische Verfahrensweise" in connection with a number of other similar projects roughly contemporary with these songs.[14]

Now, by some definition of tonality, a proof of cohesion rests ultimately in a demonstration of tonal closure. Tonicity, by Classical norm, *means* closure—a closure that is self-evident and predetermined in the immediacy of the piece. What I want to suggest here is that the very idea of a tonic as the single generating motor of coherence, in its explicit position in the temporal unfolding of the piece, seems manifestly to have undergone a fundamental redefinition in the Heine cycle and implicitly some years earlier in these Goethe settings. The inexorable pull toward a *final* tonic is rejected: better, the final tonic—the powerful close that characterizes *Willkommen und Abschied* (and, some years later, *Der Atlas*)—contradicts what we must take to be the central and generating tonic. The true tonic becomes a poetic image, a figure of ambiguity that hovers somewhere in the midst of the cycle. And that accords well with the sense of most Romantic song cycles, for it is not structural closure that they are about but rather reminiscence and longing and dissolution.

I mean further to suggest that there must be two responses to the tonal relationships described in these songs. On the one hand, we are inclined to hear them as an instance of temporal unfolding: put bluntly, as a motion between A♭ and D. On the other hand, we take the linear time of the thing to be subordinate to a deeper tonal implication, wherein beginnings and ends, and various events in between, refer to one another and even implicate tonal areas never made explicit. The tonal hierarchies of the set are deeply bound in with the complex time warp of the poetry. In this connection, think once again how the poems activate a temporal layering:

> *Der Musensohn.* Poet as god-like. The creative act as a rite of fertility. The poet engenders love, but is beyond it, does not experience it. Its unarticulated time scale suggests the infinite—and thus the poignance of the closing couplet, "Wann ruh' ich ihr am Busen / Auch endlich wieder aus?"
>
> *An die Entfernte.* Poet as *Mensch*: as lover and loser. His songs have a personal mission. Time is specific. He longs for the past from an uncomfortable present.
>
> *Am Flusse.* He longs for a cosmic future, for *Vergessenheit*, for the transfiguration from past sorrow to timeless oblivion. His songs have betrayed him, and he disowns them, returns them to the gods.
>
> *Willkommen und Abschied.* Poet as ballad maker. Past events are chronicled, recaptured and recycled from a remote point in time, outside the chronicle.

It is not easy to see how the temporal weave of such poetry might be projected in a tonal construct of Classical profile. And Schubert's construct does indeed seem pitted against the Classical process of formal closure, a notion antipathetic to the convoluted nesting of these poems within one another. The criteria by which we understand the coherence of the individual song are sim-

14. See Berke, "Schuberts Liedentwurf," 307.

ply inadequate for comprehending the larger work of which it is a part. If there is an axiom lodged in Beethoven's elegant model, it is that the subordination of the song to the cycle would issue in a design of large-scale closure even as the individual songs avoid the kinds of structural articulation that might abrogate those qualities of continuity, interdependence, and subordination that we take as predicates of the model. For Schubert, the axiom seems consumed in some other vision. The laws of deep structure must lie elsewhere.

V

> If we wish to introduce a morphology, we must not speak of form [*Gestalt*]; but rather, whenever we use the word, think of an idea, a concept, or something fixed for only the briefest moment. That which is formed is promptly reformed.[15]

Were it not known that Goethe was here writing an introduction to a group of essays (published in 1817) on plant morphology, we might have thought that music was much on his mind. We have no evidence that Schubert knew firsthand the Goethe of *Naturwissenschaft* or that he had contemplated the applicability to his own work of those theories of form and generation that Goethe was continually transferring from nature to art and back again.[16] But there are good reasons for suspecting that such ideas must have entered into the agenda of more than one meeting of the *Leseabenden* held several times weekly by a number of artists and intellectuals in Schubert's circle—the same membership, essentially, that participated in the Schubertiads.[17]

A provocative figure in that circle was the poet-philosopher Franz Bruchmann, whose friendship with August von Platen at Erlangen generated a critical dialogue on the significance of Goethe's oeuvre.[18] Years later, Bruchmann saw all this from a different perspective: "I passionately devoured all of

15. Reprinted in, e.g., *Goethes Werke: Hamburger Ausgabe*, vol. 13, *Naturwissenschaftliche Schriften*, 55–56. The translation is from Peter Salm, *The Poem as Plant: A Biological View of Goethe's Faust* (Cleveland and London, 1971), 18.

16. The interpretation of art and science is made manifest on one level in the elegy "Die Metamorphose der Pflanzen" (composed in 1798), which expresses in poetic language the ideas put forth in the essay *Versuch die Metamorphose der Pflanzen zu erklären* (published in 1790). On the relationship between the two, see Gertrud Overbeck, "Goethes Lehre von der Metamorphose der Pflanzen und ihre Widerspiegelung in seiner Dichtung," *Publications of the English Goethe Society*, n.s., 31 (1961), 38–59.

17. "Whether a discussion of literary theory followed upon such readings we do not know, but it can safely be assumed that it did," surmises Walther Dürr ("Schubert's Songs and Their Poetry: Reflections on Poetic Aspects of Song Composition," in *Schubert Studies: Problems of Style and Chronology*, 7). Dürr cites Schubert's letter of 30 November 1823—the passage given in n. 18 below—as evidence in support of the argument.

18. The power of Bruchmann's presence is evident in this passage from Schubert's letter of 30 November 1823: "If Bruchmann is not there, or even ill, we go on for hours under the supreme direction of Mohn hearing nothing but eternal talk about riding, fencing, horses and hounds" (Deutsch, *Documentary Biography*, 300–301; see also Deutsch, *Dokumente*, 207). For Bruchmann's relationship to von Platen, see Moritz Enzinger, ed., "Franz von Bruchmann, der Freund J. Chr. Senns und des Grafen August v. Platen: Eine Selbstbiographie aus dem Wiener Schubert-

Goethe's work. Following his mind, everything human and godly was exalted, overvalued, and abused; and every bit of excrement from this Dalai Lama was idolized with a truly childish veneration."[19] The breathtaking setting of *Schwestergruß* (D. 762), a meditation written by Bruchmann in July 1820 on the death of his sister, is a song whose manifest depth of feeling might be taken as a symptom of intimacy between Schubert and Bruchmann, an intimacy nourished, perhaps, in a shared devotion to some Goethean ideal. Schubert's autograph is dated November 1822.[20]

In a letter dated 7 December 1822, Schubert reported to Josef von Spaun, "Our society in Vienna is now quite pleasant. We hold readings three times a week at Schober's, and a Schubertiad, at which Bruchmann also appears."[21] Earlier in the same letter, we learn of the impending publication of three groups of songs, two of which were settings of Goethe poems. The letter continues, "I have also composed several new Lieder by Goethe, namely: Der Musensohn, an die Entfernte, am Flusse and Willkommen und Abschied."[22] To have summoned up the songs in precisely this order will set loose sympathetic vibrations, even if we cannot take Schubert's formulation as a signal with deeper implications.

It does not much matter whether Berke's "zyklische Verfahrensweise" is literally appropriate to the compositional impulse at the seat of these settings. *Cycle* is decidedly not an appropriate metaphor for how these songs are related, unless it means to invoke those simultaneous kinds of motion through which Goethe describes the growth of the plant: he writes of "spiral" tendencies in simultaneous opposition to vertical growth; he writes of metamorphosis, of *Steigerung*, of anastomosis.[23] As Peter Salm has it in his study of *Faust*

---

kreise nebst Briefen," *Veröffentlichungen des Museum Ferdinandeum in Innsbruck* 10 (1930): 117–379, esp. 136–45.

19. "Mit Leidenschaft verschlang ich alle Produktionen Goethe's; Alles Menschliche und Göttliche wurde in seinem Geiste gewürdigt, ueberschätzt und mißhandelt; und jedes Exkrement dieses Dalai Lama wurde mit wahrhaft läppischer Verehrung vergöttert" (Enzinger, "Franz von Bruchmann," 217).

20. Deutsch, *Thematisches Verzeichnis*, 459. A reflection of that intimacy is perhaps to be read in the decision, finally, to publish *Willkommen und Abschied* together with settings of two poems by Bruchmann: *An die Leier* (after Anacreon; D. 737) and *Im Haine* (D. 738) (see n. 3 above).

21. "Unser Zusammenleben in Wien ist jetzt recht angenehm, wir halten bey Schober wöchentlich 3mahl Lesungen, u. eine Schubertiade, wobey auch Bruchmann erscheint" (Deutsch, *Dokumente*, 172–73, see also *Documentary Biography*, 247–49).

22. "Auch habe ich einige neue Lieder von Göthe componirt, als: Der Musensohn, an die Entfernte, am Flusse, u. Willkommen und Abschied" (Deutsch, *Dokumente*, 173).

23. Of the enormous body of literature on Goethe's writings in the natural sciences, two studies that investigate the applicability of Goethe's conception of organic process to concepts of artistic form are Salm, *Poem as Plant*; and Thomas Clifton, "An Application of Goethe's Concept of Steigerung to the Morphology of Diminution," *Journal of Music Theory* 14, no. 2 (Winter 1970): 165–89. If Clifton's attempt to understand intervallic transformations in certain of Mozart's keyboard works as exemplifications of the Goethean notion of *Steigerung* seems forced and unconvincing, his instructive discussion of Goethe's theories is incisive and clearheaded.

(*The Poem as Plant* is his suggestive title), "The flowering process is therefore a moment of spatial and temporal concentration containing within it the ultimate distillation of all previous stages experienced in well-defined segments of time and within the context of various physical forms."[24] For "flowering process" substitute "musical process," and something akin to the spatial and temporal processes of these songs seems to have been captured.

The Goethe settings, dated December 1822 in the autograph, lie in the midst of a considerable repertory of music in which Schubert had begun to explore the deeper connections through which the pieces of a work may be related. The B-Minor Symphony, whose cyclic aspects have been the subject of more than one recent study, and the Piano Fantasy in C Major (*Der Wanderer*), whose cyclic aspects are explicit and self-evident, date from October and November.[25] The two extended "Blumen-Balladen," *Viola* (March 1823) and *Vergißmeinnicht* (May 1823), play with the tonal strategies of *An die ferne Geliebte*.[26] *Die schöne Müllerin*—the one true *cycle* among all these and yet paradoxically unresponsive and inaccessible to this deeper strain of cyclic conception—followed in October and November 1823.

At the same time, the Goethe set exhibits some of those external symptoms by which we shall learn to identify the "authentic" cycles. Again, it is the Heine cycle, arguably the most clearly integral of them all, that one might take as the measure. *Der Musensohn* behaves very much like those wanderer's songs with which the big cycles open.[27] In this respect, it has much in common with *Das Fischermädchen*, the Heine opener: both in A♭, both in 6/8,

24. Salm, *Poem as Plant*, 36–37.

25. A case for cyclic procedure in the B-Minor Symphony is made by Martin Chusid, "Beethoven and the Unfinished," in *Franz Schubert: Symphony in B Minor ("Unfinished")*, ed. Martin Chusid (New York, 1968), 98–110. Chusid's arguments resemble those in his "Schubert's Cyclic Compositions of 1824," *Acta Musicologica* 36 (1964): 37–45, the main topics of which are the String Quartet in A Minor (D. 804) and the Octet (D. 803), for in both essays a Beethoven symphony is proposed as an explicit model. Joseph Müller-Blattau hears the second movement of the *Unfinished* as an inflection ("Abwandlung") of the first ("Schuberts 'Unvollendete' und das Problem des Fragmentarischen in der Musik," in *Von der Vielfalt der Musik: Musikgeschichte, Musikerziehung, Musikpflege* [Freiburg i. Br., 1966], esp. 287–89).

26. Tovey's enthusiasm for *Viola*, not universally shared, elicited a valuable study of its formal design (see *Essays in Musical Analysis*, suppl. vol., *Chamber Music* [London, 1944], 137–41). For Maurice J. E. Brown, *Viola* is "a masterpiece" of the genre established in *An die ferne Geliebte*: "Essentially an extended song beginning and ending with the same music" (*The New Grove Schubert* [New York and London, 1983], 93).

27. Thrasybulos Georgiades had a term for it, *Gehlied*—"ein Lied, wonach man, beim Gehen singend, seine Schritte regelt" (*Schubert*, 225, 362). Georgiades holds to a distinction between an actual *Gehlied* and something like a stylized intimation of the real thing: if, for Georgiades, the opening songs in the Müller cycles are of the latter type, *Der Musensohn* meets the criteria of the former. In a quite different context, Rudolf Steglich includes *Der Musensohn* in a discussion of *Wanderlieder*, coincidentally following on a discussion of the opening songs of *Die schöne Müllerin* and *Winterreise* ("Das romantische Wanderlied und Franz Schubert," in *Musa-Mens-Musici: Im Gedenken an Walther Vetter*, ed. Institut für Musikwissenschaft der Humboldt-Universität zu Berlin [Leipzig, 1969), 272–73).

both signal ahead to the cardinal relationships that lend the two sets their internal coherence. Like its analogue *Der Atlas* in the Heine cycle, *Willkommen und Abschied* signifies closure in all the appropriate ways and at the same time manages to recall and to absorb the A♭—more pointedly, the A♭ as an uneasy neighbor to G—in a canvas the final perspective of which gains some distance from the interior anguish of the inner songs.

The Heine cycle and the Goethe set share yet another, and troubling, attribute. They both seem to have been repudiated—indeed, dismantled—by their composer, who in both cases chose to offer the songs for publication in some reordering or in groups with other, unrelated songs by other poets, obliterating any symptom of an earlier integrity. The circumstances attending the dismantling of the Heine cycle are shrouded in much obscurity, darkened finally by Schubert's death only months before its publication. If the single surviving autograph of the Heine songs is very much a part of the mystery, the Goethe set is illuminated—authenticated, rather—in just this aspect, for it is the autograph that stands as the single compelling piece of evidence for a discursive reading of Goethe's four poems that takes us deep into their resonant interiors and offers up a vision of organic form that would yield in the next months to a less radical concept of song cycle; *Die schöne Müllerin* is at once pellucid, concrete, conventional, theatrical, where the Goethe set resonates more deeply in poetic conceit, in a Romantically conceived form.

The source of the conceit, *An die Entfernte* must now be understood in this refound context. Finally, it was Beethoven's cycle that set loose the figure of an "entfernte Geliebte," and it is Beethoven's cycle that haunts the ear in the imagined music of Goethe's lyric. "Dich rufen alle meine Lieder," sings Goethe's lover and in Schubert's music is made to enact a reprise so plaintive as to evoke Beethoven's "Nimm sie hin denn, diese Lieder," a phrase that captures within itself the essence of reminiscence and nostalgia and, with it, that quality of cyclic process in which the genre would seek its definition.

5

In der Ferne: Schubert's Rellstab

Schubert in B minor is Schubert at the depths of his soul. Two songs from his last months make the point. *Der Doppelgänger* follows Heine's neurotic lover to the void. No other song has provoked quite as much hermeneutical exercise.[1] *In der Ferne*, on a poem by Ludwig Rellstab, sings forth its anguish in a different mood. Two sets of songs are comprised in *Schwanengesang* and two kinds of song as well. Where Heine provokes Schubert to the taut, compressed, declamatory speech of anxiety, Rellstab touches that other nerve in him. The Rellstab songs sing the expansive, lyrical Schubert. The Heine songs scream and groan.

I

There is a way that Schubert has of getting to the core of a poem, of getting past its superficial conceits to some essence. This is a point sometimes lost in critical perceptions of his music. It seems to have been lost in a notorious gloss that addresses just one aspect of a single passage. The gloss is by Brahms, and it refers to those brazen parallel fifths that have stigmatized *In der Ferne* ever since the passage was brought to public attention in the earliest review of *Schwanengesang*, by G. W. Fink in the *Allgemeine Musikalische Zeitung* for October 1829: an "Ohren zerreißenden Fortschritt"—an ear-splitting progression—Fink complained of the passage shown in example 5.1, fulminating against the aesthetic and even ethical implications of such license:

> Should such unseemly distortions of harmony, defiantly represented to the spite of all reason, find their impudent swindlers who would smuggle them in as the unheard of surplus of originality to the patient and astonished observers: then, in the event that they succeed, we should find ourselves transplanted into that most blessed of circumstances—the circumstance of anarchy. Oh, how glorious if each should do what pleased him most in his delirium, and were his bold

1. Studies are legion. Among them, two recent ones are Gernot Gruber, "Romantische Ironie in den Heine-Liedern?" in *Schubert-Kongreß Wien 1978*, esp. 329–34; and Lawrence Kramer, "The Schubert Lied: Romantic Form and Romantic Consciousness," in *Schubert: Critical and Analytical Studies*, esp. 218–24.

Example 5.1 *In der Ferne* (D. 957, no. 6), mm. 46–47

stroke to be his fame!—Had Schubert lived longer, he should have cleansed himself of this paroxism.[2]

For Brahms, on the contrary, ethics was not at issue. Rather, we take the citation as an acknowledgment of a grammatical problem, entered into his personal compendium of "Octaven u. Quinten" from the master literature.[3] The pursuit of fifths and octaves, more than some antiquarian diversion, stirred in him deep theoretical questioning. Alongside the infamous passage and another from *Die böse Farbe* (*Die schöne Müllerin*, no. 17), Brahms sketched out conventional solutions of his own and wondered in the margin whether the power of Schubert's effect had been sacrificed: "Apart from the fact that these progressions may be explained or justified easily enough, one may be permitted to ask the delicate question: whether the effect is weakened."[4] Whether Brahms directed his "leise Frage" at Schubert's passages or at his own alternatives—whether, that is, the grammatical weakness of the passage can be claimed to rob it of some expressive effect or whether, in alleviating the stark fifths, the proposed alternatives are weakenings in effect—is not entirely clear. Brahms himself equivocated on this point, scribbling "? dieselbe Wirkung" at his alternative to the passage from *Die böse Farbe* and another mark of interrogation to the alternative for *In der Ferne*.

In the commentary to his meticulous edition of the Brahms manuscript, Paul Mast took the occasion to suggest that "the fifths are used for the sake of the text" and, further, that "they contribute to the intended shock effect . . .

2. "Könnten solche Unziemlichkeiten, solche trotzig hingestellte Harmonieen-Zerrbilder allem Verstande zum Hohn ihre kecken Schwindler finden, die sie geduldigen Anstaunern alles Unerhörten für Originalitäts-Ueberschuß einschwärzen wollten: so würden wir, im Fall das Großartige gelänge, bald in den glückseligsten aller Zustände, in den Zustand der Anarchie, wie in den Tagen des Interregnums, versetzt werden. O wie herrlich, wenn Jeder thun dürfte, was ihm im Rausche beliebte, und sein Gewaltsschlag wäre noch sein Ruhm!—Hätte Schubert länger gelebt, von diesem Paroxismus hätte er sich selbst geheilt" (*Allgemeine Musikalische Zeitung* 31 [1829]: col. 661).

3. Originally published in facsimile as Johannes Brahms, *Oktaven und Quinten u. A.*, ed. Heinrich Schenker (Vienna, 1933), the manuscript has been published again in facsimile in a new critical edition by Paul Mast: "Brahms's Study, Octaven u. Quinten u. A., with Schenker's Commentary Translated," in *The Music Forum*, vol. 5, ed. Felix Salzer and Carl Schachter (New York, 1980), 1–196. The passage from *In der Ferne* is ex. 48, shown on pp. 62–63 and "MS page 4."

4. "Brahms's Study," 62–63.

of the chromatic progression at 'Mutterhaus hassenden.'"[5] It is precisely this view of the thing that seems inadequate and misleading as well in what it implies about how the poem is made to resonate in the music.

Consider how the poem goes:

In der Ferne	*Far Away*
Wehe, den Fliehenden,	Alas, those who flee,
Welt hinaus ziehenden!—	who go out into the world,
Fremde durchmessenden,	who travel strange parts,
Heimat vergessenden,	forgetting their homeland,
Mutterhaus hassenden,	hating their own home,
Freunde verlassenden	abandoning their friends
Folget kein Segen, ach!	—them, ah, no blessing follows
Auf ihren Wegen nach!	upon their way.
Herze, das sehnende,	Yearning heart,
Auge, das tränende,	tearful eye,
Sehnsucht, nie endende,	never-ending longing,
Heimwärts sich wendende!	homewards turning!
Busen, der wallende,	Seething breast,
Klage, verhallende,	fading lament,
Abendstern, blinkender	gleaming evening star,
Hoffnungslos sinkender!	setting without hope!
Lüfte, ihr säuselnden,	Whispering breezes,
Wellen, sanft kräuselnden,	waves, gently ruffled,
Sonnenstrahl, eilender,	sunbeam, hastening,
Nirgend verweilender:	nowhere tarrying:
Die mir mit Schmerze, ach!	ah, to her who with grief
Dies treue Herze brach,	broke this true heart
Grüßt von dem Fliehenden,	—greetings from him who is fleeing,
Welt hinaus ziehenden.	going out into the world.[6]

Every reader will be struck first off by its incessant dactyls, by the substantive planted invariably at the front of the verse and burdened with its own participle, and as well by the trisyllabic rhymes that marry each verse pair. It is the cumulative impact of these repetitive devices that Rellstab is after here, for it is not until the middle of the third strophe that the language straightens out in a formulation that clarifies the relationship of all these hanging participial phrases to a subject:

> Die mir mit Schmerze, ach!
> Dies treue Herze brach. . . .

More than that, these lines are the very crux of the poem. They speak the unspeakable that all the rest of the poem wants to conceal in its distancing of the poet from his object, the estranged, alienated wanderer—the poet himself in

5. Ibid., 167.

6. The translation is from *The Fischer-Dieskau Book of Lieder*, 332.

disguise. So it is with some discomfort that the ear is led to the egregious fifths as "Mutterhaus hassenden" and again, in the second strophe, at "Busen, der wallende." That is because the fifths are so wrenching as to cause the whole sense of the poem to hinge on their significance.

What, in fact, do they mean to signify? Here it would be good to contemplate the obdurate theoretical legacy that such a passage would incite. The seven prolix essays in Lorenz Mizler's *Musikalische Bibliothek* for 1743, in answer to the question, "Why two fifths and octaves that follow immediately one on another in direct motion do not sit well in the ear," may stand for the earnestness with which the issue was addressed in the eighteenth century.[7] Mizler had himself addressed it a year earlier in the course of his translation of Fux's *Gradus ad Parnassum*, in a monumental footnote worrying the nuances of hidden perfect fifths on the way to a diminished one.[8] To persevere through the flourished, baroque rhetoric of these seven essays, like so many legal briefs, along with the responses to them by members of Mizler's famous Societät der musikalischen Wissenschaften, is to be convinced of the profundity of Mizler's question, if not by the answers that it provoked.[9] Without wishing to labor the point, everyone senses that parallel fifths have a lesson to teach. There is in them the violation of some theoretical principle so profound as to approach the imponderable. The whole understanding of tonal music seems at stake. For Brahms, the quest is in response to this eternal question that, in Mizler's quaint phrasing, touches on the single law to which all counterpoint seemingly reduces.

Schenker, too, asked Mizler's question and pursued the answer rather more systematically, even in the course of his own annotations to the Brahms manuscript. The motion between mm. 10 and 29 was understood by Schenker in the construct shown in ex. 5.2.[10] As with so many of Schenker's graphs from these last years, the message is enshrouded, riddle-like, in a hearing impatient with the details of the surface and dismissive of such things as poetic texts. In the path of the inexorable *Quintzug* in the bass, the fifths survive, but as curiosities unexplained. This is the place not to quibble over the details of that *Quintzug*, but only to acknowledge that its assumptions about priorities and hierarchies are necessarily in conflict with what we might call the "speaking" surface of the passage. It is precisely this tension between surface and

7. "Warum zwey unmittelbar in der geraden Bewegung auf einander folgende Quinten und Octaven nicht wohl ins Gehöre fallen?" ([Lorenz Mizler,] "Sieben Schrifften [wegen der] Quinten und Octaven," in *Musikalische Bibliothek*, ed. Lorenz Mizler, vol. 2, pt. 4 [Leipzig, 1743], 1–95).

8. Johann Joseph Fux, *Gradus ad Parnassum, oder Anführung zur Regelmäßigen Musikalischen Composition*, trans. Lorenz Mizler (Leipzig, 1742; reprint, Hildesheim and New York, 1974), 89–91.

9. Mizler and the members of his society were similarly unmoved, and, in the preface to these seven essays, Mizler announced that the contest would be extended into 1744 (see Mizler, "Sieben Schrifften," 3–4).

10. Example 5.2 is taken from Mast, "Brahms's Study," 149.

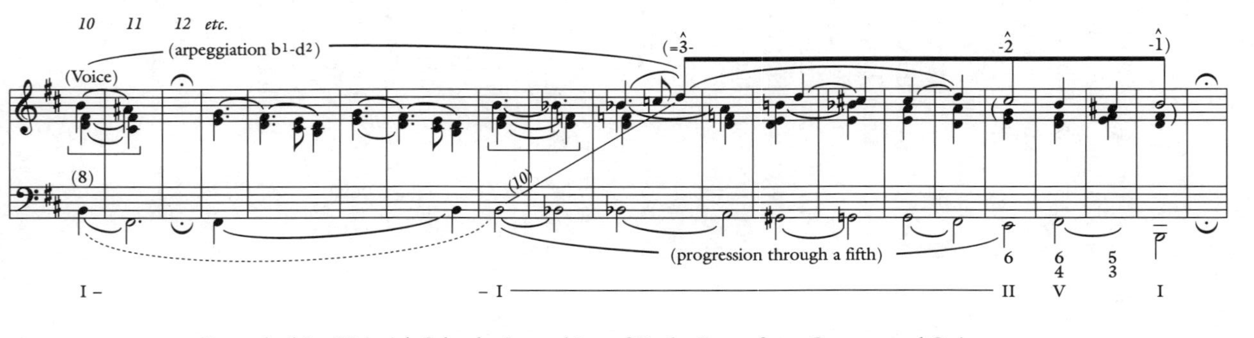

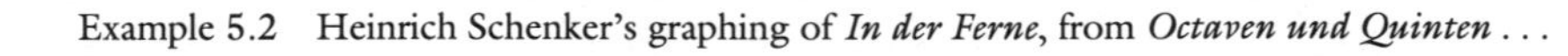
Example 5.2 Heinrich Schenker's graphing of *In der Ferne*, from *Octaven und Quinten* . . .

infrastructure that may be said to generate much of the expressive power of such passages.

It was characteristic of Schenker to hear in the motion between B and B♭ an "analogue" to the motion between B and A♯ at mm. 10 and 11, by way of justifying the octave doubling between voice and bass. But syntax is not a matter of evidence and argument. There can be no compensation to weigh against a breach in syntax. In this case, the essence of the solecism is situated less in those octaves, which, taken alone, might be heard as decorative reinforcement—a doubling, that is—than in the fifths, where the ground rules of counterpoint are at issue.

The model of voice leading that would govern a chromatic descent in the bass from the tonic through to the dominant is a common one. Schenker himself described it on a number of occasions in various contexts, perhaps most tellingly in his graphing of the opening measures of Mozart's *Dissonance* Quartet (K. 465).[11] Clearly, this is not a model for *In der Ferne*, for its bass does not move to the leading tone of the triad on the dominant (as is the case in the opening measures of K. 465). Rather, the B♭ will be heard at once as an upper neighbor to A, in turn a passing harmony to the $^6_5$ chord on G♯ (as shown in ex. 5.3). But the surface of the music—the way in which it is articulated and inflected—fights tenaciously against that hearing. The B♭ is made to sound ponderously like an *end* accent, a harmony in its own right. The fifths are real.

Example 5.3 *In der Ferne*, mm. 46–53, linear abstract

And this brings us round again to those critical lines—

Die mir mit Schmerze, ach!
Dies treue Herze brach. . . .

—invoking their analogues at lines 5 and 6 in the first two strophes. But now there is a turning away, epode-like, from the subject of those strophes. The conventional agents of nature are sent forth bearing the obligatory message—a *Liebesbotschaft* gone sour. Even the naive reader—or perhaps only he—will have grasped the intent of Rellstab's estranged wanderer. In the familiar Romantic fantasy, she who provokes the suffering must be made to bear wit-

11. Heinrich Schenker, *Free Composition (Der freie Satz)*, ed. and trans. Ernst Oster (New York and London, 1979), suppl., *Music Examples* (unpaginated), fig. 99/3. For a reading by Oswald Jonas of this graph, see Heinrich Schenker, *Harmony*, ed. Oswald Jonas, trans. Elisabeth Mann Borgese (Chicago, 1954), 346–47.

ness to it. The poem regulates the timing of these lines—a gradual homing in on the moment of revelation, from the remote, objectifying description of alienation in the first strophe, where the wanderer is the *object*, generalized in the plural ("Wehe, den Fliehenden"), to the expression, in the second strophe, of subjective anguish. The turning outward, in the consoling language at the outset of the third strophe, has an ominous tinge.

If Rellstab's tender images are enhanced in the turn to the major mode here, Schubert has in mind a deeper strategy. The music hews to the harmonic course of the earlier strophes. That is a simple enough matter in the modal conversion of the first quatrain, whose harmonies oscillate between tonic and dominant. But the ear is stretched to anticipate what this turn to major might signify for the music that follows, where the lover's dark secret is finally revealed, for it is precisely here that the music touches to the core of the poem, probing at the source of those perplexing fifths that earlier hinted at some deeper angst. The syntax proposed in example 5.3, and earlier obscured by those fifths, comes clear.

Schubert's autograph (shown in fig. 5.1) for once betrays the composer engaged—even *listening*—in some intimate reversal of the play between text and author now further complicated by a confusion of author, protagonist, and performer.[12] The play is captured in the new reverberations in the piano after "Schmerze, ach" and "Herze brach," afterthoughts interpolated in the manuscript, that feign reaction to this chilling confession. In sympathy, the pianist (the composer disguised) allows the singer (the lover—but here, too, the composer in deeper disguise) a moment to catch a breath. In the interval, we listen for—conjure up in the inner ear—those attendant fifths, whose earlier implications deepen now in that they pointedly do not sound.

II

The echoing in the piano brings to mind a very similar passage, also in B minor, in another Rellstab song. In the last strophe of *Ständchen*, the music finally breaks away from an incessant idling between modes—now D minor, now D major—and breaks loose from the controlling metaphor, the nightingale, its painfully erotic songs, and so forth (see ex. 5.4):

> Laß auch *Dir* das Herz bewegen,
> Liebchen, höre mich!
> Bebend harr' ich Dir entgegen!
> Komm', beglücke mich![13]

12. The autograph is now at the Pierpont Morgan Library in New York (see *The Mary Flagler Cary Music Collection*, comp. O. E. Albrecht, H. Cahoon, and D. C. Ewing [New York, 1970], item 188, p. 44). A facsimile of the autograph is published as *Franz Schubert: Schwanengesang: 13 Lieder nach Gedichten von Rellstab und Heine, D. 957*, ed. Walther Dürr (Hildesheim, 1978).

13. In Schubert's autograph, in Haslinger's edition of *Schwanengesang*, and in all subsequent editions, Rellstab's "das Herz" becomes "die Brust," and the emphasis on "Dir" (typographically

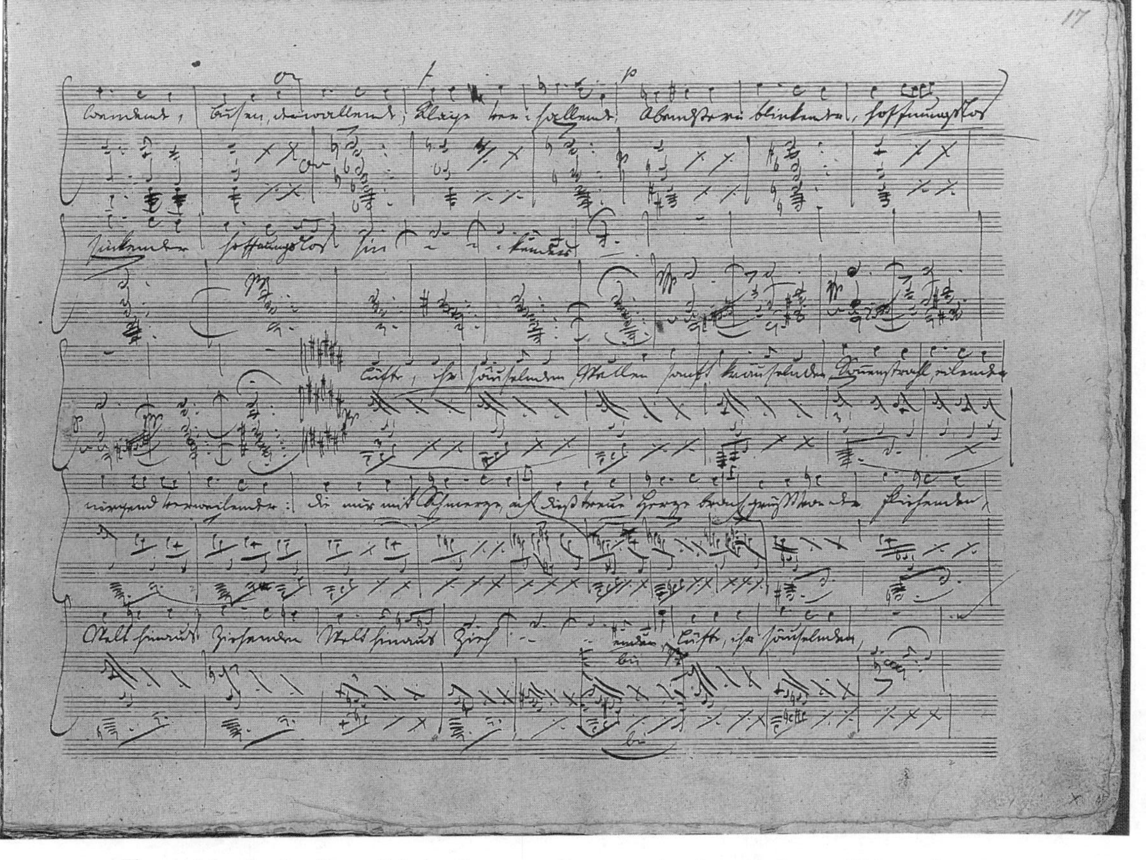

Figure 5.1 *In der Ferne*, Schubert's autograph score, showing the later addition of m. 76. Courtesy Mary Flagler Cary Music Collection in the Pierpont Morgan Library, New York.

Example 5.4 *Ständchen* (D. 957, no. 4), mm. 59–72

> (Let your heart, too, be moved; beloved, hear me! Trembling, I await you! Come, make me happy!)

Trembling, he awaits her. In this otherwise strophic setting, these lines are unique. A momentary affliction, the music throbs in B minor. The blithe, matter-of-fact regaining of composure, at "Komm', beglücke mich," as if nothing had happened, only points up the aberrant aspect of the passage. The memory of it, eros and anxiety together, seems to smolder still beneath the moment of revelation in *In der Ferne.*

---

gesperrt) is lost. Rellstab's text, otherwise hard to come by, may be studied in *Franz Schubert: Die Texte seiner einstimmig komponierten Lieder und ihre Dichter*, ed. Maximilian Schochow and Lilly Schochow, 2 vols. (Hildesheim and New York, 1974, 2:474). The discrepancy (unreported by the Schochows and in the *NGA*) owes either to Schubert's misreading or to a distinction between the text of the poems as Schubert may have received them and the version published in Ludwig Rellstab, *Gedichte* (Leipzig, 1827), vol. 1.

Here it will be good to recall that the two songs belong to *Schwanengesang*, Tobias Haslinger's designation for a collection, published two months after Schubert's death, that includes settings to seven poems by Rellstab and six by Heine. The authority for this uncomfortable marriage rests with Schubert, for the two sets were written out discursively in a single and integral holograph whose central fascicle, a gathering of four "nested" bifolios, runs the last two songs of the Rellstab set on into the first five songs of the Heine set. The ground for construing the Heine set as a cycle in and of itself is in the hypothetical rearrangement of the songs to follow the order in which the poems are revealed in Heine's *Heimkehr*. The arguments in its support are made in the chapter that follows. Decoupled from the Heine songs—from a Heine *cycle*—the Rellstab songs consequently take on a life of their own. Do they lay claim to some similar design of narrativity and coherence?

The obstacles to such a reading are formidable. The poems were evidently those offered to Beethoven during Rellstab's visit to Vienna in 1825. Schindler—not an agent who inspires confidence in the transmission of evidence—was a player in what followed. As Rellstab told it, "Some years ago, Prof. Schindler retrieved [the poems] for me from Beethoven's *Nachlaß*. Several were emended with pencil markings in Beethoven's own hand. They were those which he liked best, and which he then gave to Schubert to compose, for he himself felt too unwell."[14] A contradiction lurks, for how can Schindler have retrieved the poems from Beethoven's *Nachlaß* when at the same time it is claimed that Beethoven had himself given them to Schubert? Schindler, we know, exercised a not quite legal privilege shortly after Beethoven's death in sifting through the *Nachlaß*, some of the contents of which he did in fact share with Schubert.[15] That, at any rate, is how Schindler himself explained the matter.[16] In this instance, and from what can be pieced together of Schindler's tendency to implant Beethoven's remains in Schubert's workshop—to mediate in some lurid reincarnation of his hero—perhaps we are right to follow him here.

Unlike the Heine poems, which in effect have a story to tell (elliptical as it may be), the Rellstab poems make no pretense to a prevailing narrativity. Nor does Rellstab encourage us to seek any. "I picked out eight or ten of the lyrical poems, each cleanly written on its own leaf," Rellstab wrote, recalling

14. "Herr Professor Schindler hat sie mir vor Jahren aus Beethovens Nachlaß zurückgestellt. Einige waren mit Bleistiftkreuzchen versehen von Beethovens eigner Hand; es waren diejenigen, welche ihm am besten gefielen und die er damals an Schubert zur Komposition gegeben, weil er selbst sich zu unwohl fühlte" (Otto Erich Deutsch, *Schubert: Die Erinnerungen seiner Freunde* [Leipzig, 1957], 348; another English translation can be found in *Schubert: Memoirs by His Friends*, trans. Rosamond Ley and John Nowell [New York, 1958], 303).

15. For something on the mistrust with which Schindler was viewed during those months after Beethoven's death, see Clemens Brenneis, "Das Fischhof-Manuskript: Zur Frühgeschichte der Beethoven-Biographik," in *Zu Beethoven: Aufsätze und Annotationen*, ed. Harry Goldschmidt (Berlin, 1979), 90–116, esp. 98.

16. Deutsch, *Erinnerungen*, 367–68; *Memoirs*, p. 319.

his offering to Beethoven many years after the event.[17] This suggests that Schubert acquired a portfolio of separate leaves, randomly ordered, from which it must follow that the order in *Schwanengesang* is Schubert's, not Rellstab's. Yet, when the songs are sung as Schubert sets them forth, intimations of some cyclic process are pronounced and suggestive.

Such intimations seem almost the central message of *Liebesbotschaft*, the song that sets the process in motion. After *An die ferne Geliebte*, it would be difficult indeed to read Rellstab's poem without conjuring the image of Jeitteles's (and Beethoven's) *entfernte Geliebte*, a response that Rellstab may well have hoped to excite in giving the poems to Beethoven. The connection would not have been lost on Schubert. *An die ferne Geliebte*, it must again be suggested, touched his work in various ways, overtly and subliminally.

And Rellstab's "rauschendes Bächlein" will have put Schubert in mind of an earlier cycle of his own. The agency of the brook—its personification—is so central to *Die schöne Müllerin* that the cycle may be said fully to engage only with its second song. *Wohin?*, in G major as well, sings forth in the innocence of Müller's *Volkston*, an intimation of the more sophisticated conceits of *Liebesbotschaft*. Coincidently, *Liebesbotschaft* was also to have been a second song. In a preliminary draft for the first few of these Rellstab settings (described in the "Postscript" below), it is preceded by an unfinished *Lebensmut*; like *Das Wandern*, it too is cast strophically and in B♭ major, a robust out-of-doors song. Here, too, the cycle is not yet engaged.

In *Liebesbotschaft*, the distancing of the parted lovers is conveyed in a characteristic tonal plotting: from the tonic G major, a casual motion away by thirds through E minor, C major, A minor, and (for an instant) F major, and then a shift of focus to B—first as a dominant, then tonicized as B major—when, in the erotic cliché, the image of the beloved is conjured nodding off on the bank. Here is the gist of the poem:

Tröste die Süße
Mit freundlichem Blick,
Denn der Geliebte
Kehrt bald zurück.

(Console the sweet one with a friendly glance, for then the beloved will soon return).

The brook, eternal symbol of fertility, is again the surrogate lover. The physical, spatial distancing between the lovers (the *Entfernung*) is synonymous with a more powerful motion in the opposite direction, toward the vicarious embrace—she, he imagines, nods off to sleep, her thoughts embracing him ("*meiner* gedenkend das Köpfchen hängt"). The "taking" of B major suggests something of that paradox: by logical modulation, it is plotted out as the key of greatest remove from the tonic, while, in the acoustic *senario* from

17. "Jedes auf ein besonderes Blättchen sauber geschrieben" (Ludwig Rellstab, *Aus meinem Leben* [Berlin, 1861], 244–45).

G, B holds a privileged position, embedded in the tonic unfolding. In a song given to phrases of ecstasy and bliss, the quatrain in B major is heart stopping—not that its phrases are in themselves more ecstatic, but only that B major makes them seem so. It is an apostrophe in itself, closed off. In a phrase of wrenching poignance, the music is coaxed finally back to G. The lover is again distant.

It is a good long while before B major is again sounded. When it is, at the turn to the third strophe of *In der Ferne*, the evocation of that lost moment of ecstasy, locked in cyclic association with B major, is hard to resist. The strategy of modal play within *In der Ferne* seems to have something to do with a convoluted signaling of some psychoanalytic self-revelation. Even as it is proclaimed in those opening, hortatory measures in which the piano intones its octaves F♯-G♮-F♯, we may want to ponder how the key itself—B minor/major—is meant to contribute to that revelatory process.[18] Does the B major of *Liebesbotschaft* play into the memory of *In der Ferne*? Is B major itself thematic?

Consider again those confessional lines, "Die mir mit Schmerze, ach! / Dies treue Herze brach," from which the music seems to gather its deepest inflections. The telling inflection, that which captures the piercing revelation of the poem, is the direct, even contradictory, passage from B major to B minor. Those onerous fifths, their prophetic mission now revealed, fall away. The music probes the differences between B major and B minor on many levels. At one level, the D♯ is cast as a prolonged appoggiatura to D♮, poised to resolve at "Schmerze." *In der Ferne* is in B *minor*, its final measures emphatically remind us. The B *major* that sets off its third strophe is as exotic, in its way, as is the B-major quatrain in *Liebesbotschaft*. And it is only in the expansive peroration to the song, set to a repetition of the text of the third strophe, that this conflict between modes is played out, even to the two thwarted cadences that exercise once again the F♯-G♮ of the opening, and much else. Here, too, the bonding with *Liebesbotschaft* is palpable.

If *Liebesbotschaft* is a song to set a cycle in motion, *Abschied* (as its name implies) is a song to close one off. Its bluff E♭ acts as an antidote to the somber B minor with which *In der Ferne* closes. There is a sheer, physical exuberance to *Abschied* that dispels the pathological brooding that precedes it. In its six long strophes, the parting seems to go on forever. Toward the end, the music makes its inevitable turn to the flat submediant, but with a difference. C♭ major is prolonged, tonicized, and made more substantial than seems justifiable in the song itself, where C♭ has otherwise no role to play. It evokes a nostalgia for those past musics in B major, no matter that Rellstab's lines here might bear only the faintest poetic relevance to the passages in *Liebesbotschaft*, *Ständchen*, and *In der Ferne* awakened in this music:

18. Joseph Kerman hears another function for these opening measures: "The semitone step and the suggestion of parallels prefigure *inter alia* the grating juxtaposition of B-minor and B-flat-major root-position triads later in the song" ("A Romantic Detail" [rev. ed.], 56).

Ade, Ihr Sterne, verhüllet Euch grau! Ade!
Des Fensterleins trübes, verschimmerndes Licht
Ersetzt Ihr unzähligen Sterne mir nicht.

(Adieu, stars, veil yourselves in gray. Adieu! You numberless stars cannot replace for me the dim, fading light in the window.)

But the "Verhüllung"—the enshrouding—that is the final sentiment is morbidly apropos. The stars take on a mourning aspect. We think for a moment of the final song in Schumann's *Dichterliebe*—the final poem in Heine's *Lyrisches Intermezzo*—that watery *Begrabung* in which are entombed all those "alte, böse Lieder," and the poet's love and suffering with them.

III

Do these Rellstab settings then constitute a song cycle? Even as the poems are formulated in Schubert's ordering of them, they miss the unities of time, of place, of narrative continuity, and even of poetic species that are the minimal prerequisites to cycle making in the prototypes established by Jeitteles and Müller. A story literal in all its details is not at issue here. The poems do not pretend to that. But when we give ourselves up to its accents, the music seems to draw from each poem what is essential to the plotting of some inner, psychological journey. That the poems together were designed to invite such plotting we may wish to infer from a letter by Rellstab believed to have been written to Beethoven: "I send you herewith some songs which I have had copied fairly for you; some others, written in the same vein, will shortly follow. They have perhaps this novelty about them, that they form in themselves a connected series, and have reference to happiness, unity, separation, death, and hope on the other side of the grave, without pointing to any definite incidents."[19] Sensitive to such traces of consanguinity, Schubert would have drawn the invitation from the poems themselves. Better external evidence—a title, for example, in Schubert's manuscript or in some text of the poems—might satisfy the orthodox conditions for attributing cyclic status to these songs; but internal evidence—the semantics and the syntax of the songs as text—makes eloquent claim to another kind of coherence, one not easily aligned with the more conventional modes of cyclic process yet not at odds with its conventions.

The positioning of *Liebesbotschaft* at the beginning of the set and *Abschied* at the end is clue enough of an intent to enclose the set in some meaningful way. And then there are all those signals that flash back and forth from one song to the next. The most portentous of these is the brutal C-minor triad,

19. That, at any rate, is how it is reported in Heinrich Kreissle von Hellborn, *Franz Schubert* (Vienna, 1865; reprint, Hildesheim and New York, 1978), 446–47 (translated by A. D. Coleridge as *The Life of Franz Schubert* [London, 1869], 2:134). For a discussion of the letter, see Rufus Hallmark, "Schubert's 'Auf dem Strom,'" in *Schubert Studies: Problems of Style and Chronology*, 44.

Example 5.5 *Aufenthalt* (D. 957, no. 5), mm. 118–30

Example 5.6 *Aufenthalt*, mm. 127–29, harmonic abstract

struck in root position, in the final strain of *Aufenthalt* at m. 124, and sustained intact for four complete bars (see ex. 5.5). This is a harmony without antecedent—with no apparent justification, no syntactic "cover." To hear it merely as a disfiguring of the cadential formula ♭VI-V—an interpretation buoyed by the A (fleeting but essential) in the voice at m. 127, where the E♭ is understood to anticipate the D♯ in the dominant (see ex. 5.6)—is to miss the catastrophic knell of the harmony. And, because the harmony insists on C as a root (contradicting its sense as an appoggiatura), the move to the dominant has more than a whiff of parallelism about it. The fifths at "Mutterhaus hassenden" seem to sound in direct response to this passage; registral identity only clinches the connection (see ex. 5.7).

A non sequitur, its symbolic aspect brazenly displayed, the C-minor triad sounds forth in isolation as if to seek out a cognate, a referent. The opening bars of *Kriegers Ahnung* spring to mind. In the disposition of its pitches, the opening chords form a template for the piano part in *Aufenthalt* at mm. 124–26 (see ex. 5.8), whose pointed rhythm, isolated *fortissimo*, now suggests a willful play with the rhythm of the device with which *Kriegers Ahnung* begins and ends.

Example 5.7 *a*, *Aufenthalt*, mm. 124–29. *b*, *In der Ferne*, mm. 17–20

Example 5.8 *a*, *Kriegers Ahnung* (D. 957, no. 2), opening measures. *b*, *Aufenthalt*, mm. 124–26

One other passage in *Kriegers Ahnung* is to the point here. At the innermost recesses of the poem—

> Hier, wo der Flammen düstrer Schein
> Ach! nur auf Waffen spielt,
> Hier fühlt die Brust sich ganz allein,
> Der Wehmut Träne quillt.

(Here, where the somber glimmer of the flames, alas, plays only on weapons; here the heart feels utterly alone; a tear of sadness wells up.)

—the music recedes as well, to remote regions a tritone from the tonic, and traces in serpentine motion a descent back to its dominant (see ex. 5.9). The A-minor triad at "ganz allein" (m. 50), struck ***fp*** in root position, is at once a

Example 5.9 *Kriegers Ahnung*, mm. 41–61

bold and unexpected harmony and a devious passing chord that countermands any sense of true root—much like the C-minor triad of similar affect in *Aufenthalt.* Again, we are put in mind of the critical phrase in *In der Ferne,* at "Die mir mit Schmerze, ach!" The two passages are of course very different, yet the chromatic evasion at "Hier fühlt die Brust sich ganz allein" seems to trouble this motion in a way that evokes the obfuscation at "Mutterhaus hassenden." Here, too, parallelisms abound. Deviant syntax strains the limits of intelligibility, even as the greater motion in the bass, casting A♭ as ♭VI to the dominant, redeems the passage (see ex. 5.10).

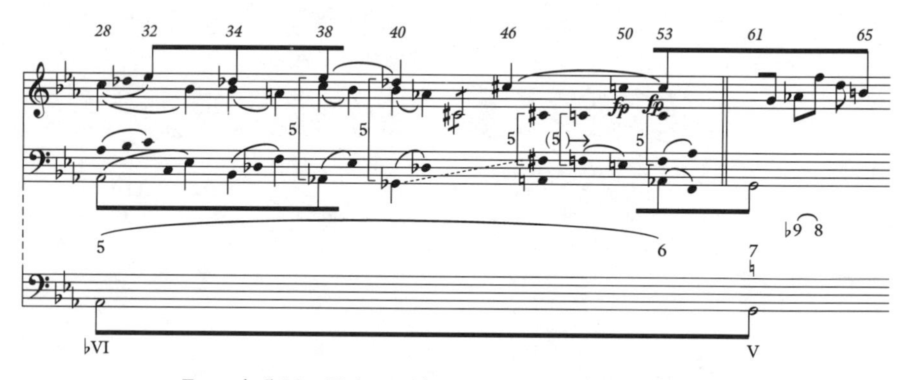

Example 5.10 *Kriegers Ahnung*, mm. 28–65, analytic sketch

In the end, Schubert's ordering of the poems allows a characteristic scenario to emerge:

> *Liebesbotschaft.* The distant beloved. Messenger as surrogate.
>
> *Kriegers Ahnung.* Distance of time and place reinforced.
>
> *Frühlingssehnsucht.* Eroticism intensified: "Nur du befreist den Lenz in der Brust, Nur du! Nur du!"
>
> *Ständchen.* The lovers are very close now: "Bebend harr' ich dir entgegen! Komm', beglücke mich!"

In *Aufenthalt* comes the catastrophe. If the sentiments in the poem allow some latitude of interpretation, the central conceit is clear enough:

> Wie sich die Welle an Welle reiht,
> Fließen die Tränen mir ewig erneut.
>
> (As wave follows upon wave, so my tears flow, ever renewed.)

The lines play on the paradox of the moment at which love is consummated and lost. The flow of tears is at once metaphor for the love act and symbol of the sorrow that must follow from it. *Aufenthalt*: the title itself bespeaks a sense of time stopped, the journey broken. The signal harmony at mm. 124–27, wrenching the music back to some distant past, seems a mutation of the title itself, a view encouraged in the deliberate omission of "Mein Aufenthalt," the text that ought to have sounded at just these bars. The fusion of poem and music is complete.

A denouement of sorts is played out in *In der Ferne* and *Abschied* and, at the same time, a receding to some remote point equivalent to the measure of distance established in *Liebesbotschaft*, but irreversible in its temporal aspect.

IV

"Schubert in B minor," perhaps too boldly asserted at the outset, means to suggest in its topological way that in the key itself lies some impenetrable essence of substance and expression—that the composer so to speak inhabits the key. So to assert is to raise thorny epistemological questions. How can we *know* that specificity of key denotes meaning in and of itself? Is "B minor means *X*" the kind of assertion that can be verified? And, in such a formulation, how precisely might "B minor" be said to "mean" or even to contribute to meaning?

Whether or not B minor can be shown to enjoy some immanence of universal appeal, the evidence for "how B minor means" must be rigorously scrutinized in those single cases that seems intuitively to be the right ones. The process has a tautological ring to it, but that is in the nature of the thing. In the end, we might allow that something approaching "impenetrable meaning" is wrung out of the music at the lines "Die mir mit Schmerze, ach / Dies treue Herze brach," at the instant of self-revelation where the striking repercussion of B minor is the catharsis enacted, the powerful moment that seems to draw up within itself all those other moments that collectively signal what this Rellstab cycle means in its deepest sense to convey. To argue that the passage loses none of its eloquence transposed to some other key—further, that in manifold instances Schubert sanctioned such transposition—is to miss the point: *B minor* is where *this* passage is situated, and its situation, whether or not we can summon a proper sensitivity to it, must remain at the core of the message.

In a similar way, *Der Doppelgänger*—about torment at some deeper psychological plane—acquires a kind of gravitational magnitude in the set of Heine songs, even to the manner in which the outer songs in that cycle pay homage to its centricity. At the beginning is *Das Fischermädchen* in A♭ major, its middle strophe set to music in C♭ major. *Der Atlas*, at the end, is in G minor, so the setting of its middle strophe in B major must be construed as an act intended to point up the thematic relevance of the key itself. The coincidence of all this with tonal plotting in the Rellstab set is provocative. The B major in the midst of *Liebesbotschaft* and the C♭ major in the midst of *Abschied* stand in much the same relationship to the B minor of *In der Ferne* as do the skewed mediant relationships in the outer songs of the Heine set to the B minor of *Der Doppelgänger*.

Winterreise is a cycle of a radically different kind, but perhaps it is not beside the point to recall that B minor has—or, rather, had—a fundamental role to play in its transmission. Its final song, *Der Leiermann*, where the concept of expression is itself driven to a vanishing point, was to have been declaimed in B minor. The circumstances surrounding its transposition to A minor are considered in chapter 8. To anticipate, it can be said here that no hard evidence is at hand to support the contention that Schubert authorized the transposition. Nor is this the place to speculate on the senses in which B minor intrudes in the grim Odyssey traveled in *Winterreise*—that, too, is a topic for later chapters. Here we can only contemplate for a moment its last, chill phrase, a glimpse into the void, frozen forever on a final high F♯.

Nor is *Die schöne Müllerin* immune. The inside-out reversals of "liebe Farbe / böse Farbe," a salient opposition in the cycle, are manifest in a pairing of exceptional pathos. The bleak B minor of *Die liebe Farbe*, its obsessive F♯s suggestive of similar (and later) obsessions in *Der Doppelgänger* and *Der Leiermann*, gives way to the B major/B minor of *Die böse Farbe*. It is tempting to speculate that this was the connection that led Brahms, in his notebook "Oktaven u. Quinten," to couple a climactic, fifths-ridden phrase from *Die böse Farbe* with the disquieting passage from *In der Ferne*.[20]

V

One other cycle from just these years seems worth invoking in this context. "Ciclus von Kleinigkeit[en]," Beethoven called it in an early draft, referring to what we know as the six Bagatelles, op. 126, published in 1825 and reviewed enthusiastically in two principal critical journals in Berlin and Leipzig, in 1825 and 1826.[21]

In its rough outline, op. 126 adumbrates the tonal plan that characterizes the Rellstab set: a first number in a tender G major, *Liebesbotschaft*-like, and a last in an E♭ struck with vehemence in effect much like the alfresco E♭ of *Abschied*; there is even something *Abschied*-like in all those farewell clichés in the slower, middle music of this final piece. And in one other aspect, op. 126 is kin to the Rellstab cycle, for here as well the piece of greatest weight is in B minor, as the Berlin critic was the first to note.[22]

"H moll schwarze Tonart," Beethoven mused, in a sketchbook from 1815.[23]

20. Example 47 in Paul Mast's edition (see "Brahms's Study," 60 and MS page 4).

21. Both pieces are reprinted in *Ludwig van Beethoven: Sechs Bagatellen für Klavier* Op. 126, ed. Sieghard Brandenburg, 2 vols. (Bonn, 1984), 2:72–73. For Beethoven's inscription, see 1:52, 2:27. But his orthography is ambivalent, and one might do better to transcribe "Cüclus" or even "Cÿclus."

22. Ibid., 2:72. For an interesting discussion of the piece, see Edward T. Cone, "Beethoven's Experiments in Composition: The Late Bagatelles," in *Beethoven Studies 2*, ed. Alan Tyson (London, Oxford, and New York, 1977), 97–98.

23. "B minor black key." See Gustav Nottebohm, *Zweite Beethoveniana: Nachgelassene Aufsätze*, ed. E. Mandyczewski (Leipzig, 1887), 326; and Lewis Lockwood, "The Beethoven Sketch-

It is a key that he avoided like the plague. There is the Goethe song *Sehnsucht* ("Was zieht mir das Herz so"), op. 83, no. 2; the funeral march for Friedrich Duncker's *Leonore Prohaska*, transcribed from the Piano Sonata, op. 26 (where it is in A♭ minor); and another "bagatelle," this one written in Ferdinand Piringer's *Stammbuch* in 1821. For Schubert, on the contrary, B minor seems to have inspired its own vocabulary of tropes and images, and it is tempting to reach for an even more intimate, autobiographical code of signification.

The appeal of Beethoven's op. 126 as some paradigmatic ideal is irresistible. A. B. Marx seems to have been the first to comprehend the deep originality and infinite promise of the new genre. He captures something of its essence in a remarkable piece on the Bagatelles, op. 119, in the 1824 *Caecilia*: "As favorable as sonata form is for the complete development of a musical idea . . . it is as little suited for freer effusions or for the expression of impulses that surely appear worthy of preservation in an artistic form as such.[24]

Common sense will dictate that op. 126 cannot have served as a concrete model for the Rellstab settings. In their pithy eccentricity, the Bagatelles are the benchmark of Beethoven's last music. The elliptic wiring in their circuitry is incompatible with Schubert's manner. Yet precisely this novelty of expression must have claimed privilege for op. 126 as an inspiration in some deeper theoretical sense: the Classical verities that control conventional large-scale works surrender to the ambiguities immanent in the nesting of thirds that describes the tonality of op. 126. And that does seem to the point in construing how these songs map an idiomatic coherence of their own.

One final thought on those parallel fifths. In answer to Mizler's naive question, one wants to suggest that, when two perfect fifths are consecutively sounded, they have the power to launch, by their implication, two alien tonal fields. Schubert's fifths reach back to similarly contradictory motions in *Kriegers Ahnung* and *Aufenthalt*. And while one may wish to hear in them a spasmodic response to Rellstab's "Mutterhaus hassenden," the fifths vibrate deep into the final strophe of *In der Ferne*, where, for good reason, they must not actually sound. In their absence, they yet signal beyond, to those cognate moments in other songs that together suggest the true, the inner cycle. In some mode not conducive to concrete description, the trajectories set forth in Beethoven's final, eccentric "Kleinigkeiten" make themselves felt among the play of contingencies in the Rellstab songs. The two works together forge a provocative new model for the conceiving of Romantic form.

---

book in the Scheide Library," *Princeton University Library Chronicle* 37 (Autumn 1976): 139–53, esp. 150–52. For more on the sketchbook, see Douglas Johnson, Alan Tyson, and Robert Winter, *The Beethoven Sketchbooks: History, Reconstruction, Inventory* (Berkeley and Los Angeles, 1985), 241–46.

24. "So günstig die Sonatenform ist, eine Idee musikalisch vollkommen zu entwickeln . . . so wenig eignet sie sich doch für freiere Ergüsse, oder für die Aussprache von Anregungen, welche schon als solche der Aufbewahrung in einer künstlerischen Gestaltung werth erscheinen" (*Caecilia*, 1 [1824]: 140; reprinted in Brandenburg, ed., *Beethoven: Sechs Bagatellen*, 2:59).

Postscript

A preliminary draft for the setting of three Rellstab songs—a single bifolio containing *Lebensmut* (D. 937), *Liebesbotschaft*, and a textless eleven-measure fragment that agrees with a possible scansion of *Frühlingssehnsucht*—is witness to an earlier concept of some grouping of Rellstab poems.[25] The manuscript is rich in the symptoms of compositional process. *Lebensmut*, complete in all the detail characteristic of what O. E. Deutsch would have described as an "erste Niederschrift," breaks off inexplicably at the bottom of folio 1r with the final B♭ in the voice tied over to some missing postlude. Presumably, the opening measures in the piano were to have assumed that function, but the manuscript is mute on this point. *Liebesbotschaft* is drafted out complete in the voice part, with text underlaid, and in the piano right hand between strophes. The bass is given only at m. 44, at "tröste die Süße," where the harmony, in the midst of its address in B major, inflects a D♯ in the bass. The notation is sparse: D♯ in the bass, a double-sharp (without notehead!) scribbled in the F space on the treble staff, and nothing more.

If the draft for *Liebesbotschaft* is the essence of the song that was finally published, the sketch for *Frühlingssehnsucht* (see fig. 5.2) bears no resemblance to the finished version. It begins straight away with the voice part, leaving no space for the obligatory piano preamble. There seems little margin for error in assuming that the sketch is in fact a setting of the opening lines of *Frühlingssehnsucht*: "In consideration of the complicated prosody of the draft, only *Frühlingssehnsucht* comes into question," as Walther Dürr puts it.[26]

Schubert responds avidly in the setting of such strophic parallelisms to close off each of the five strophes in *Frühlingssehnsucht*:

. . . Wohin? Wohin?
. . . Hinab? Hinab?
. . . Warum? Warum?
. . . Und du? Und du?
. . . Nur du! Nur du!

Tellingly, the draft breaks off just before the setting of this final line, as though stopped before the problem of finding the perfect music for these twice-asked questions and, simultaneously, some emphatic confirmation at "Nur du!" that would respond syntactically to those questions. Further, it breaks off at a high A, an overly ecstatic pitch that, by the summer of 1828,

25. The manuscript has the signature A 236 in the collection of the Gesellschaft der Musikfreunde in Vienna. For a description, see chap. 6 below; and *NGA*, ser. 4, vol. 14b, where the manuscript is given in transcription on pp. 284–89.

26. "Bei der komplizierten Metrik des Entwurfs kommt da nur *Frühlingssehnsucht* in Frage" (*NGA*, ser. 4, vol. 14b, p. 328). E. Mandyczewski seems to have been the first to come to this conclusion, and he penciled an identification at the top of the page. It is more than a little suggestive that *Frühlingssehnsucht* was to have followed directly on *Liebesbotschaft*, for the two poems are very close in tone and imagery.

Figure 5.2 Unused draft, putatively for *Frühlingssehnsucht* (A236 from Archiv der Gesellschaft der Musikfreunde in Wien).

ought to have triggered in Schubert noises of censorship from singer and publisher.[27] Its sense of peak will perhaps have obscured the way to an appropriate device at "Wohin?"

In the end, Schubert rejected this music for a very different view of *Frühlingssehnsucht.* We cannot of course know with any certainty why Schubert abandoned the draft. Arguments for its banality will sound forced and self-serving. But perhaps an answer is to be sought in the more intriguing decision to replot the cycling of the Rellstab poems that form the set—a decision born in the recognition of *Liebesbotschaft* as the characteristic song with which to open a cycle and yoked to a simultaneous decision about *Lebensmut.* Why was *it* abandoned? Not simply—as has been argued—because its tessitura would make it an uncomfortable song to sing.[28] Rather, the poem itself, in its rough bravado, strikes a tone incompatible with the seven poems that finally consti-

27. On ambitus and transposition, see Georgiades, *Schubert,* 194–99; Arnold Feil, *Franz Schubert: Die schöne Müllerin; Winterreise* (Stuttgart, 1975), 30 (translated into English by Ann C. Sherwin as *Franz Schubert: Die schöne Müllerin; Winterreise* [Portland, Oreg., 1988], 27–28); and Anthony Newcomb, "Structure and Expression in a Schubert Song: *Noch einmal* Auf dem Flusse *zu hören,*" in *Schubert: Critical and Analytical Studies,* 168–70.

28. *NGA,* ser. 4, vol. 14b, p. 347. Richard Capell, on the other hand, thought that there was a flaw in the strophic concept: "The tune . . . is impossibly jaunty for the last stanza" (*Schubert's Songs,* 69).

tute the set. Its closing couplet—"Neu gläntzt ein Morgenroth: / Muthig umarmt den Tod!"—is an exhortation that speaks to nothing in the poems that follow, which are all in some sense about a *lover* pursued and remembered.

Abandoned, but not forgotten—for in the new *Frühlingssehnsucht* much of *Lebensmut* continues to sound. Its key is recycled. More than that, *Lebensmut* played up an ambivalence between B♭ major and D minor, an ambivalence that enlivens the final strain in each verse of the new *Frühlingssehnsucht* and forecasts the opening measures of *Ständchen*. Even that troublesome high A of the draft finds its place, now husbanded for the final "Nur du!" at the end of the song. Finally, the new *Frühlingssehnsucht*—unlike the old—will be heard to echo the distant tones of *Kriegers Ahnung*, the song that now precedes it. The music continually slips away toward A♭. "Wohin? wohin?" the poet asks, and the music darkens, alluding faintly to the labyrinth at "hier fühlt die Brust sich ganz allein."

6
Schubert's Heine

Among the Schubert controversies of the past twenty years, perhaps the most disquieting stems from a hypothesis that contradicts the authority of a primary text. The hypothesis was conceived by Harry Goldschmidt, who proposed that the order of Schubert's Heine settings, as it is transmitted in the autograph score (itself the engraver's source for the *Schwanengesang* that Haslinger published some months after Schubert's death and the text from which all subsequent editions have been drawn), is the wrong one.[1] In the haphazard order in which they appear in the *Schwanengesang*—indeed, by the very fact of their publication in a collection that has the look of a miscellany—the six Heine settings can make no claim to the autonomy of a self-contained work. But when the songs are withdrawn from *Schwanengesang* and their sequence revised, an integral cycle is reinstated so elegant in concept as to force us to a revision of the idea of cycle itself and, by extension, to a rethinking of its history as genre.

What inspiration led Goldschmidt to so visionary a rehearing? To recognize that the text of *Schwanengesang* is by its nature problematic is preliminary to any such hypothesizing. That a single publication should comprise *two* sets of songs (the Heine songs following from the group of seven Rellstab songs with not a single sign of articulation between the two), each with strong claims to an integrity of its own, is in itself confounding—intentionally so, one might believe. And then, striking and indisputable musical associations across and within the Heine songs speak to the kinds of deeper relationships that can be ascribed to the pieces of a single work. With the luxury of hindsight, the next step seems inevitable. When the songs are rearranged according to the order in which the poems appear in Heine's *Die Heimkehr*—a collection of eighty-eight poems, of which Schubert set numbers 8, 14, 16, 20, 23, and 24—a poetic narrative, coherent both in its temporal aspect and in what might loosely be called its plot, is shown to emerge. Further—and here is the clinching point—an eloquent musical discourse falls into place, at once an expression—a rewriting in music—of Heine's narrative and, in the pure language of musical discourse, a narrative in its own right. Thus redefined, the six songs in the *Schwanengesang* form a single coherent work.

Goldschmidt's claims have not been widely accepted. While performances

1. Harry Goldschmidt, "Welches war die ursprüngliche Reihenfolge in Schuberts Heine-Liedern," *Deutsches Jahrbuch der Musikwissenschaft für 1972* (1974), 52–62.

of the newly proposed Heine cycle seem only to reinforce the power of those claims, the editors of the *Neue Ausgabe* have been cautiously reluctant to move beyond the orthodoxies that such primary evidence as the autograph score sets in the way.[2] At the same time, Goldschmidt did not always serve his cause with analytic acumen. Is there a Heine cycle? The question is far from trivial. A proper understanding of Schubert's last works hangs in the balance, and so too does our broader theme, this evasive "distant cycle" that seems always to hover in the midst of Schubert's engagement with poetry of a certain magnitude. Is there a Heine cycle? Even if we could claim to know the answer to this question, the issues that it raises are sufficiently perplexing to demand that the question itself be readdressed. In the language of the philosopher, How can we know that we know?

I

Poetic narrative in Heine's *Heimkehr* is a convolution, a whorl not readily disentangled.[3] Whether a single narrative, a single cast of personae, can be identified here is surely not the real issue. Rather, it is how the poems play against one another, individually and in all those various subsets and strata that together constitute the lucid, dense texture of the collection.[4] To accept Goldschmidt's proposal to reorder Schubert's six settings according to the order in which they would appear in *Heimkehr*—taking Heine's order as inviolable—is to contend with narrative at another level, for an intense love story—more about its ironic bitter aftertaste than its ecstasy—is now distilled from it. But the distillation is Schubert's, not Heine's. The rich poetic ambivalence of *Heimkehr* is necessarily filtered out. There may even be some cause

2. Walther Dürr leaves the issue unresolved. Goldschmidt's reordering "ergebe sich für die sechs Lieder nicht nur ein klarer novellistischer Faden, sondern auch eine charakteristische tonartliche Ordnung und eine gewisse Folgerichtigkeit in der musikalischen Konzeption. Die Lieder verbänden sich zu *einem wirklichen Zyklus*" (yields not only a clear, novel-like thread for the six songs, but a characteristic tonal ordering as well, and a certain logical consistency in the musical conception. The songs bond into a genuine cycle [*verbänden sich zu einem wirklichen Zyklus*]), he writes, as if to compensate for the seemingly intractable view expressed some lines earlier (n. 59): "Da Entwürfe für die Heine-Lieder nicht erhalten sind und der Handschriftenbefund eindeutig ist, muß dies jedoch Vermutung bleiben" (Since drafts for the Heine songs have not survived and the state of the autograph is unambiguous, this must nevertheless remain conjecture). (See *NGA*, ser. 4, vol. 14a, p. xxiv; my emphasis). The songs are published in the *NGA* following the ordering in the autograph and the first published edition.

3. Thirty of them were published earlier, in 1824, in a quite different order, along with three poems subsequently dropped from the collection, as *Dreiunddreissig Gedichte von H. Heine. Die Heimkehr* was first published in *Reisebilder von H. Heine: Erster Theil* (Hamburg, 1826) and then in *Buch der Lieder* (Hamburg, 1827). For more on matters of publication, see Heinrich Heine, *Historisch-kritische Gesamtausgabe der Werke (Düsseldorfer Ausgabe)*, ed. Manfred Windfuhr, vol. 1, pt. 2, *Buch der Lieder*, ed. Pierre Grappin (Hamburg, 1975), 870–74.

4. For one way of understanding the set, see Urs Wilhelm Belart, *Gehalt und Aufbau von Heinrich Heines Gedichtsammlungen* (Bern, 1925), 46–62. For summaries of still others, see Heinrich Heine, *Werke*, ed. Stuart Adkins (Munich, 1973), 1:764–65.

to suspect that this inevitable distortion of Heine's plot lay behind what seems to have been a deliberate act to dismantle the cycle, a matter to which we must return.

A synopsis of Heine's narrative in Schubert's redaction might go this way:

Heine 8. Das Fischermädchen (D. 957, no. 10). Poet, on the make, offers up his heart in an ironic simile for the sea.

Heine 14. Am Meer (D. 957, no. 12). Love consummated. Or, rather, a love that has been consummated ("Wir *sassen*"). Tears as the mysterious elixir of the act. In the third strophe, he drinks the tears. That literal act strains a conventional metaphor.[5] In the fourth strophe, the consequences of the act: love as synonym for spiritual and physical decay and dying.

The third, fourth, and fifth songs reflect on a love now past. The more remote in time, the closer the image is drawn:

Heine 18. Die Stadt (D. 957, no. 11). He sees her town from the water.

Heine 20. Der Doppelgänger (D. 957, no. 13). He stands before her house and sees a figure of himself.

Heine 23. Ihr Bild (D. 957, no. 9). He stares at an image of her. Here again, the ironic coming to life of her image, a neurotic projection of fantasy on reality, is written in tears: "Und wie von Wehmutstränen / Erglänztze ihr Augenpaar. / Auch meine Tränen flossen" (And her eyes glistened as though from tears of melancholy. My tears also flowed).

Heine 24. Der Atlas (D. 957, no. 8). He internalizes the affair, reasons from it, and moralizes. She—her image—is now expunged. He rebukes his "stolzes Herz," which plays on the offerings of the first song ("Leg an mein Herz dein Köpfchen . . . Mein Herz gleicht ganz dem Meere" [Lay your little head on my heart . . . My heart is just like the sea]).

I do not mean to convey in such a reading anything more than the surface of the poems, as a demonstration that a narrative of sorts is etched in it. Schubert's music *reads* the poems as well, but in a rather different sense. It fixes the poetry, whether as narrative or in its suggestive metaphoric sense, and glosses it in a rigorous harmonic transliteration that conveys and deepens its ambiguities—makes them resonant, one might say. And it imposes on the poems a structural identity that regulates their relationship to one another beyond what is explicit in the poems taken alone.

5. On tears as a symbol for the love act, see *Tränenregen*, from Wilhelm Müller's *Die schöne Müllerin*, at what is arguably the point of climax in the affair (*Mein!*, which follows it, is the exultant response to the act); and (Heine, again) two songs from Schumann's *Dichterliebe*: "Aus meinen Tränen sprießen / Viel blühende Blumen hervor" (the fertility of tears) and, most evocatively, in the fourth song, "Doch wenn du sprichst: 'Ich liebe dich!' / So muss ich weinen bitterlich." Two songs later, in the unexpurgated version, Heine reads "Lehn' deine Wang' an meine Wang', / Dann fließen die Tränen zusammen." The metaphor is pursued with gusto elsewhere in *Die Heimkehr*: in no. 19, "Wo einst ihre Tränen gefallen, / Sind Schlangen hervorgekrochen"; and in no. 27, "Was will die einsame Träne?"

II

The famous opening sonority of *Am Meer* (shown in Ex. 6.1) is a case in point. In a penetrating study of one aspect of Schubert's harmony, Joseph Kerman writes of it,

> It does not signal ahead to a later event in the song, nor does it anticipate figuration or melody. It simply recurs; the song begins and ends with an oracle framing or glossing the poetic statement, rather than playing in to it. From the Classical point of view the introduction is non-functional; it illuminates nothing. But from the Romantic point of view it suggests everything—everything in the world that is inward, sentient, and arcane.[6]

The opposition between Classical illumination of function and Romantic non-functional suggestion is perhaps too trenchant, for when *Am Meer* is set in its broader narrative context, an isolationist view of the opening sonority will not hold.

Example 6.1 *a*, *Das Fischermädchen* (D. 957, no. 10), closing measures. *b*, *Am Meer* (D. 957, no. 12), opening measures

That sonority embodies a complicity of function, for it must be understood to convey the passage of time and action between the scenes of *Das Fischermädchen* and *Am Meer*: the sense of separation in *Das Fischermädchen* and the togetherness, at least for a fleeting moment, already past, in *Am Meer*. Kerman is surely right to think of this sonority as holding some symbolic meaning. And it is in the nature of Romantic symbol to suggest more than it

6. Kerman, "A Romantic Detail," 40 ([rev. ed.] 52).

reveals. But it is not quite so simple to divorce symbol from function. The two are not categorically opposed; the semantics of a passage depend on its syntax, and that very dependence nourishes the symbol.[7] Syntactic position catches it at the moment of redefinition: A♭ is recast, from the careless naïveté that it supports in *Das Fischermädchen* to the poisoned kiss that it seems to represent as troubled appoggiatura at the outset of *Am Meer*. The symbol, in any case, is Schubert's, and because it adjusts the balances between the explicit and the implicit, meddling in the play of ambiguity innate in the poems themselves, it can be said to impose an interpretation on the poems. But the musical symbol is itself a poetic artifact, so what might be perceived as interpretation must yet be understood as poetic speech in its own right.

Example 6.2 *a*, *Am Meer*, closing measures. *b*, *Die Stadt* (D. 957, no. 11), opening measures

The splayed diminished seventh with which *Die Stadt* opens (see ex. 6.2) and its bearing on the tonality of the song are among the perennial topics of music theory.[8] Here, too, the meaning of Romantic sonority is couched in its power as symbol to suggest and as function to assert. If the oracular augmented sixth that frames the music of *Am Meer* insinuates itself into the song in no obvious way, the diminished seventh that frames the music of *Die Stadt* feeds directly and literally into its middle strophe, which is haunted by that harmony and by no other. The chord has no grammatical position, no ostensi-

7. Goldschmidt, too, makes the distinction here between syntactic and semantic function, noting that the latter lies in "der Zerstörung der Vordergründigkeit, in Aufreißen des Konfliktes" ("Welches war die ursprüngliche Reihenfolge," 55).

8. Among the more provocative discussions is one by Robert P. Morgan, "Dissonant Prolongations: Theoretical and Compositional Precedents," *Journal of Music Theory* 20 (Spring 1976): 49–91, esp. 57–60.

ble context. But the aura of *Am Meer* lingers, and the lingering is enhanced by the bare octave tremolos with which *Die Stadt* begins. The memory of *Am Meer* imposes a context and, consequently, an inflection on this fickle harmony.[9] The tremolos seem virtually to shake C loose, and the fresh harmony only forces the issue, flexing toward a resolution of the kind shown in example 6.3. In either case, the C in the bass pulls toward B. That tension is not released in *Die Stadt*, for the song contains no harmony based on that pitch. The diminished seventh stands opposed to the blatant C minor that is the key of the outer strophes.

Example 6.3 *Die Stadt*, opening sonority and two implied resolutions

The song plays on these irreconcilable harmonic fields: on the one hand, the diminished seventh—a kind of *Hauptklang* that suggests resolutions toward C major and E minor—and, on the other, a contradictory, too stable C minor. The sense of the poem gives this as well. The deceptive stability of the town is seen from the bottomless water, in a boat as nearly rudderless as the diminished seventh that enshrouds it. The third strophe probes the irony. When the sun illuminates the town, to the poisoned lover it illuminates his barren inner world. The stability of the town is false, just as the C minor associated with it is rendered unstable by the prolonged diminished seventh the implied resolutions of which are not answered in the song itself and could not be answered logically without some playing out of C *major*.

In *Der Doppelgänger*, an answer comes. For one, the opening fifth might be construed as a skeleton of the principal harmony toward which the diminished seventh in *Die Stadt* tends. That the low Cs at the end of *Die Stadt* (and, by extension, the song itself) are to be understood as an appoggiatura to the Bs of *Der Doppelgänger* (as suggested in ex. 6.4) seems echoed in the continual turning of the bass to an otherwise grammatically difficult C♮ at "Schmerzensgewalt" and "eigne Gestalt": grammatically difficult because the C♮ at both places corrupts evident dominant harmony and undermines the tonic stability of B. That tendency echoes into the hollow postlude, where C♮ now supports its own bare harmony and clinches the transformation of B into

9. Morgan's view (ibid., 57) that the diminished seventh is "triadic in structure (. . . an extension of the diminished triad)" is at odds with tonal theory after Rameau, where the diminished triad has no authority, for it has no root. The 7 of the diminished seventh is generally understood as a local appoggiatura (in the sense 9-8) to the root of a plain dominant seventh, the actual root determined by the context.

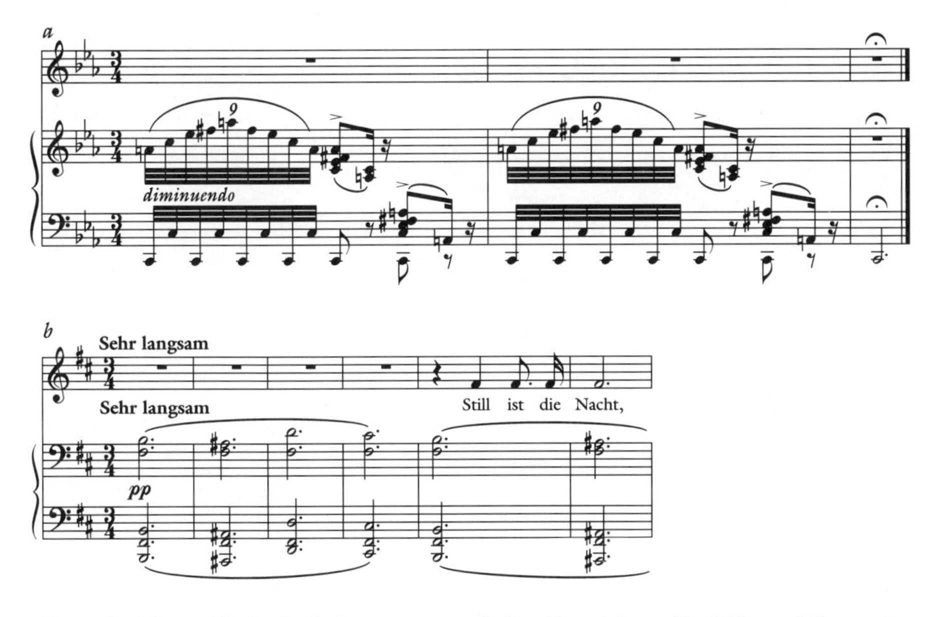

Example 6.4 *a*, *Die Stadt*, closing measures. *b*, *Der Doppelgänger* (D. 957, no. 13), opening measures

a dominant. It offers up a literal dominant seventh of B that sounds right through to the end of the song.[10]

What I am proposing, then, is that, taken together, *Die Stadt* and *Der Doppelgänger* do not so much elaborate a relationship between two keys (C minor and B minor) as formulate a kind of harmonic model: a diminished-seventh chord whose bass, C, moves to a true root, B, which in turn identifies a dominant seventh (ex. 6.3a above).

But there is more at stake in *Der Doppelgänger* than the playing out of implications left unanswered in *Die Stadt*. The gist of its own inner conflict is captured in the brutal augmented sixth, *fortissimo*, at "so manche Nacht in alter Zeit," which establishes finally and for once an unequivocal cadence in B minor—the very first F♯ in the bass. The bass motion G♮-F♯ is decisive. It responds to, and in a sense resolves, the shrill G♮ at "eigne Gestalt" that the voice, straining at the top of its range, will not resolve (see ex. 6.5).

The eloquence of that final augmented sixth to illuminate some central conflict in the song is drawn from its function to contradict the ironic tonic-dominant dance around D♯ minor at "Was äffst du nach mein Liebesleid." The true augmented sixth and the true cadence gain in significance as a con-

10. Goldschmidt hears a concealed ("verdeckter") Neapolitan in the low C at the end of *Die Stadt* the hidden function of which is disclosed "in der Akkordauflösung des plagal erweiterten Schlußritornells" ("Welches war die ursprüngliche Reihenfolge," 57). But Neapolitans are invariably sixth chords the functional power of which derives from the root of the minor subdominant. Schubert's C-major triad may hint at a Neapolitan ancestor, but its effect is very different.

Example 6.5 *Der Doppelgänger*, mm. 36–52

tradiction to the false cadencing around the mediant. Those root-position dominants to D♯ minor play on the local neighbor motion B-A♯ with which the song begins. For a moment, this fixation on B minor (itself a key with neurotic implications in Schubert) is put in the shade. The true tonic is reconceived as an upper neighbor to a dominant, as scale-degree 6 to scale-degree 5. And that brings us back to the synoptic view—the cyclic view—of these songs, for one aspect of the motion from *Am Meer* and *Die Stadt* to *Der Doppelgänger* is as scale-degree 6 to scale-degree 5.

The reversal about B♮ and A♯ looks ahead and, indeed, directly into *Ihr Bild* (see ex. 6.6). It was Schenker's fantasy on the meaning and function of its opening octaves that in turn inspired Kerman to pursue the question as a model for all those other cryptic openings in which two harmonies, one neighbor-like and ambiguous, the other a tonic, adumbrate something essential in the piece.[11] Kerman noted how these opening octaves are fleshed out with "relevant" harmonies prior to the third strophe and noted, too, that Schenker was not inclined to dwell on the relationship beyond its immediate

11. See Heinrich Schenker, "Schubert: *Ihr Bild*," *Der Tonwille* 1, no. 1 (1921): 46–49.

Example 6.6 *a*, *Der Doppelgänger*, closing measures. *b*, *Ihr Bild* (D. 957, no. 9), opening measures

poetic significance.[12] Doubtless intrigued by the conceptual problem of the octaves as motivic and substantive, Schenker probes beneath their gestural significance, struck by their power to get us into the soul of the poet.

Yet when they are heard to respond directly and pathetically to the closing measures of *Der Doppelgänger*, the octaves gain in nuance and texture what they lose in innocence. *Der Doppelgänger* has prepared us to hear A♯ (even if it must be spelled B♭) either as a leading tone or as the root of a dominant in D♯ minor. At its close, the tonic, B minor, has been inflected as a kind of dominant seventh. This complicates the hinge to B♭, for conditions have been set to reinterpret dominant sevenths as augmented sixths. One tendency of those octave B♭s, then, is as dominant to E♭ minor, and another is as leading tone in a dominant seventh on G♭. It is the implication of the latter that is invoked prior to the third strophe, where the first octave now sounds the augmented sixth that is enharmonically equivalent to the dominant seventh on G♭ that we might have been led to hear at the very beginning of the song. The case for hearing that augmented sixth as a dominant on G♭ has in the meantime been bolstered because the middle strophe of *Ihr Bild* sits squarely and ironically in the key of G♭ major. I shall want to return once more to the significance of this other meaning of the harmony: as true dominant seventh to a tonic C♭.

This idiosyncratic harmonic device at mm. 23–24—the augmented sixth, encased in the tonic to which it resolves directly, without the mediation of a dominant—echoes the powerful ellipsis in which the opening bars of *Am Meer* are cast. The metaphoric significance captured in the motion between *Das*

12. Kerman, "A Romantic Detail," 43–44 ([rev. ed.] 57).

Fischermädchen and *Am Meer* is consequently evoked at this moment where finally the consuming love act is recapitulated in sorrow, even to the imaginary and suggestive flowing of tears in tears (see ex. 6.7). Here, too, the psychology of events *in time* is mapped in the music of the cycle.

Example 6.7 *Am Meer*, closing measures, and *Ihr Bild*, mm. 23–24, together with linear abstract

III

The inner action of the cycle is now past. As musical action, it conveys a continual, one is tempted to say pathological, dissolution of harmonic focus, a playing out of those lines toward the end of *Am Meer*: "Seit jener Stunde verzehrt sich mein Leib, / Die Seele stirbt vor Sehnen" (Since that hour my body wastes away, my soul dies of longing).[13] Dominants are liquidated and reduced to neighbor harmonies. Evident tonics are at once tinged with the implications of their own dissolution.

For Goldschmidt, the musical continuity is clearer still. Overwhelmed by the topos of an unbroken chromatic descent and of what might be called chromatic closure, he argues that *Der Atlas* is misrepresented as it stands in G minor. We know of other cases, contemporary with the Heine settings, in which Schubert, in deference to his singers and publishers, seems to have agreed to the transposition of a song down one or two semitones.[14] Goldschmidt wants to hear *Der Atlas* in A minor, for that would run out a chromatic descent and fill the gap between the A♭ of *Das Fischermädchen* and the C of *Am Meer*. Repositioned in A minor, the final, precarious phrase with

13. Belart (*Gehalt und Aufbau*, 48) senses the pivotal position of *Am Meer* (*Heimkehr* 14) in its broader context: it closes off a series of *Seebilder* initiated in "Wir sassen am Fischerhause . . ." (*Heimkehr* 7), while the third strophe ("Seit jener Stunde . . .") points ahead to those following poems "die der verlorenen Liebe gewidmet sind" (which are dedicated to lost love).

14. Goldschmidt, "Welches war die ursprüngliche Reihenfolge," 62, n. 15.

which *Der Atlas* closes now lies just beyond orthodox vocal range, more precarious still. And so it would have been transposed.

The argument is ingenious and yet hollow. To insist that the large motion of the cycle must plot out an unbroken chromatic descent is to argue from a false premise, for it takes as axiomatic that there is some innate tonal logic in the chromatic scale. To imagine *Der Atlas* in A minor, as Goldschmidt would have it, is to allow the cycle to run its course unarticulated, without benefit of a definition that would distinguish the inner action of the cycle from its frame. Further, to insist that the song was conceived in A minor is necessarily to dismiss all the significance special to *Der Atlas* in G minor.

That significance speaks out at every level. One aspect of it is tied to the text "Du stolzes Herz! du hast es ja gewollt!" (You, proud heart, you willed it so!). This final apostrophe to the heart calls back to the middle strophe of *Das Fischermädchen*: "Leg an mein Herz dein Köpfchen. . . ." One in B major, the other in C♭ major, the two map out cognate areas that together propose a secondary tonic at some subliminal level. The world of *Das Fischermädchen* is further evoked in the abrupt turn to triplets—disruptive in *Der Atlas* taken by itself, nostalgic in the context of the full cycle.

We might dwell for a moment on the meaning of C♭, or its enharmonic equivalent, as a kind of tonal linchpin in the cycle. The C♭ in these outer songs does not offer itself in easy answer to the question, What is the key of the cycle? Rather, it intimates a tonal reverberation (the before and after) of the moment of psychic self-revelation that is *Der Doppelgänger*, where the key is B—but *minor*. Its essence is projected in the extreme cadence at "So manche Nacht in alter Zeit"; its fallout reaches deep into *Ihr Bild*, to the augmented sixth on G♭ before the final strophe. The motivic significance of that augmented sixth—its harmonic recasting of the opening octaves of the song—only reinforces its rhetorical position in the cycle. The ambivalence inherent in the chord—the tendency implicit within it to behave as a dominant seventh whose root is G♭—is played up as the inflection of a middle strophe where G♭ is taken as the classic example of "♭VI" and taken again as a phenomenon with a message of its own. The sense of this augmented sixth as a frustrated dominant to C♭ is strong indeed.

Carried one step further, the opening motive of *Der Atlas* is skewed just enough to allow a faint tendency toward B minor (as in ex. 6.8).[15] The attack at the outset of *Der Atlas* has a crucial role to play, for the area of the attack—G minor—as well as the force of the downbeat, is meant to break out of the syndrome of disease with which the inner songs are infected and to establish the larger time frame of the cycle, to establish, that is, a tonal perspective. To invoke the concept of perspective is to signify something of that hierarchy of relationships that controls the work and ensures its coherence. *Das Fischermädchen* and *Der Atlas*—distant states of mind through which the real

15. Kerman ("A Romantic Detail," 45) hints at this: "The powerful motive . . . controls the song measure by measure until the end."

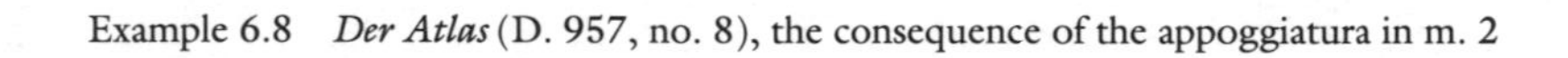

Example 6.8 *Der Atlas* (D. 957, no. 8), the consequence of the appoggiatura in m. 2

action is viewed—stake out a teleology of the whole: a neighbor motion between A♭ and G that at some level of abstraction must mean $\hat{6}$-$\hat{5}$. That intervallic model has generated much of what happens at critical moments in the inner songs. The outer songs magnify it and thus imply a tonic around C, now a figure of memory. The cycle gathers its coherence from an encompassing neighbor motion that freezes the tonic at the elusive moment of ecstasy. Example 6.9 sketches some of these governing motions.

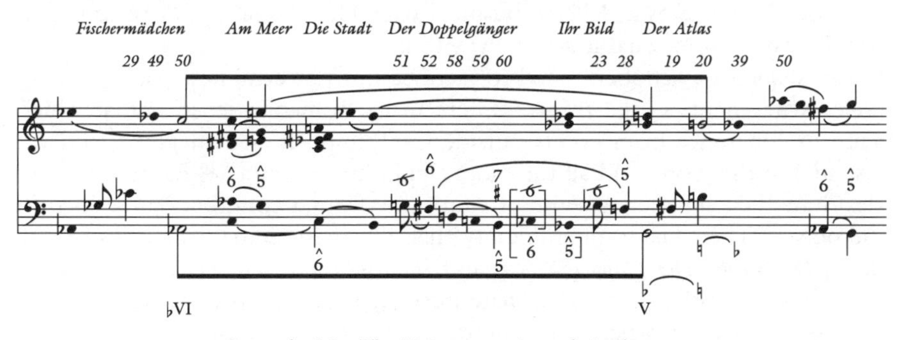

Example 6.9 The Heine songs in analytic abstract

In its very last phrase, *Der Atlas* heaves up one final, violent allusion to this cardinal relationship. The neighbor motion A♭-G, *fortissimo*, at "Schmerzen" brutalizes the close in a way not entirely supported by the events of the song itself. The phrase alludes as well to the deflection away from the tonic at "Ich trage Unerträgliches." The rhythm of the two phrases makes this clear. A♭ is meant to ground the volatile tendency of G♯, but it does not have that effect. The dissonance is too piercing, too extreme, too near the end. It wants to be heard as the final agonized memory of that elusive moment of love evoked in *Am Meer*. And it recalls, too, and in a sense neutralizes the prolonged dissonance at "eigne Gestalt" that is the crux of *Der Doppelgänger*. The dissonance is tonicized, grounded.

IV

At the outset, I suggested that Goldschmidt's hypothesis flies in the face of a perfectly clear piece of documentary evidence. How do we reconcile these two antithetical transmissions of the Heine songs? The hard evidence by which the authority of the text is established speaks clearly here. The autograph score, the primary document in this case, tolerates no revisionary criticism. But internal evidence—the meaning that burns through both poem and song—argues fervently that this cold exterior evidence is a cover-up.

When two bodies of evidence—evidence fundamentally different in kind—contradict one another in this way, there can be no reconciliation in a clean, legal sense. Yet the historian wants some construct to explain how the one became the other. I think that we must suppose that there *are* two versions here and that the cycle, as I have been describing it, was ultimately rejected in favor of the sequence, inconsequent in effect, that has come down to us. It is tempting to consider whether this rejection was provoked by a failure of nerve, for it must have struck Schubert that he had profoundly violated Heine's text, infusing an intimacy into these six poems, imposing a psychological drama, and finally distorting the fragile, ambivalent web of connections in *Die Heimkehr*. The fixing of narrative tone in Heine's cycle is no simple matter. Poetic "voice" is a delicate business with Heine, and it can be said that Schubert plays somewhat indelicately with it.

Consequently, Schubert is led to sacrifice this powerful new concept: song cycle as fragment. I take *fragment* here in its Romantic sense as that which gains in coherence from events outside itself, implicit and imagined, and yet essential to the work, and all the more significant therefore.[16] Earlier song cycles draw their immediate sense of continuity from a continuity prescribed in the poems. That quality of ambiguity that allows the initial sonorities of *Am Meer*, *Die Stadt*, *Der Doppelgänger*, and *Ihr Bild* each to inflect its antecedent, their final sonorities each to resonate into what follows, is cultivated to a degree quite beyond what is encountered in *Die schöne Müllerin* and even *Winterreise*. It is a quality unsought in *An die ferne Geliebte*, whose sophisticated lines of continuity have little to do with the eloquence of Romantic harmony.[17] What these earlier cycles share is a poetry that sustains the eighteenth-century definition of the Lied as essentially folk-like and a music that by and large conveys that sense of folk. But there is a complex psychological inner tone to Heine's poetry and a sardonic, cosmopolitan edge that cuts through its simple folk-like facade.

In a provocative, sometimes exasperating study of Schubert's Heine settings, Jack M. Stein sought to demonstrate Schubert's insensitivity to the irony at the core of much of Heine's poetry. To suggest, as Stein does, that poetry of such advanced sophistication was beyond the cognitive grasp of a Schubert is to write off the sense in which any art can be said to speak to its contemporaries. Yet, when Stein contends that "songs are automatically interpretations [that] fix the poem in a mode which cannot adjust to changing insights or deepened perspectives," he touches a raw nerve in the aesthetics of Romantic song, for it is in the nature of Romantic art that idiosyncratic, per-

16. Nor was this the first time that Schubert seems to have backed off from such an enterprise. Dietrich Berke has proposed that the fragmentary setting of Ludwig Tieck's *Abend* (D. 645) may have been intended for yet another cyclic project as early as 1819 ("Schubert's Liedentwurf," esp. 313).

17. All the same, *An die ferne Geliebte* cannot have been far from Schubert's mind. Pointedly ignored in the two Müller cycles, its shadow hovers over the Heine cycle, an elusive model to which Schubert pays elusive homage—most strikingly, in the tonal hinge between the first two songs. As Maynard Solomon reminds us, the cycle was performed "on Easter Monday 1827, . . . as a memorial to Beethoven" on a program that opened with Schubert's Octet (on this and, more broadly, for new ideas on Schubert's ambivalence toward Beethovenian models over the years, see his "Schubert and Beethoven," *19th Century Music* 3 [November 1979]: 114–25, esp. 119).

sonal style is a deep part of the message.[18] The rhetoric of irony, darkly stained in Heine's language, does not easily translate into music. One might even suggest that irony is a quality of thought that music is incapable of expressing. It is at any rate a quality foreign to Schubert's profound, pathetic naïveté. Romantic harmony and declamation remake the poem—at odds, perhaps, with our own reading of it *as poem.* But everyone understands that, in Romantic song, poem and music cannot be separated. Heine's poem is no longer his own. Fusion of this sort can never be the case in critical readings, whether exegetical or simply declamatory, for these are meant not to penetrate the text and become a part of it but only to illuminate and enliven the text and then to recede from it.

The conceptual vision in Schubert's Heine cycle is breathtaking. The vision itself burns so brightly and with such intensity as to have shone through the overt dismantling of the concept. Despite the disarray, a powerful cyclic undercurrent controls these songs, much like the mysterious magnetic field that reconstitutes the iron filings no matter how we disarrange them. More mysterious still, and destined to remain so, is the internal dialectic that led Schubert, finally, to disengage. *Retreat* and *withdrawal* are words that come to mind—suggestive words that allude to a weakness of resolve. A probe further into Schubert's obscure character, were it more vividly accessible to us, might tell us better of such vulnerability. This putative dismantling of the cycle is of a piece with other, similar acts, described in earlier chapters, in which a primary, intuitive, and genuine concept is forfeited for some less daring configuration. The autograph of *Schwanengesang* is such an artifact. There is nothing else like it in Schubert's portfolio, no other manuscript of like dimension containing thirteen songs in two groups each of a single poet. It is *as though* the intention were to obscure the indelible configurations in which the Rellstab and Heine songs were conceived. That Schubert could not bring himself to designate in the autograph that there are two groups of songs here: this, together with an evident *mis*ordering of the Heine songs, must signal a deeper ambivalence about the making of these songs into cycles.

What can have been the motive beneath such self-betrayal? The figure of the poet intrudes in the dialectic. With Müller's two cycles, there was no inner conflict. Schubert enacts Müller's script. In the Heine cycle, Schubert writes his own script. We may disagree as to the nature of the enterprise, but there can be no denying that, if we accept the narrative teased from the six poems in Schubert's cycle, the integrity of Heine's *Heimkehr*—the authority of its tangled narrative—is in the process violated, the poet's work traduced. We have come to accept such appropriation, perceiving it not as an act of aesthetic im-

18. Jack M. Stein, "Schubert's Heine Songs," *Journal of Aesthetics and Art Criticism* 24 (Summer 1966): 566. The attack is softened, but the arguments remain essentially unchanged, in Stein's *Poem and Music in the German Lied from Gluck to Hugo Wolf* (Cambridge, Mass., 1971), 80–91.

propriety but rather as admissible under the ground rules that dictate how the games of Romantic art are to be played.

Ready as we may be to exonerate Schubert of malicious tinkering, the telling question is whether Schubert can have held so dispassionate a view of the matter—whether this entanglement with Heine was not seen in the end as a transgression. The power of music to obliterate the subtleties of poetic language, those fine connections *between* the poems of *Heimkehr*, cannot have been lost on Schubert. The setting of poem to music—of the individual poem, isolated from its broader context—is an enterprise honored in tradition: the struggle between word and tone is the essence of which music is born, one might claim. But the setting together of poems to figure in music a narrative not explicit in the text of those poems is quite another issue. It is tempting to locate the failure of nerve precisely here, in the retraction of a cycle that would forever contradict the integrity of *Heimkehr*. The evidence for such retraction is not of the verifiable kind. Schubert leaves nothing behind except the traces of an ambivalence that masks a deeper conflict.

Postscript: On the Autograph of *Schwanengesang*

In the structure of its fascicles and how it serves to record the thirteen Rellstab and Heine songs, the autograph score of *Schwanengesang* has been taken as the imposing obstacle to the view that the Heine songs were conceived as a self-contained cycle.[19] The autograph is not a perfectly clean one. It is not, for example, like the autograph of *Winterreise*, part II, which is written in a fine public hand, free of correction and emendation, from which the engraver might work. But it is even less like the autograph of *Winterreise*, part I, a working score in which large sections of some songs are seen to have undergone radical revision, where, in some instances, one may rightly speak of an earlier version on which the final one has been inscribed and where, in other instances, the earlier version has been torn from the manuscript and discarded.[20]

The autograph of *Schwanengesang* was written in evident haste. The Heine songs, perhaps more so than the Rellstab songs, needed emendation along the way. Revision nearly always attends to detail: the piano echo in mm. 13–14 of

19. The autograph is now at the Pierpont Morgan Library in New York (see *The Mary Flagler Cary Music Collection*, item 188, p. 44). For a facsimile edition of the autograph, see *Franz Schubert: Schwanengesang*. See also *NGA*, ser. 4, vol. 14b, pp. 327–35.

20. The autograph of *Winterreise* is also at the Morgan Library (see *The Mary Flagler Cary Music Collection*, item 191, p. 45). For a description of the manuscript, see Georg Kinsky, *Manuskripte, Briefe, Dokumente von Scarlatti bis Stravinsky: Katalog der Musikautographen-Sammlung Louis Koch* (Stuttgart, 1953), item 159, pp. 171–74. The facsimile edition, published as *Franz Schubert: Winterreise: Faksimile-Wiedergabe nach der Originalhandschrift* (Kassel and Basel, 1955; reprint, 1966), does not clearly distinguish the two shades of ink that correspond, in part I, to the earlier and later entries. For more on the autograph, see *NGA*, ser. 4, vol. 4b, pp. 299–316; and the introductory essay by Susan Youens in *Franz Schubert: Winterreise: The Autograph Score* (New York, 1989).

Der Doppelgänger, evidently an afterthought; the disposition of the piano tremolos in *Der Atlas*; or the orthography of the opening sonority of *Am Meer* (the D♯ was originally spelled E♭—a spelling not without its own significance). *Nearly* always, for the most striking revision affects what is arguably the psychological crux of the cycle: the distended *Geschrei* at "Der Mond zeigt mir meine eigne Gestalt." The original reading is shown in example 6.10. To observe that this earlier version is perfectly coherent, that it rhymes with "Schmerzensgewalt," and that it preserves what Heine surely intended as the crucial sense stress on "eigne" (for that is precisely where the irony twists) is to report the obvious. The revision captures a breathtaking leap beyond all that. The new phrase has become almost an emblem of *Der Doppelgänger* itself, the phrase that invariably springs to mind when we picture the song. It is difficult to imagine the song without it, but that is just what the autograph proposes.

Example 6.10 *Der Doppelgänger*, mm. 38–42, earlier version, canceled in the autograph MS

Yet, for all their significance, none of these revisions identifies a stage during which the songs were not already complete in a form very close to the final one. That is decidedly not the case in the autograph of *Winterreise*, part I.

How did Schubert get a song from concept to *Reinschrift*? Sketches survive, but in magnitude and species they are not on the order of the Beethoven sketches, where incessant rewriting at a preliminary stage might yield a dozen or more drafts for a single song. For the most part, Schubert's sketches consist of continuity drafts on two staves, very different from the clusters of discontinuous entries, improvisation-like, and the weighing of options that characterize the Beethoven sketches. And while Beethoven carefully husbanded his sketchbooks, we must reckon with the probability that Schubert routinely discarded those papers that were no longer of any practical value. Those that have survived are the exceptions.

John Reed noted a marked change of habit around 1828: "It was now Schubert's normal practice to sketch out a new work, and then to go back to it after an interval. Sketches exist even of minor works."[21] The truth of the matter is probably more complex. Sketches and drafts from 1827 and 1828 may have survived in greater number simply because the time to dispose of them ran out. Yet there are reasonable grounds for supposing a change of

21. John Reed, *Schubert: The Final Years* (London, 1972), 214.

habit in the spring of 1827. Beethoven's death on 26 March of that year led to the gradual revelation of his private workshop papers to what was at first a small coterie of Viennese appointed to put the estate in order and to advise how to dispose of it. That task carried over into the autumn of 1827, up to the auction on 5 November.

It is now well known that Schindler, ostracized by those empowered to sort out Beethoven's library and papers, absconded with a substantial horde of manuscripts, presumably in the brief interval between Beethoven's death and the securing of the *Nachlass* under lock and key.[22] Schindler, we know, possessed the bulk of the autograph papers for *Leonore* and *Fidelio* (which he claimed to have received from Beethoven himself), all the conversation books, many of the odd lots of literary manuscripts, and a number of sketchbooks containing work on the last quartets.[23]

The evidence that Schubert saw some of these things rests with Schindler himself, who left us two descriptions of this extraordinary engagement. The first concerns the autograph of *Fidelio*: "Shortly after Beethoven's death, [Schubert] wished to examine the manuscript of *Fidelio*. After he had been occupied with it for a long while and had scrutinized at the piano the many alterations in harmony, instrumentation, and rhythmic construction, he remarked that under no circumstances would he accede to such drudgery and that moreover he finds the first idea to be just as good as the emendation." The second concerns the literary manuscripts: "In the summer of 1827, I often had the satisfaction of observing Schubert at my home, 'unbuttoned' à la Beethoven. During these visits, certain parts of Beethoven's literary *Nachlaß* occupied him quite in particular, among them all kinds of lyric poems that had been sent to the great master."[24] And here Schindler recounts how Schubert came on the Rellstab poems—among them, those that would be included in *Schwanengesang*—in a manuscript given to Beethoven by the poet.[25]

22. The matter was broached above, in chapter 5 (see Brenneis, "Das Fischhof-Manuskript," esp. 98).

23. "Die Skizzen dazu [of op. 132] könnten Sie mir wohl schenken, denn sie verlieren sich doch mit der Zeit, wie alle andern" (You could very well make me a gift of the sketches [for op. 132], for with time, they will otherwise disappear like all the others), Schindler has himself say to Beethoven in one of those fictive conversations that he invented in the 1840s; in this case, as Dagmar Beck and Grita Herre observe, "wollte Schindler seinen Besitz an Beethovenschen Manuskripten legitimieren" (Schindler wished to legitimize his posssession of Beethoven manuscripts) ("Anton Schindlers fingierte Eintragungen in den Konversationsheften," in *Zu Beethoven: Aufsätze und Annotationen*, 11–89, esp. 83–84). Most of Schindler's collection went to the Königliche Bibliothek at Berlin in 1846; other items are now at the Bibliothèque Nationale (Paris), the Beethovenhaus (Bonn), and the Österreichische Nationalbibliothek (Vienna).

24. Otto Erich Deutsch, *Erinnerungen*, 363, 367. Schindler's account first appeared in the *Niederrheinischen Musik-Zeitung für Kunstfreunde und Künstler*, 7 and 14 March 1857.

25. Deutsch, *Erinnerungen*, 367–68. In *Aus meinem Leben*, 244–45, Rellstab, who reacquired the manuscript from Schindler, noted pencil markings in Beethoven's hand. The manuscript has not survived. For a review of certain aspects of the Rellstab-Beethoven-Schubert connection, see Hallmark, "Schubert's 'Auf dem Strom,'" 42–45.

Schindler's testimony constitutes the single bit of evidence that Schubert ever came face to face with Beethoven's sketches. We read Schindler circumspectly these days and do not readily count his testimony as admissible evidence. Still, there is a ring of truth to these accounts. For one, they square with what we know Schindler to have owned at the time. For another, the rough chronology must be right:[26] by 15 September, Schindler had left—fled, one might imagine—Vienna for Budapest. And, for a third, it would have been just like the man to use those possessions—evidence of his intimacy with Beethoven—as a means of entry into an intimacy with Schubert.[27]

The picture of Schubert absorbed in the study of the *Fidelio* papers is a touching one. He can hardly have come away unmoved. And it is fair to assume that, during those "unbuttoned" sessions with Schindler, Schubert saw a good deal more: the sketchbooks for the late quartets would surely have aroused his curiosity.

Among the projects of the summer of 1827, work on the opera *Der Graf von Gleichen* (D. 918) looms very large. What has survived of it is a substantial draft—very nearly the complete opera in *particella*—on two kinds of paper, each comprising a run of thirty-six leaves.[28] This second run is of an unusual paper type: small pocket-size sheets of eight-stave paper, with entries in pencil. Moreover, drafts for two unknown piano pieces, D. 916B and 916C, were recently discovered, lurking unsuspected among the opera papers.[29] Without laboring the point, these drafts look very much like Beethoven's. The paper and its format are familiar to those who have worked with the sketchbooks for the late quartets. The barely legible pencil entries, rare among Schubert's papers, are the very picture of a Beethoven manuscript in the 1820s.[30]

26. Of Schubert's visits, that is. When Schindler reports that "only two days later he brought me *Liebesbotschaft*, *Kriegers Ahnung*, and *Aufenthalt* set to music" (Deutsch, *Erinnerungen*, 368), he cannot have been telling the truth. On stronger evidence, we must take the summer of 1828 to be the date of a preliminary draft (discussed below) for *Liebesbotschaft* and for two other Rellstab settings, and, on the basis of the draft, we must assume that *Kriegers Ahnung* and *Aufenthalt* were not among the very first to have been composed.

27. Perhaps it was a similar motive that led Schindler to make gifts to Ignaz Moscheles of the score of the Scherzo of the Ninth Symphony and of a pocket sketchbook for op. 131 (now Beethovenhaus, BSk 22/70). The parcels were dispatched with a letter dated 14 September 1827, one day before Schindler's departure for Pest. The letter to Moscheles is given in Stephan Ley, *Beethoven als Freund der Familie Wegeler–v. Breuning* (Bonn, 1927), 243–44.

28. For a discussion of the paper, see Winter, "Paper Studies," 244–45. The draft is now published in facsimile (see *Franz Schubert: Der Graf von Gleichen: Oper in zwei Akten (D 918)*, ed. with commentary by Ernst Hilmar [Tutzing, 1988]). For some reflections on it, see my "Posthumous Schubert," *19th Century Music* 14 (Fall 1990): esp. 202–16. See also Hilmar, *Verzeichnis*, 28–29.

29. The discovery was first announced in Hilmar, *Verzeichnis*, 102–3, and more thoroughly described in Otto Brusatti, "Zwei unbekannte Klavierwerke Franz Schuberts," in *Schubert-Studien: Festgabe der Österreichischen Akademie der Wissenschaften zum Schubert-Jahr 1978*, ed. Franz Grasberger and Othmar Wessely (Vienna, 1978), 33–41.

30. For an example, see the facsimile of one page of D. 916C in *Franz Schubert: Ausstellung der Wiener Stadt- und Landesbibliothek zum 150. Todestag des Komponisten*, ed. Ernst Hilmar and Otto Brusatti (Vienna, 1978), 287; and also Brusatti, "Zwei unbekannte Klavierwerke," unpaginated plate.

Yet it would be naive to conclude that the encounter with Beethoven's workshop papers can have inspired no more than a studied negligence in Schubert's sketching script. We cannot know what sort of lesson Schubert drew from the encounter. Beethoven's workshop habits, which we have come to take as paradigmatic of a more general theory of compositional engagement, were in fact highly idiosyncratic. The ghost in Schubert's machine was of a different character; those offhand remarks to Schindler seem to express Schubert's recognition of this basic difference. But the monumental aspect of the Beethoven sketchbooks—the sheer bulk of all that writing, even—must surely have left its mark.

Preliminary drafts for the Heine songs have not survived. Circumstantial evidence argues that such drafts must have existed. The evidence is provided by contemporary manuscripts of two different kinds. The bifolio, discussed earlier, containing drafts for three Rellstab settings—*Lebensmut*, *Liebesbotschaft*, and an untexted song whose prosody implicates a setting of *Frühlingssehnsucht*—is a document of the first kind.[31] As witness to some preliminary concept of a Rellstab cycle, it is not altogether unequivocal in its signals. In the draft for *Liebesbotschaft*, we have evidence of the kind of draft from which a complete setting could have been developed without transfer to another score. The layout is designed to accommodate a complete setting. But Schubert elected to leave the draft unfinished, for he used folio 2v not for the completion of *Liebesbotschaft* (which would have required eight additional measures) but for another song. And because the potential of this bifolio for finished copy had now been removed, the draft for the new song begins directly with the voice entry. Space for a piano opening is omitted altogether. It is a draft by prior definition.

The *Lebensmut* fragment is something of a puzzle. I think that we must imagine it to have existed originally on the page as a skeletal draft, similar to those for *Liebesbotschaft* and *Frühlingssehnsucht*: the three drafts would have been made consecutively, almost cursively. That Schubert subsequently returned to the draft for *Lebensmut* and in effect completed the piece is irrelevant to the argument here.[32] The three fragmentary drafts give evidence of a way of working: they were likely conceived in a single compositional thrust. The final autograph, then, stands in contradiction to that original concept.[33]

31. Vienna Gesellschaft der Musikfreunde, A 236; its contents are described in some detail in chapter 5 above.

32. "Das Fragment ist zwar offensichtlich nicht in einem Zuge mit den Entwürfen niedergeschrieben" (The fragment was quite apparently not written in a single dash of the pen with the other drafts), writes Walther Dürr (*NGA*, ser. 4, vol. 14a, p. xxix). But it is unclear why he believes so, except to serve an assumption that *Lebensmut* can never have been conceived as a member of a Rellstab cycle.

33. Of other such fragmentary groupings, two might be mentioned here. (1) A gathering of two bifolios (Vienna Stadtbibliothek, MH 182/c) contains the drafts for three Leitner songs. The text to *Fröhliches Scheiden* (D. 896) is underlaid, but the drafts that follow are without text or title. For something more on these, see Reinhardt van Hoorickx, "The Chronology of Schubert's

The other sort of preliminary document is exemplified in a draft for the setting of Seidl's *Die Taubenpost* (D. 965A).[34] It is on two staves, comprising a principal voice and, now and again, the bass. Its format and a hand that tends toward the illegible (especially in the piano interludes) define it at once as the kind of draft from which a complete version cannot be developed without transfer to another sheet. The autograph score of *Die Taubenpost*, now bound in at the very end of the *Schwanengesang* manuscript, is written on two consecutive bifolios.[35] Because the two are of different kinds of paper, Robert Winter was led to suggest that the second bifolio may replace an earlier form of the continuation.[36]

Such two-stave drafts, fairly common for large-scale instrumental works and for works requiring extended performing forces, are decidedly uncommon among preliminary documents for the songs.[37] That Schubert felt the need to draft out a song as apparently simple in concept as *Die Taubenpost* gives rise to the suspicion that drafts of this kind were routine and that they were just as routinely discarded.

If these preliminary documents, and others like them, cannot of themselves support an elaborate hypothesis on Schubert's working habits, they at least flash warning signals. We must not rush to the conclusion that a manuscript worked over even to the degree evident in the autograph of the Heine settings necessarily represents a first writing down. If the autograph looked a bit more like *Winterreise*, part I, we might fairly say that it records the effort to conceive. But it does not.

The Rellstab fragments and the draft for *Die Taubenpost* constitute the pieces of evidence from which, along with the autograph of *Winterreise*, part I, a mode of working may be pieced together. This in turn helps us imagine what ought to have preceded the autograph of the Heine songs: a draft for the set, at once cursive and fragmentary, and a working autograph developed from it in situ or in a parallel score.

In a letter dated 2 October 1828, Schubert wrote to the Leipzig publisher Heinrich Albert Probst, "I have also composed several songs by *Heine* of

---

Fragments and Sketches," in *Schubert Studies: Problems of Style and Chronology*, 324–25. The dating is refined in Winter, "Paper Studies," 251; and Reinhardt van Hoorickx, "An Unknown Schubert Letter," *Musical Times* 122 (1981): 291–94. (2) A bifolio enveloping four additional single leaves (Vienna Stadtbibliothek, MH 180/c) contains drafts for three of the four settings from Goethe's *Wilhelm Meister* eventually published as op. 62. On their dating, see Winter, "Paper Studies," 238.

34. Vienna Stadtbibliothek, MH 4100/c. A facsimile of the recto side is given in Hilmar and Brusatti, *Ausstellung*, 203.

35. For a facsimile of the first page, see *The Mary Flagler Cary Music Collection*, plate 39.

36. Winter, "Paper Studies," 255.

37. Another such document is the draft for *Der Unglückliche* (D. 713), Vienna Stadtbibliothek, MH 187/c, published in *NGA*, ser. 4, vol. 4b, pp. 257–59. For a thoughtful study of it, see Walther Dürr: "Entwurf—Ausarbeitung—Revision: Zur Arbeitsweise Schuberts am Beispiel des Liedes 'Der Unglückliche' (D 713)," *Musikforschung* 44 (1991): 221–36.

Hamburg that have pleased here quite out of the ordinary."[38] No mention of Rellstab, and more than a hint that the Heine songs had had a hearing. How do the implications of this letter to Probst square with the condition of the *Schwanengesang* autograph? Schubert dated the autograph "Aug. 1828" at the front of the manuscript, above the first of the Rellstab songs. If we hold to the view that Schubert began to compile the autograph in August, we must contend with the peculiar structure of the manuscript (shown in table 6.1). Midway through the copying of the Rellstab songs—in the midst of *In der Ferne* at the very latest—Schubert took up a last gathering of four double leaves, enough to accommodate the Heine songs (all six, presumably, although an additional single leaf was needed at the end). The structure of the manuscript suggests, if it does not establish unequivocally, that Schubert had the Heine songs clearly in mind before the Rellstab songs were fully entered in the autograph. Just how clearly and how long before are matters for conjecture. We cannot know, then, whether to read "Aug. 1828" as the date by which the manuscript had been begun or whether to take it as one of those retrospective datings that may mean any number of things regarding the *Entstehungsgeschichte* of two groups of songs as complex as these.

Were the Heine songs performed during Schubert's lifetime? None of those witnesses whose accounts loom large in Schubert's biography recalls such a performance. In one case, the omission is worth pondering. Carl Freiherr von Schönstein, the tenor-baritone who seems to have performed with Schubert from as early as 1818, did in fact reject the implication that the Heine songs were "Schwanengesänge." His argument, given in a memorandum dated January 1857, hinged on the finding of Heine's *Buch der Lieder* during a visit to Schubert "many years before his death." Some years later, having in the meantime learned that the *Buch der Lieder* first appeared in October 1827, Schönstein had to temper his account. But he held obstinately to the view that Schubert's settings could in no sense be construed as "Letztlinge."[39]

What is odd in this is that Schönstein, arguing his point in slavish detail, says nothing about a performance of the songs. There were, of course, other singers among Schubert's intimates. But late in September 1828, Schönstein and Schubert seem again to have made music together, for, in a letter dated 25 September 1828, Schubert wrote to Johann Baptist Jenger, "I accept the invitation to Dr. Menz's with pleasure, for I am always very glad to hear the Baron von Schönstein sing."[40] Deutsch presumed that the evening *chez* Menz must have been Saturday, 27 September. The following Friday, Schubert wrote to Probst about his Heine settings.

38. "Auch habe ich mehrere Lieder von *Heine aus Hamburg* gesetzt, welche hier ausserordentlich gefielen" (Deutsch, *Dokumente*, 540).

39. Deutsch, *Erinnerungen*, 120, 383.

40. "Die Einladung zu D. Mens [*sic*] nehme ich mit Vergnügen an, da ich Bar Schönstein immer sehr gern singen höre" (Deutsch, *Dokumente*, 537–38).

TABLE 6.1
Fascicle Structure of *Schwanengesang* Autograph

Folio	Content
1	*Liebesbotschaft*, 1r–1v
2	*Kriegers Ahnung*, 2v–4r
3	
4	*Frühlingssehnsucht*, 4v–5v, stave 9
5	*Ständchen*, 5v, stave 11–6v, stave 9
6	*Aufenthalt*, 6v, stave 11–8r
7	
8	*In der Ferne*, 8v–9v, stave 9
9	*Abschied*, 9v, stave 12–12v
10	
11	
12	
13	*Der Atlas*, 13r–13v
14	*Ihr Bild*, 14r
	Das Fischermädchen, 14v–15r
15	*Die Stadt*, 15v–16r, stave 6
16	*Am Meer*, 16r, stave 9–17r, stave 3
17	*Der Doppelgänger*, 17r, stave 6–17v
18	*Die Taubenpost*, 18r–20r
19	
20	
	(20v–21v blank)
21	

Note: Folios 1–19 are of paper type (Winter) VIId, folios 20–21 of VIIIa (see Winter, "Paper Studies," 253–55).

The fact remains that we do not know what Schönstein sang that evening, If he ever sang the Heine songs in Schubert's presence, it is hard to understand why he should have failed to bring this to bear in his protest against the Haslinger edition. Schönstein, it seems clear, did not know the autograph from which Haslinger worked.[41] This, together with the letter to Probst, contends against the view that the autograph can have been completed before 2 October. Admittedly, the evidence is circumstantial. But that often is the most persuasive kind.

41. When Schönstein returned to this matter in 1875, he conjured up the Heine songs as "nämlich: *Ihr Bild*, *Das Fischermädchen*, *Die Stadt*, *Am Meer*, *Der Doppelgänger*, *Der Atlas*" (Deutsch, *Erinnerungen*, 383)—a free association, perhaps, the implications of which will not be lost on readers sympathetic to the ideas put forth in this chapter.

IV

The Cycles in *Winterreise*

❄

7
Winterreise I

How is *Winterreise* a cycle? To ask the question might seem heretical in the presence of what is gravely taken as the ultimate song cycle. Yet the quest for answers, beyond the trivial ways in which *Winterreise* meets the criteria by which cycles are commonly defined, bumps up against profound uncertainties in how its text is to be established. For it is reasonably clear that Schubert conceived the first twelve songs as a cycle in itself and that the decision to transpose *Einsamkeit*, the final song in this first cycle, from D minor to B minor was motivated by a prior decision to extend the cycle to include twelve new songs—a "Fortsetzung," as Schubert puts it at the top of the autograph of part II.

We now know that this new vision of the cycle as something grander owes to the unusual circumstances in how Schubert came on Müller's poems. Müller himself published the first twelve poems as a self-contained cycle in 1823, titled *Die Winterreise: In 12 Liedern*. This was Schubert's original text. A continuation of ten poems appeared in the same year, in an *Almanach* (Breslau, 1823) that Schubert evidently did not see. Finally, the full twenty-four poems were published in 1824 in the second volume of *Gedichte aus den hinterlassenen Papieren eines reisenden Waldhornisten* (Poems from the remaining papers of a traveling horn player), with the last four poems in part I now removed to positions late in part II and four of the new ones interlarded in a new part I. This was the source of Schubert's text for part II. But Müller's effort to integrate the two parts is defeated, for Schubert was evidently disinclined to tamper with the ordering of the songs in part I. Rather, he took up the new poems in the order in which they appeared in the complete run, so that *Die Post*, which Müller now inserted between *Der Lindenbaum* (5) and *Wasserflut* (6), became the first song in Schubert's part II.[1]

This determination to keep the poetic narrative of the earlier cycle intact, in sublime disregard for Müller's efforts at an integral text, must give us pause. Schubert cannot have been blind to the obvious ways in which Müller sought to amplify the narrative—to sustain for twice its length his grim, obsessive journey into the void. How Schubert's original cycle endured this redefinition—how the twelve songs constituting part I are transformed from a self-

1. The complexities in the transmission of the Müller poems are described in Feil, *Franz Schubert: Die schöne Müllerin; Winterreise*, 26–28 (Sherwin, trans., 24–25). The poems in their original form are given on 163–71 (143–51).

contained cycle into something subordinate to a greater whole—is a theme that underlies much of what follows.

I

The autograph score, in fact a compilation of two kinds of document, testifies to the conceiving of the cycle in two distinct phases. The manuscript for part I has survived in the main as a rough, working score of which the earliest discernible layer, when it can be separated out from the different ink with which later entries on the page were inscribed, resembles those rare surviving drafts that remained incomplete.[2] The manuscript for much of part I is then witness to a *Winterreise* in its earliest conception.

In some instances, the complicated act of composition has left its residue on the page. This must at times have gotten beyond acceptable legibility, for Schubert was prompted to write out a clean score for *Gute Nacht*, *Rückblick*, the second leaf of *Gefrorne Tränen*, the last page of *Auf dem Flusse* (presumably because its verso contained the first page of the original version of *Rückblick*), and the final page of *Einsamkeit*. Schubert yet found it necessary to have a clean text prepared to submit for publication. This engraver's copy of part I, carefully scrutinized by Schubert, records a good number of critical revisions in his hand.[3] The autograph for part II is clean all the way through, so an engraver's copy was not necessary. On the other hand, we may be reasonably certain that a working version of part II, resembling what has survived of part I, did once exist. It has not survived.

Dating the manuscript has its own problems. The autograph comprises two kinds of paper. The paper used for all the earliest strata of part I (with the exception of a single leaf in the *Rückblick* manuscript) has been found in other manuscripts the earliest of which can be dated October 1826, a date that gives us a preliminary bearing for the *Entstehungszeit* of part I.[4] The "Februar 1827" that Schubert inscribed on the first page of the autograph must be factored into this history as well, but precisely how is a question not confidently answered. As Georg Kinsky observed (in his catalog of the Koch collection), the date was written on the first page of the *Reinschrift* for *Gute Nacht*, and because this *Reinschrift* seems to have been prepared only after some of the later songs had been drafted out—not, that is, immediately following the preliminary draft for *Gute Nacht*—the date may well flag a later stage in the composition of part I, not the first taking of pen to paper.

2. The autograph, now housed at the Pierpont Morgan Library in New York, was published in facsimile as *Franz Schubert: Die Winterreise: Faksimile-Wiedergabe* and as *Franz Schubert: Winterreise: The Autograph Score*, the latter less well reproduced but with a detailed description of its structure in a fine introductory essay by Susan Youens.

3. The *Stichvorlage* to pt. I is described in Hilmar, *Verzeichnis*, 77–78. A study of certain aspects of the document is undertaken in Julian Armitage-Smith, "Schubert's *Winterreise*, Part I: The Sources of the Musical Text," *Musical Quarterly* 60 (January 1974): 20–36.

4. The dating of the paper is based on Winter, "Paper Studies," 240–41.

October 1827 is a month twice significant in the history of *Winterreise*. The censor's stamp on the title page of the engraver's copy of part I is dated 24 October 1827.[5] And the date at the top of the autograph of part II reads "Oct. 1827" in Schubert's hand. Here again, autograph datings have an allure of invincibility that may as easily cloud the investigation of a chronology as clarify it. Again, Schubert's "Oct. 1827" very likely confirms the month during which the clean autograph was prepared, not the month in which the composition of part II was originally undertaken. The censor's stamp certifies a latest possible date for the transposition of *Einsamkeit* to B minor, from which (as will be argued below) it may be inferred that Schubert had begun to think about the setting of part II some months earlier.

II

Auf dem Flusse has excited its share of analytic and critical discourse in recent years.[6] To take it as a point of entry into *Winterreise* is at once to acknowledge its special properties and to suggest at the outset that all those idiosyncrasies that have drawn the theorists to the song may have something to tell us about the cycle as well.

The simplest and most profound of its idiosyncrasies is lodged in its opening phrases. The chill motion between the phrase in E minor and its sequel in D♯ minor, much written about, is universally admired as the musical mimesis of an inner psychological stirring in the poem. At the sight of the frozen brook, Müller's saturnine lover imagines the very moment at which it has frozen over—the transfiguration from liquid to solid—seizing the image as a metaphor for the freezing over of his sensibilities. But in its power to choreograph such moments, the music goes beyond simple image making. As the poet sings, something internal does actually happen at the moment of transfiguration. The recognition that there is a metaphor to be read in the brook triggers a stopping of the heart, a moment of psychic "voiding" when the process of feeling is briefly lost. Unique and memorable, the event stakes its claim in the topography of gesture in which the cycle will find its definition.

At the outset, two points need to be stressed. The first has to do with the syntax of the opening phrase. On the evidence of these initial twelve measures of music, there is more than a hint that the music in E minor is to be understood as an upper neighbor leaning ponderously, appoggiatura-like, on D♯.[7] The cadencing toward m. 12 affirms D♯ minor as a tonic so emphatically as to

5. Hilmar, *Verzeichnis*, 78.

6. To cite the most provocative, David Lewin, "*Auf dem Flusse*: Image and Background in a Schubert Song," *19th Century Music* 6, no. 1 (Summer 1982): 47–59 (reprinted, slightly revised, in *Schubert: Critical and Analytical Studies*; and Newcomb, "Structure and Expression," 153–74. It is the focus as well of Armitage-Smith, "Schubert's *Winterreise*, Part I.

7. Tellingly, the autograph gives evidence that Schubert's impulse was to hear this music not in D♯ minor but rather in E♭ minor, a hearing that plays down the subsidiary relationship of D♯ to E. The point needs further elaboration.

put E minor in the shade. Not until the powerful root motion deep in the bass at mm. 59–62 is the priority of E finally and resolutely confirmed.

The second point is a corollary to the first. The relationship between E minor and D♯ minor, negotiated without any conventional explanatory motion, is in essence a contradictory one. Even the grammar of the passage is in question: The telltale scent of parallel motion is pronounced. The legitimacy of the passage is covered in a conventional mode: the dominant on A♯ is delayed through a suspension of the D♯/F♯, the $^6_4$ on A♯ posting the obligatory 5-6-5 motion that Schenker is so often at pains to describe. Strict parallel fifths are avoided. But the underlying relationship is of the troubling, contradictory kind that generates the most disturbing class of parallel fifths. A deep-rooted parallelism governs the music of mm. 1–12. However one thinks to understand the poetic image here, a structural dissonance is at play, and the playing out of its consequences is the business of much of the rest of the song.

I want to dwell for a moment on the manner in which E minor is reclaimed at the outset of strophe 2. If, by convention, some explanatory, conciliatory gesture is called for here, the stark retaking of the dominant before E minor only plays up the breach between the two keys. The autograph (here and at the parallel spot before m. 23) is revealing. Two earlier stages are shown in example 7.1. The final form rejects any mediating harmonies that might hint at the return from a distant D♯ to a comfortable E. Following the reprise of E minor at m. 41, tactics are dramatically altered. Now the cadences in D♯ minor are gradually subsumed in a larger harmonic scenario in which a final approach to E minor is positioned so as to redefine its place in the hierarchies of the song.

Example 7.1 *Auf dem Flusse*, m. 13, autograph score

The first step in this unfolding is the mutation whereby D♯ is made a local dominant. That is at m. 47, a place that is itself the subject of some controversy.[8] Example 7.2 shows how it reads in the autograph. For the first edition, the passage was revised to read as in example 7.3. An intermediate stage, preserved in the engraver's copy and expunged there, records the sequence of alterations toward the published version.

8. See Armitage-Smith, "Schubert's *Winterreise*, Part I," 26–31, on this very measure.

Example 7.2 *Auf dem Flusse*, m. 47, autograph score

Example 7.3 *Auf dem Flusse*, m. 47, 1st ed.

All this uncharacteristic fine-tuning attends the moment at which D♯ minor, the powerful imposter tonic, is at once unmasked and liquidated. Now the root of a dominant ninth, the D♯ impels the harmonic wheel back on itself, inexorably, toward the true tonic. The clash between right hand and left, between the tenacity of the right hand to cling to D♯ minor as an exotic tonic and the left to return the song to its place in the cycle, gives the sense of some metaphysical confrontation. The clash is grammatically illicit, for it entertains at once two contrary functions for D♯. Yet to understand the passage as a casualty of fast writing—an oversight lost in the heat of composition—is to misread the manuscript, for, whether or not negligence might have its claim here, the more interesting question is how Schubert could have allowed himself a lapse at this pivotal turn. Something deeper is at issue.

Indecision at this critical bend in the piece may itself be taken as a symptom of the significance of the moment, for it is precisely the inflection at m. 47 that reifies the abstraction immanent in the relationship between E minor and D♯ minor. To return to an earlier point, the manner of negotiation between these two pitches favors D♯ in the positing of some hierarchical tonal relationship between them. The setting of stanzas 3 and 4 in E major responds to this conflict in two senses. On the one hand, it tends to corroborate a commonsense reading of the opening measures of the song as "in the tonic": E, as the root of privilege, is enhanced with an acoustically "better" third. On the other hand, the G♯ that distinguishes this beginning from the others is heard in direct response to D♯. But the fact remains that, in the syntax of the opening strophes, E minor is the soft partner in relationship to D♯ minor, whose priority is affirmed as the locus of cadencing.

From the inflections at m. 47, the music begins its turn toward a reversal of these priorities. The moment is coincident with a powerful inflection—a literal turning inward—in the poetic text. Breaking out of his icy metaphoric reflections frozen in the past tense, the poet sings an apostrophe to the heart—

"*Mein* Herz! Erkennst du nun dein Bild?"—a painful entry into one's own psyche. The inflection at m. 47, and the turning of D♯ back the long, hard way (and from the theorist's view, the only true way) to E minor, is the playing out in tone of these probing questions of self-scrutiny, of *Erkennung*.

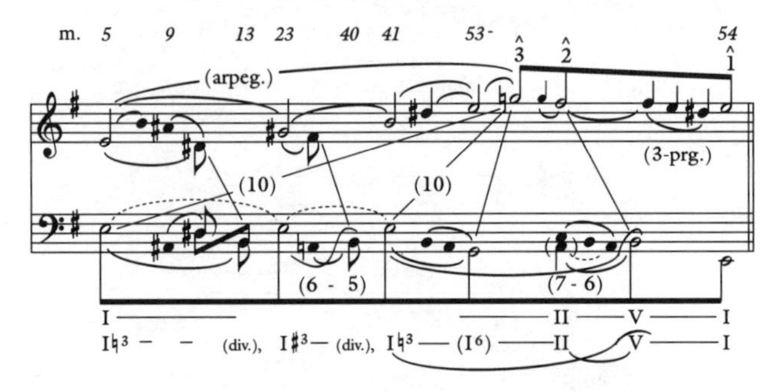

Example 7.4 *Auf dem Flusse* in Schenker's graphing

Indeed, the quality of the downbeat on G♯ minor at m. 48 has come under heavy theoretical and critical scrutiny. Much maligned, Schenker's famous graphing of the song (shown as ex. 7.4) remains a provocative attempt to translate the expressive subcutaneous power of the music into an explanatory model, an exemplum of *reinen Satz* that silently disregards the G♯ in the bass at m. 48 and, indeed, all that follows from it.[9] As an illustration of bass arpeggiation, Schenker's graph has a didactic message. Lewin even suggests that Schenker, "repelled on principle by the idea of [modal] mixture in the *Bassbrechung*," would in any case have taken pains to avoid the G♯ as a constituent of the fundamental arpeggiation in the bass.[10] Further, both Lewin and Newcomb worry about an *Urlinie* (the fundamental descent from a *Kopfton* in the "structural" descant) that begins at m. 53 and closes at m. 54.[11] But surely it is in the nature of such graphings—and an implication ingrained in Schenkerian thought—that the internal process through which the high G♮ in m. 53 is posted as the *Kopfton* is heard simultaneously (synchronically, even) and in dialectical conversation with the work as it unfolds in greater and lesser detail. "It seems dramatically essential that an *Urlinie* . . . should begin exactly with the opening G-natural in the right hand. . . . A *Kopfton* in bar 1 could, of course, later be transferred into the voice at bar 53," writes Lewin. But Schenker, for whom the definition of *Kopfton* in this or that work is an altogether consuming issue, must surely have anticipated the thrust of Lewin's argument. Had Schenker furnished graphings of more detail, the *Kopfton* would no doubt have been shown in some incipient stage. But that is not the

9. Schenker, *Free Composition*, vol. 2, fig. 40, no. 2. The graph illustrates arpeggiation in the upper (structural) voice toward the first tone (the *Kopfton*) of the *Urlinie*, a phenomenon characteristic of the middle ground.

10. Lewin, "*Auf dem Flusse*," 151.

11. Ibid., 150–51; Newcomb, "Structure and Expression," 173, n. 16.

real point. As Lewin elsewhere observes, the doubling of voice and bass, and the subsequent separating of the two at critical moments, is a thematic idea, governing much of the stage action of the song: "The singer seems to be saying, "I am, at this point, only a bass line, *unter der Rinde*; I have nothing to do with that terrible minor *Kopfton* in the right hand.'"[12] What, then, legitimizes the G♮ in the very first simultaneity as *Kopfton*? Schenker himself is reasonably clear in distinguishing the first symptoms of a *Kopfton* from the positioning of the *Kopfton* itself as the goal of an ascending motion and, at the same time, as the onset of the fundamental line (the *Urlinie*).[13] The notion of obligatory register, a key criterion in the conceiving of *Urlinie*, is very much to the point here. Newcomb senses this, so that his dismissal of Schenker's graphing suggests, in spite of itself, a very strong argument for Schenker's hearing of the *Kopfton* at m. 53. "A linear analysis," Newcomb insists, "should . . . acknowledge the exceptional nature of the case when a single, continuous vocal line resolves to a tonic an octave higher than the one from which it started."[14]

A more troubling aspect of Schenker's graph lies in the motion of the *Urlinie*—the timing of its descent—following on the posting of the *Kopfton*. In establishing closure at m. 54, the graph relegates everything that follows—more than a quarter of the song—to afterbeat, by definition inessential to the unfolding of structure. In the abstract, these proportions are in themselves objectionable. But, in this instance, Schenker seems oblivious of a subtle, if profound, signal for formal interruption between m. 53 and m. 54. The sudden *pianissimo* at m. 54 suggests an analogue at the breach between m. 39 and m. 41, where the *pianissimo* in the piano left hand at the upbeat to m. 41 reinforces the sense of a new beginning—not, that is, of a dominant resolved. Similarly, the implied articulation between m. 53 and m. 54 means to suggest a breached cadence, in the manner of a first ending. One might even suppose the music to have gone as in ex. 7.5, had the text allowed it.

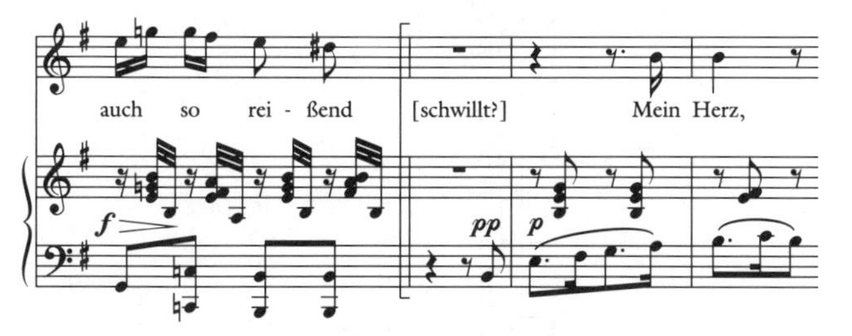

Example 7.5 *Auf dem Flusse*, m. 53, with hypothetical continuation

To reinstate mm. 54–70 as essential to the structure of the song is to recognize in the denouement from m. 47 a deliberate harmonic plotting from G♯ minor in which the dissonant ambivalence in the relationship between E and

12. Lewin, "*Auf dem Flusse*," 150, 137.
13. Schenker, *Free Composition*, pars. 93, 113, 115, 121.
14. Newcomb, "Structure and Expression," 173, n. 16.

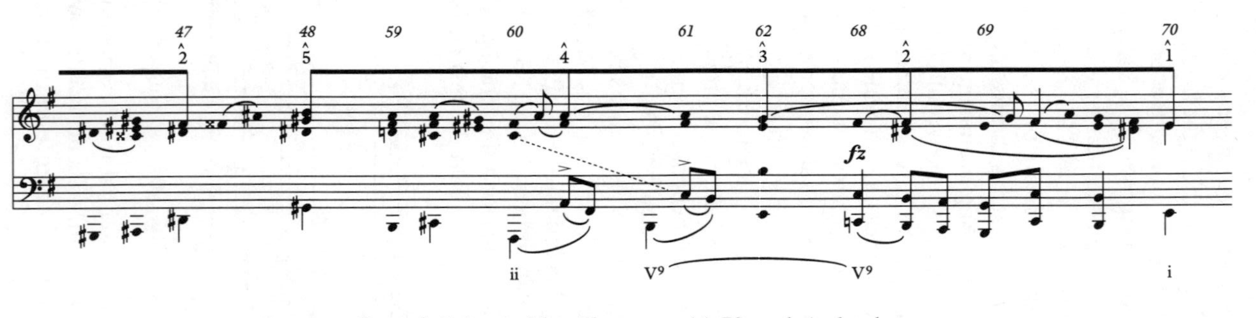

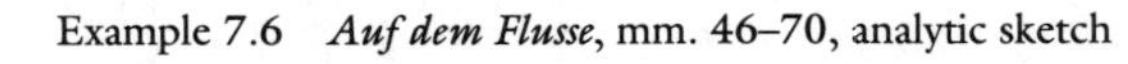

Example 7.6 *Auf dem Flusse*, mm. 46–70, analytic sketch

D♯ is finally set in equilibrium (see ex. 7.6). The deep F♯ at m. 60 seems especially critical here, seizing the connection with m. 47 and grounding the bass in a fundamental motion by fifth that firms up E minor as the true tonic. The very depth of this F♯ in complicity with an unequivocal cadence in E minor powerfully grounds those upper scale degrees essential to closure in the Schenkerian sense. Whether these upper tones are precisely in place seems beside the point. One readily accepts the displacement of upper tones; indeed, the position of an "abstract," unsounded structural tone in the descant is a common phenomenon even in Schenker's most convincing analyses. But the manipulation of the bass, of the kind that plagues Schenker's efforts to establish a structural "II" on the second eighth note of m. 53, as a reinforcement of $\hat{2}$ in the *Urlinie*, is *theoretically* troubling.

The modulatory adventure of *Auf dem Flusse* is extreme. No other song in *Winterreise* is endowed with a tonal graph anywhere near as complex. The putting of D♯ minor in conflict with E minor is a gambit that sets in vibration the music beginning at m. 47 and that resonates well beyond the song itself.

III

All this theorizing about *Auf dem Flusse* takes the song on its own terms, as something self-contained. The arguments for hearing it that way, compelling as they may be, tend to obscure the position of the song as a subordinate member in a complex grouping of songs that bear on one another in ways that everyone acknowledges to be significant, even as the specific nature of their relatedness has proved to be elusive in the extreme. By any rigorous theoretical criteria, efforts to construe *Winterreise* as a song cycle in a purely musical sense have not been wholly satisfying.

The establishing of criteria is itself a problem of some magnitude. In a valuable study of *Wanderlieder* cycles mostly from the 1820s, Barbara Turchin is led to this understanding of Schubert's *Winterreise*: "Choice of key in relation to poetic content has priority over choice of key in relation to an abstract or functionally logical scheme. Adjacent poems of related contents most often are tonally related in the first or second degree, while far more distant key relationships are reserved for moments of poetic discontinuity."[15] On its face, the claims for tonal continuity and discontinuity as a reflection of continuities and discontinuities in the sequence of poems seem unobjectionable. Yet there is a troubling aspect to this supposed opposition between "poetic content" and an "abstract or functionally logical scheme" as a determinant in which key relationships might be mapped. Why, after all, should we suspect that tonal relationships deployed in the service of poetic expression are by their nature antithetical to whatever tonal abstraction might appeal to Schubert? Conversely, and perhaps more to the point, on what evidence might we argue that Schubert's tonal abstractions are inherently antipoetic?

15. Turchin, "The Nineteenth-Century *Wanderlieder* Cycle," 514.

Further, to suggest of two songs related as tonic to dominant, or tonic to relative minor, or some such relationship "in the first or second degree," that they play out some aspect of poetic continuity is to risk generalizing (and thus trivializing) the relationship of music to poem.[16] What, finally, is the place of this "abstract or functionally logical scheme" against which tonal continuities and discontinuities, as a reflection of poetic discourse, must struggle? What does it mean to say that the latter has "priority over" the former? Turchin's formulation seems to address a concern of compositional process: the composer begins with some "abstract" tonal scheme, logical and functional by all the conventional criteria; but in the process of composition, pursuit of the content of the poetry (unsuspected in the contemplation of the scheme) diverts him from the scheme, which is then simply readjusted to fit these digressions.

The quarrel with this view of the thing is that it discourages a concept of the whole in which the poetry, read into the music, may be said to hold a fundamental and significant place. Can we imagine that Schubert would devise an abstract and "functionally logical scheme" for a cycle of songs without having contemplated the poetry? A *Winterreise* in which the meaning of the poems is secondary? On the contrary, we know very well that the first step for Schubert is always an intense saturation *in the poem.*[17]

Then, too, there is an antiorganicist ring to "functionally logical scheme" that signals trouble if we are casting about for some model of continuity in *Winterreise* that will not stand in utter repudiation of what we have come to know of continuity and coherence within the great instrumental works of the 1820s, not to speak of the inner coherence of individual songs. In Schubert's music, one speaks better of a poetics of tonal harmony, of tonality as expressive and signifying. If an opposition may be said to exist between a tonality that is poetically inspired and one that is "functionally logical" (if by that is meant the fundamental symmetries of the Classical tonal system), it is an opposition deeply rooted in Schubert's language. It does not reside on the surface.

In the case of *Winterreise*, the saturation in the poetry, and the conceptualizing of some whole, will in the beginning have comprised only the first twelve poems in what we now know as the complete cycle of twenty-four. This is simply to state a fact in the genesis of the work, but it is a crucial one for an understanding of the idea of *Winterreise* as a cycle.

16. The idea for relationships expressed in this way is borrowed from Gottfried Weber, *Versuch einer geordneten Theorie der Tonsezkunst zum Selbstunterricht, mit Anmerkungen für Gelehrtere* (Mainz, 1817), vol. 1. Weber's theoretical posture is taken by Turchin as close in time and spirit to these cycles.

17. The few eyewitness accounts of Schubert, poem in hand, before the act of composition are suggestive. Walther Dürr retells them in "Schubert's Songs and Their Poetry," esp. 9–10. And there is Schober's recollection of the composer stumbling on what must have been the first installment of *Winterreise* poems in Schober's little library: "Sich von denselben angezogen gefühlt und sie, so wie viele andere Gedichte, in seiner Weise musikalisch stimmungsvoll wiedergegeben" ([He] felt himself drawn to them, and, as with so many other poems, rendered them full of genuine expression in his music) (cited in Kreissle von Hellborn, *Franz Schubert*, 482).

Plotted out in a shorthand notation of their original keys, the twelve songs in part I constitute a whole in the sense represented in the graph shown as example 7.7. Reading a graph of this sort begs of the reader a leap of faith. Keys of songs are represented synoptically. Key becomes tone. To the collection of tones in the synopsis is imputed a coherence requisite in the notation of the graph but only vaguely surmised in the actual notation of the songs. Tones that in the first instance represent tonics of individual songs effectively closed off from one another are now endowed as roots of triads that, by implication, are induced into interaction with one another, mapping out an array that unfolds from a fundamental tonic. Conversely, the songs themselves may now be understood to "personify" and consequently to individualize the elements that in the graph are shown to be subordinate to a greater design. The process is a mutually dependent one, and because the condition for "reading" art demands that we move from the individual to the abstract—from the sounding text in all its detail to the silent engine that must be inferred to be at work beneath it—one tends to dismiss such inference as speculative and even pernicious, when in reality the infrastructure shown in the graph, *however we may think to construe it*, is no less an aspect of the work—and in no sense secondary in the conceiving of the work—than are the phrases of this or that song.

The motion of roots in the graph plays out some Ramellian teleology in which a path from the most remote key would chart a return by descending fifth to a home tonic—a fundamental model in which the entirety of the bass is displayed as a "Brechung" of the tonic triad, the more remote tones as dissonances of lesser priority. All the while, the ear picks out configurations in the bass that suggest something akin to motivic play.[18] This contradictory tendency of the bass to be governed by a motion of roots related by fifth, and at the same time to seek the linear properties of "voice," is a universal one, and I draw attention to it here only as a way of opening the possibility that, in this array, certain tones are to be understood as lesser functions of others. Not all of them are to be understood as roots in quite the same way. That the relationships embedded in the graph may seem in conflict with one another is itself a symptom of some innate disposition in the construct—more an emblem of Romantic tonality than an argument for various and independent modes of coherence. So that while the graphing of tonality in *Winterreise*, part I, displays a complex elaboration around a tonic D, the *place* of tonic has less to do with the calibrated dramatic equipoise of Classical form—of tensions held in check—than with the flight away to remote and exotic regions from which the tonic is itself viewed as distant and inexorable, the undesirable but necessary "other self."

"Der Klassiker Schubert" (to borrow from Walther Vetter) inhabits the de-

18. Something of the dialectic, manifest in the theoretical work of Schenker and Schoenberg, between a bass conceived as a coherent thread of pitches, even thematically conceived, and as a system of "tonal centers" is suggestively explored in David Lewin, "Inversional Balance as an Organizing Force in Schoenberg's Music and Thought," *Perspectives of New Music* 6, no. 2 (Spring–Summer 1968): esp. 2–4.

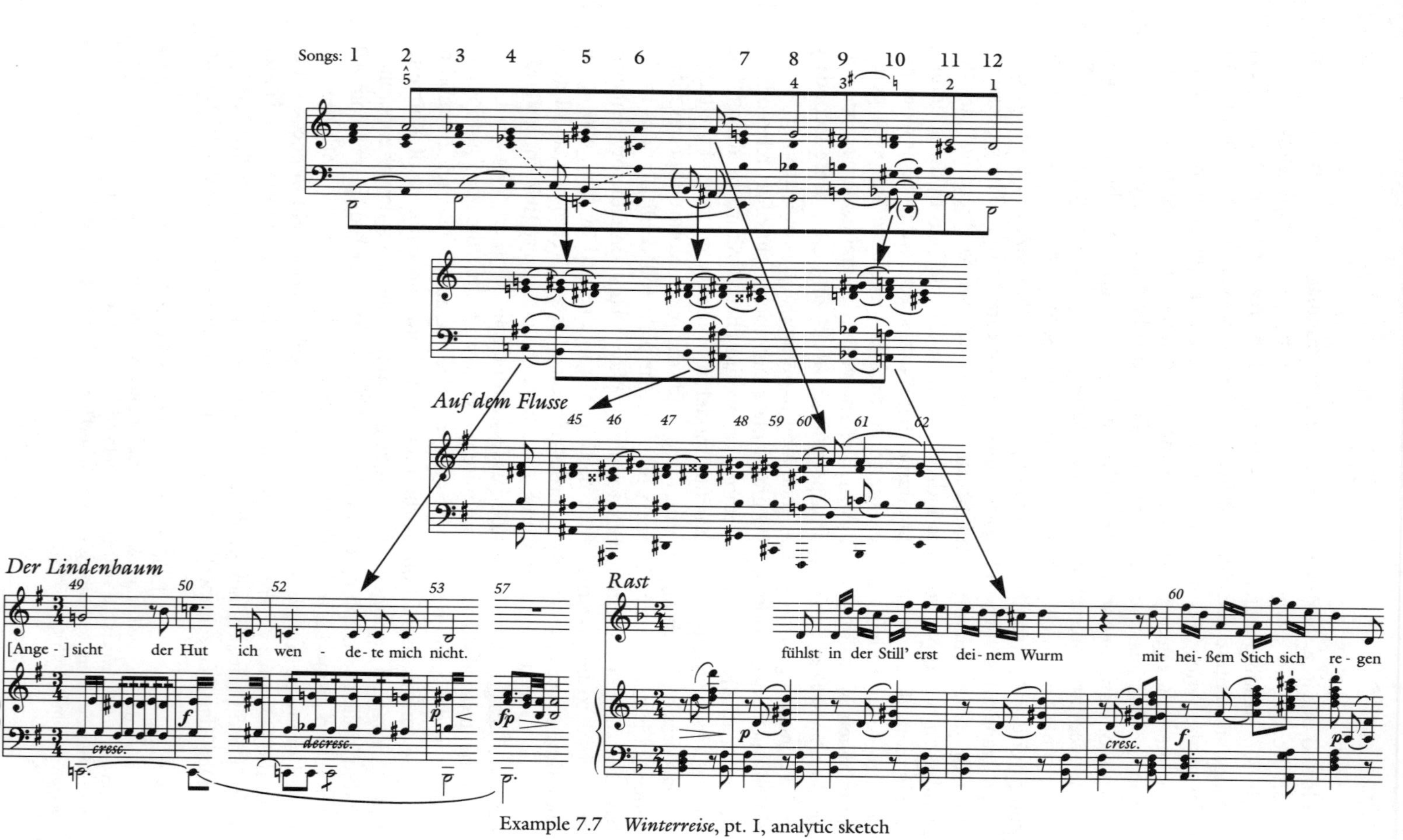

Example 7.7 *Winterreise*, pt. I, analytic sketch

sign as well, and, in the positioning of the tone E in the array, may be heard in conflict with the Romantic in him, for, while E occupies and envelops the center of the cycle in a manner to suggest some centripetal symmetry out from a distant antipode, it stands as well for "dominant-of-the-dominant" in a sonata-like plot in which the next move is to the dominant itself. Characteristically, the resolution of this dominant-of-the-dominant, now transformed into the subdominant (first minor, then major) and prolonged in the B minor of *Irrlicht*, is delayed until the very end. In an *Urlinie* of the whole, the obligatory *Terzzug*—or *Quintzug*, or indeed both—closes with the final songs.

The positioning of E as some limit in the structural underpinnings of the cycle lends weight to the grouping of *Lindenbaum*, *Wasserflut*, and *Auf dem Flusse*, which together might be said to form a tonal outpost toward which the journey makes its way and from which it plots out a reluctant return.

IV

Wasserflut is one of several characteristic songs in *Winterreise* in which bare harmonies serve to set off one or two piercing gestures that are all that remain when we conjure the song in memory. The singular gesture in *Wasserflut* is the chilling *Geschrei* at m. 12. It came to Schubert only in a second pass. And there was some uncertainty as to its notation (see ex. 7.8). Virtually the same pitches—yet another *Geschrei*, at the apex of a song, set off in relief by similarly austere harmonies—are at issue in the climactic phrase in *Der Doppelgänger;* again, the autograph registers the investment in dissonance, the high G grating against F♯. In *Wasserflut*, the final phrase returns the singer to that strident region—"*stark*," Schubert added to the engraver's copy. It is a phrase that one hears as an obligatory confirmation of the *Geschrei*, at once an affirmation of its pitch region and a grounding of its extreme dissonance.

The autograph is again telling, for it shows that, on second thought, Schubert took back a more comfortable alternative ending (see ex. 7.9). He insisted, that is, on these difficult pitches that by 1826 would have augured trouble with singer and publisher.

Example 7.8 *Wasserflut*, m. 12, autograph score

Example 7.9 *Wasserflut*, mm. 27–28, showing deletion in autograph score

Such phrases, not readily effaced, seem to reverberate beyond the actual moment, to invade the pitched space of other songs, and thus to assume a significance that has much to do with the deeper questions of cycle making. No singer will strain to find the dyad F♯-A in the final phrase of *Auf dem Flusse* without sensing echos from *Wasserflut*. Further, this simple analogue in final phrases suggests a more daring leap beyond conventional thematics (shown in ex. 7.10), where similarly placed dominant ninths buttress a deeper connection between the two songs.

Example 7.10 *a*, *Wasserflut*, m. 12. *b*, *Auf dem Flusse*, mm. 68–70

Here, too, at the end of *Auf dem Flusse*, an alternative to the high pitches in the final, climactic phrase has found its way into the literature. But its credentials are suspect, for there is no evidence of it either in the autograph or in the engraver's copy. The rejected alternative in *Wasserflut* is instructive for what it tells us of Schubert's instinct to hear his most expressive phrases in that precarious region for the voice and to take them back in the service of a more pragmatic mission.

The relationship between *Flut* and *Flusse* is manifest in the harmonic unfolding that characterizes the cycle as a whole. And that brings us back to the nature of harmony in *Wasserflut*: a song *about* F♯ minor in a degree approaching the metaphysical, its harmony seems to get caught up in the bold modulatory apparatus of *Auf dem Flusse*, where the cadence in F♯ minor at m. 60, sounding the deepest possible F♯, displaces D♯ minor and establishes the larger root motion whereby the tonicity of E minor is once and for all confirmed. *Wasserflut*, the embodiment of F♯ minor, is drawn into the harmonic design, invoked at a moment of revelation, where the ambiguities that have threatened the coherence of *Auf dem Flusse* are set in some prevailing context.

To propose *Wasserflut* as an embodiment of F♯ minor is to force out into the open a much vexed issue in *Winterreise*: the investment in a theory of absolute pitch seems contradicted in the transposition of fully five songs down from the keys in which they appear in Schubert's autograph. The evidence, on its face, is plain enough. For reasons that often seem irrefutably clear, Schubert stood prepared to sanction these transpositions and may even in some instances have promoted them. But a harder issue remains unaddressed. Does it follow from this readiness to transpose from some original key that the concept of key, pure and absolute, has no primary place in Schubert's aesthetic but lies only at its periphery? And if this is the case, what are the consequences of this view—a commonly held one, after all—for a coming to grips with the idea of tonal coherence in the song cycles?

The answers to these questions do not come easily because the evidence bearing on the aesthetic of absolute pitch is of no concrete, palpable kind. What we know about *meaning* we must learn from a controlled repertory of works. To remind us of but one example, B minor is made an element of expression in both the Heine and the Rellstab songs, shrewdly positioned in each set, aligned with the poetic instance of greatest anguish. The key itself acquires topos-like status. No argument about the shifting standards for the measurement of pitch is to the point. Whatever *B minor*—in all is specificity and as some abstraction tied in with the tonal system and the repertories of music that endow the keys with their complexity of association and character—can have meant to Schubert, the key itself invades his expressive vocabulary, informing, however subconsciously, all those aspects of the music that, conversely, define the key for us. To put it more aggressively, in the conceiving of the song, the poetic idea and the idea of key belong to the inchoate creative impulse from which the song will emerge.

How, then, are we to understand the transpositions in *Winterreise*? The two transpositions in part II, affecting *Mut!* and *Der Leiermann*, may be set aside for the moment; the slender documentation surrounding them points more readily to Haslinger than to Schubert. Of the three in part I, two—the transposition of *Wasserflut* from F♯ minor to E minor and of *Einsamkeit* from D minor to B minor—must have been authorized in a separate instruction to the copyist before the engraver's copy was prepared, for the songs appear in their new keys in that manuscript; the autograph gives no hint of these transpositions.[19] The case is rather different for *Rast*, which survived the engraver's copy in its original key. But Schubert wrote "NB Ist ins C moll zu schreiben" in both the autograph and the engraver's copy, suggesting that the decision to transpose it was made while Schubert was checking the engraver's copy against his autograph.[20]

In more than one sense, the transposition of *Einsamkeit* from D minor to B minor has a troubling aspect. On the face of it, the decision must have been coincident with the undertaking of the composition of part II; the transposition away from D minor "negates the closed tonal circle of the original twelve-song cycle," as Susan Youens puts it.[21] Considerably more than the "closed tonal circle" is affected, for *Einsamkeit* plays on earlier songs on various levels. The affinity with *Gute Nacht* extends beyond the shared D minor. In its opening chords, staggered between the hands in just that way, *Einsamkeit* seems to suggest a final disintegration of the "gehender Bewegung" that characterizes the very same chords at the outset of *Gute Nacht*.[22] Further, the continual stress on E in *Gute Nacht* as a dissonance of various kinds—now an unprepared ninth against the bass D, now the prominent added sixth to a minor subdominant, finally translated stunningly to the root of a seventh chord in 4-2 position (m. 73)—is echoed in *Einsamkeit*, even if the stress is less prominently displayed.

Affinities vanish when the song is transposed. New ones are gained, for the final phrase—*not* a transposition, but a new phrase—sounds a memorable F♯ that will sound again at the analogous place at the end of part II, the last, dying pitch in the voice at the end of *Der Leiermann*. There will be more to say about that, for *Der Leiermann*, too, suffered a transposition that does great damage to the tonal hard wiring in the cycle. Here it might only be noted that the F♯ in the new phrase in the B-minor *Einsamkeit* agrees enharmonically with the G♭ that is the highest pitch in the D-minor *Einsamkeit*.

In its position at the end of the original cycle, *Einsamkeit* plays out another aspect of tonal bonding. Like *Wasserflut*, this is a song where spontaneity of gesture enhances the incisive grip of its phrases. Unlike *Wasserflut*, harmonic discourse is elevated here to an expressive language so powerful that in the

19. Susan Youens ("*Wegweiser* in *Winterreise*," *Journal of Musicology* 5, no. 3 [Summer 1987]: 378) wants to believe that the transposition of *Wasserflut* from F♯ minor to E minor was intended to clinch a motivic relationship with the piano figuration in *Der Lindenbaum*. That is implausible on many counts. For one, it cannot be maintained that similarities in piano figuration of this kind are enhanced through pitch equivalence. If that were established as a principle in the flow of the cycle, it would continually tend toward the perfect case, absolute equivalence in both pitch and motive—a single song. Nor can one imagine Schubert's second thoughts in this direction: a conscious transposition merely to point up the similarity in figuration. Too much else is at stake.

20. Youens (ibid., 359, n. 6) seems to have misread the evidence, for it is clear that Schubert wrote his instruction in both the autograph and the engraver's copy and that Haslinger's entry is simply an additional memorandum to the engraver.

21. Ibid.

22. A point noted as well by Youens (ibid., 367).

setting of its third strophe the explanatory agency of ordinary formal syntax is stretched to the limits of common discourse. Strophes 1 and 2 are simple enough in this regard, but the motion between m. 23 and m. 24 is a motion between two diminished seventh chords masking two dominant ninths whose implied roots (A and G) are both strongly felt. While the motion in all four voices contrives a simple sliding *up* by semitone, the unheard roots imply a more powerful motion *down* by a whole tone (see ex. 7.11). Still, the ear accepts the chromaticism as a passing harmony in a device that sets up C as the dominant in a modulation toward the relative of D minor.

Example 7.11 *Einsamkeit*, mm. 23–25, in harmonic abstract

But the modulation to F is stopped cold. The *tremolando* aggravates the breach, healed in the chromatic return to A in the bass at m. 28. The motion between A and B♭, readdressed, now yields the desperate phrase at "Als noch die Stürme tobten." Everything is at loose ends. The triplets in the piano are new and unprepared. The trajectory of the upper voice in the piano traces nearly two octaves, as if in search of the dominant seventh on B♭ found at its end. Struck ***ffz*** on a weak beat, the sheer force of it only quickens the riddle of the harmony, for, in its context, the seventh on B♭ must ultimately explain itself away as an augmented sixth: G♯, not A♭.

The consoling phrase that follows, a hymn to misery, gains in poignance in that the inexorable descent of the B♭ in the bass to the true dominant seems a very long time in coming. At the repetition, from the arpeggiation in mm. 34 and 35, the diminished seventh first heard at m. 24 is now approached more logically. But the unhinged passage returns intact.

Schubert's manuscripts, even those that have all the characteristics of a rough draft, rarely give witness to the electricity of decision making at a higher power. So the survival of an abandoned page in the rough draft for *Einsamkeit* (shown in fig. 7.1) is of special value for what it captures of an early concept of this third strophe.[23] The page is spectator to the process of mind where in-

23. The draft concept is given in transcription in *NGA*, ser. 4, vol. 4b, p. 278.

choate idea and image burn through with an intensity at the edge of comprehensibility.

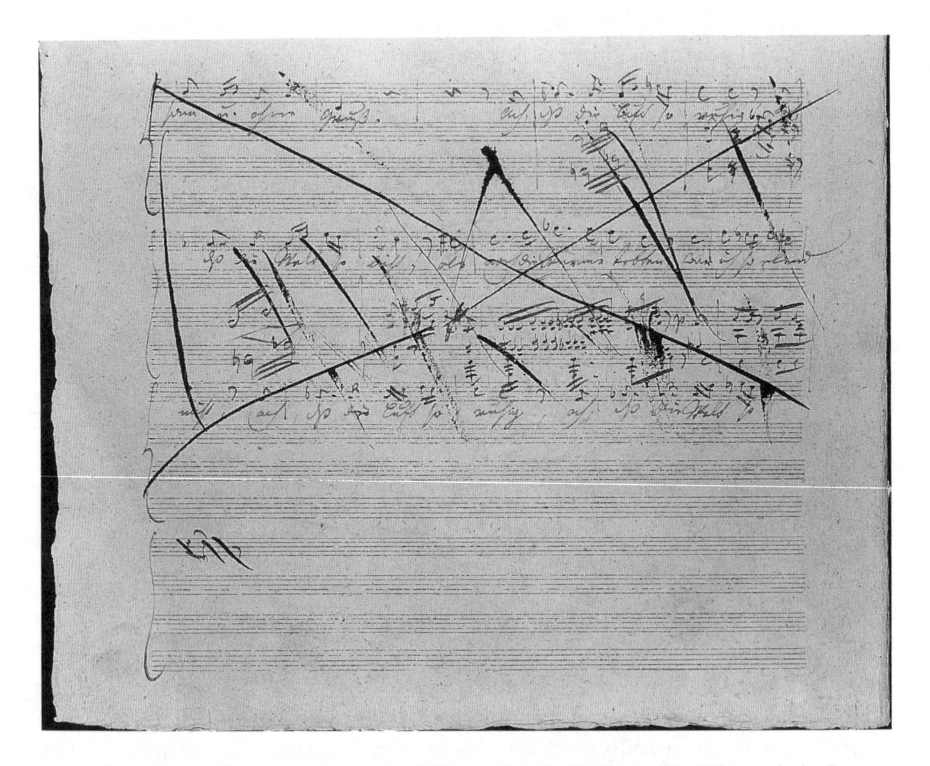
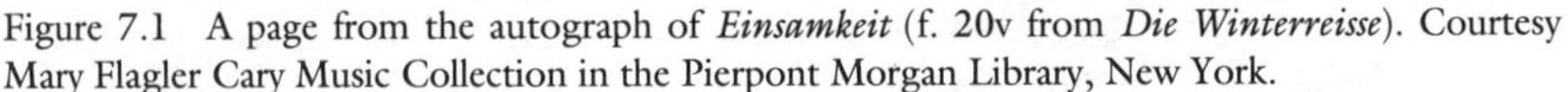

Figure 7.1 A page from the autograph of *Einsamkeit* (f. 20v from *Die Winterreisse*). Courtesy Mary Flagler Cary Music Collection in the Pierpont Morgan Library, New York.

In this earlier concept, the cadence at m. 22, at the end of the second strophe, closes in the tonic, suggesting of the third strophe something yet more detached. Perhaps the opening figuration in the piano was to have interceded in these empty measures, a notion suggested by the voice, which begins to unfold the diminished seventh on an F, a pitch that presupposes some other harmony than the anterior diminished seventh at the upbeat to m. 24 in the final version. The hypothetical reconstruction in example 7.12 shows how this passage may originally have sounded in Schubert's mind.

Knowing, as we do, the opening of the third strophe in its final version, it is something of a shock to be confronted with the tritone-vexed contortion that Schubert conceived in the original draft for the lines "Ach, daß die Luft so ruhig, ach, daß die Welt so licht!" The revision probes at the troubled opposition in these lines: "Alas, that the air is so calm, the world so bright, for when the storms still raged, I was not so miserable." When the world is at peace, his alienation is yet more pronounced. In heavy weather, the elements rage with

Example 7.12 *Einsamkeit*, mm. 21–25, hypothetical reconstruction from autograph fragment

him: he is at one with them. These barometric readings—the world now mirrored in the soul, now alienated from it—are reflected in a paradoxical music divided between what is sung and what is played. In the revision, the *tremolando* diminished sevenths now suggest a longing for the storm, while the wanderer sings his lines with a touch of sangfroid, composed and detached, rather less engaged.

But it is at the interstice between m. 29 and m. 30 (and to a lesser degree between m. 27 and 28) that the grandest mystery of the piece is concealed. The conceptual leap from an earlier version to this final one is quite beyond the grasp of analysis. In a single luminous measure of music, a fresh vision is conceived. The second chord in m. 29 (m. 30 in the final version), now struck *ffz* (and no longer rolled), is revoiced with a doubled seventh. This new inflection inspires a broad new phrase, embracing E♭ major, seemingly born from the terse cadential phrase that comprises the whole answer in the draft. The new phrase, this brief lingering on the dominant of E♭, conjures an expanse of space and time and a nostalgia for past events. In its basic syntactic alignment, not much has been altered in the revision. The augmented sixth at the last eighth of (draft) m. 29 is prolonged. Yet there is more at stake here than the mechanics of syntax in *Einsamkeit.* The prolongation evokes time outside the confines of the song. In the breadth of the cadence, other songs are remembered. The cadence seems now to speak for the cycle.

How is this so? Most notably, in the appeal to *Auf dem Flusse*: not, of course, to its thematic surface, but to the modulatory device that drives it to the brink—to the provocative gambit in which the true dominant masquerades as ♭VI, suggestive of an augmented sixth folding out to the dominant A♯. Much of the song is an elaboration of just that harmonic conceit, tuned to a conceit in the poem.

This device that drives *Auf dem Flusse* lodges uncomfortably in the mind. So the apotheosis with which *Einsamkeit* closes—again, a prolongation having to do with an augmented sixth reinterpreted as a dominant seventh (now the inverse of the conceit)—awakens the memory of it. Powerful signifiers of one another, the two passages reciprocate in something like the construct shown in ex. 7.13. In their reciprocity, the two together bond into an even more powerful metaphrase. An archetypal harmonic motion is forged that may be

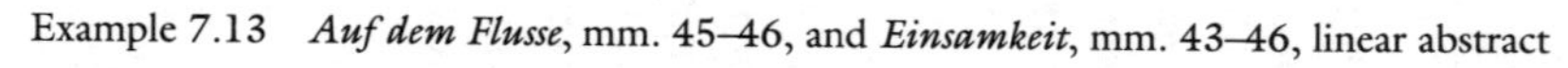

Example 7.13 *Auf dem Flusse*, mm. 45–46, and *Einsamkeit*, mm. 43–46, linear abstract

said to stand for the cycle. *Einsamkeit*, it is good to recall, was conceived at once as the final song in a cycle and as a music of final alienation. On its surface, it is not a song that effects the accents of closure very powerfully. Yet in its infrastructure a deeper quality of closure is ingrained.

Transposed to B minor at the inception of a new "Fortsetzung," *Einsamkeit* loses its sense of ending. The fine intricacy of structural closure is dissolved. That, no doubt, was the intent. The consequences are severe, for the eloquence with which the extreme phrases of the inner songs in the cycle were heard to resonate within one another is now muted. The original cycle is sprung and must find its eloquence elsewhere.

8
Winterreise II

The publication of the twelve new poems for Müller's *Die Winterreise* happened in two stages. Ten of them appeared in 1823.[1] Schubert seems not to have known this publication or, at any rate, did not begin his work on the *Fortsetzung* on the basis of its text. In 1824, the full twelve poems were published, but decidedly not as a discrete *Fortsetzung*. The new poems are fed into the cycle in ways that suggest that Müller was thinking less of a continuation than of a fleshing out of the narrative sketched in the twelve original poems (see table 8.1).[2] *Einsamkeit* is now the antepenult in the full set, followed only by *Mut!* and *Der Leiermann*; the sense of extreme alienation denoted in its position at the end of the original cycle of twelve poems is here amplified. And the poems that, in the original twelve, sing of increasing delusion—*Irrlicht*, *Rast*, and *Frühlingstraum*—are consequently kept in close proximity to *Einsamkeit*, suggesting that, for Müller, this sequence of three poems, now magnified in the perplexing, astigmatic *Die Nebensonnen*, must lead ineluctably to *Einsamkeit*.

The action of *Winterreise* is interior, a play of the mind caught in the inexorable trudge toward solitude and alienation. Devoid of interaction, of direct communication between a protagonist and some other sentient being—until the final quatrain of *Der Leiermann* (although even these lines are perhaps better understood as willed than actually spoken)—the process is of gradual dissolution. Perhaps it is this timeless quality, without the palpable articulation of concrete event, that permits us to accept Schubert's reordering of the poems less as a violation of whatever dramatic unities might inhere in Müller's story than as an infringement on the authority of Müller's text. Schubert's reordering has even been defended.[3] This is troubling, for it seems clear that the revised *sense* of poetic narrative in Schubert's reordering (the exchange between

1. In *Deutsche Blätter für Poesie, Litteratur, Kunst und Theater* (Breslau, 1823). See *Gedichte von Wilhelm Müller: Vollständige kritische Ausgabe*, ed. James Taft Hatfield (Berlin, 1906; reprint, Nendeln, Liechtenstein, 1968), 463–64.

2. In this form, they were published as *Die Winterreise* in the collection titled *Gedichte aus den hinterlassenen Papieren eines reisenden Waldhornisten . . . zweites Bändchen* (Dessau, 1824). For the complete texts, see *Gedichte von Wilhelm Müller*, 111–23. They are given as well in Feil, *Franz Schubert: Die schöne Mullerin; Winterreise*, 163–71 (Sherwin, trans., 131–51).

3. Most recently, by Susan Youens (see her "*Winterreise*: In the Right Order," *Soundings*, no. 13 [Summer 1985]: 41–50, and her introduction to *Franz Schubert: Winterreise: The Autograph Score*, xv, n. 11).

TABLE 8.1
Ordering of the Poems in Müller's *Winterreise*

Urania (1823)	*Gedichte* (1824)
1 "Gute Nacht"	
2 "Die Wetterfahne"	
3 "Gefrorene Tränen"	
4 "Erstarrung"	
5 "Der Lindenbaum"	
	13 "Die Post"
6 "Wasserflut"	
7 "Auf dem Flusse"	
8 "Rückblick"	
	14 "Der greise Kopf" (1)
	15 "Die Krähe" (3)
	16 "Letzte Hoffnung" (2)
	17 "Im Dorfe" (4)
	18 "Der stürmische Morgen" (5)
	19 "Täuschung"
	20 "Der Wegweiser" (7)
	21 "Das Wirtshaus" (8)
9 "Irrlicht"	
10 "Rast"	
	23 "Die Nebensonnen" (6)
11 "Frühlingstraum"	
12 "Einsamkeit"	
	22 "Mut!" (9)
	24 "Der Leiermann" (10)

Note: The numerals before the poems refer to the order in which a poem appears in Schubert's manuscript. The numerals in parentheses refer to the order in which the ten new poems were published in the *Deutsche Blätter für Poesie, Litteratur, Kunst und Theater* (Breslau, 1823).

Mut! and *Die Nebensonnen* excepted) can have arisen only as an accident of the formula through which Müller's poems are mechanically transposed into their position in part II of the cycle. Whether or not Schubert was engaged in some deliberate effort to make Müller's story more convincing, the reordering makes plainest sense when it is understood to have been provoked by a determination to keep intact the original design of part I and to pick up in order the *new* poems from Müller's newly integral cycle of twenty-four. As as result, the order of the poems in Schubert's part II is true to Müller only in the abstract, for it is an order derived by a process in which the sense of narrative is not itself the determinant, *even if* the resultant narrative can be said to tell its tale coherently.

I

Whether by design or by accident, the second part of Schubert's *Winterreise* establishes a fresh start. Consequently, the urge toward recapitulation will be strongly felt. *Die Post* comes as a new beginning. Its music, not meant to sustain the narrative with which part I ends, rather suggests a breach: the dying strains of *Einsamkeit* are put out of mind. The choice of key—E♭ major, after the B minor with which *Einsamkeit* is now made to end—is the defining agent, fixing a schism that extends even to the temporal canvas of the cycle.

In the conception of the original cycle, the allusion to E♭ major at the end of *Einsamkeit* (in D minor) has a nostalgic aspect. This evocation of distance is seized on at the outset of part II. Everyone who has given thought to tonal relationships in *Winterreise* will have been struck by the nesting of songs 13–16 around E♭ major. What is the *sense* of this E♭ in the cycle? That is the more difficult issue, one of signal importance to an understanding of the cycle both in its semantics and in its genesis.

The evocation of distance in *Die Post* is manifest at every level. Again, Beethoven springs to mind—the post horn signaling "les adieux" and the post chaise signaling "le retour" in the Piano Sonata in E♭ Major, op. 81a. Closer to home, the key itself concretizes what was only suggested at the end of the original *Einsamkeit*—seems to respond, if subconsciously, to the brazen and ineffable dominant seventh on B♭, even as the late transposition of the song eradicates it.

The harmonic display in *Die Post* is singular. The music veers off at once toward its subdominant side. The address to the heart—"Was hat es, daß es so hoch aufspringt, mein Herz?"—calls to mind the last such address—"Mein Herz, in diesem Bache erkennst du nun dein Bild?"—and the plangent music in *Auf dem Flusse* that it inspires. The inflections of the harmony in *Die Post* jog the memory in a similar way. In the second strophe, the inflections draw closer still. At "was drängst du denn so wunderlich, mein Herz?" the music touches on G♭—a precarious G♭ that hints at a tonicity that dissolves almost as it is formed. (One admires the seamless quality of the harmony, at once suggesting G♭ major, at the same time effecting a motionless return to the dominant in E♭: the plaintive diminished harmony at mm. 34 and 36, seemingly an appoggiatura to G♭, gently hints at its ultimate function, the dominant of the dominant in the cadence at m. 44.)

The troubled tonal deployment of *Auf dem Flusse* is mirrored in two ways: (*a*) in the fleet recapitulation of its tonal stations (the sag toward D♯ minor in *Auf dem Flusse*, echoed in the E♭ minor of *Die Post*) and (*b*) in the suggestion of a more complex process of inversional balance, in which E and E♭ are suspended against one another as the extreme poles of a tonal axis (see ex. 8.1). In the one—what we might call the diachronic—it is the chronology of tonal event that is recapitulated; in the other—the synchronic—time and the temporal are suspended. By its nature, the first appeals to the aesthetic *feel* of the music—to how it is perceived. The perception of inversional balance appeals less to the senses than to some deep-rooted intuition that the tonal strategy of the one, in its motion along the sharp side, suggestive of ascent by dominants, is now checked through a motion in the opposite direction, along the flat side, descending by subdominants. In short, the E♭ of *Die Post*—and of the brace of songs through *Letzte Hoffnung*—is itself a complex sign, touching back to earlier moments of anguish and evoking tonal distance at several levels.

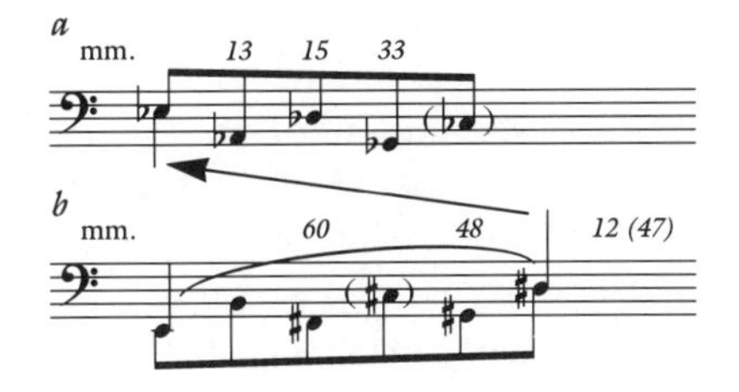

Example 8.1 *Die Post* (*a*) and *Auf dem Flusse* (*b*) in inversional balance

Where the deft tonal maneuvering of *Die Post* is draped in pastoral innocence, the harmonic strategy in *Letszte Hoffnung* is obsessive, focused, and decidedly not naive. Something of its strategy is evident in the much-admired piano introduction, its pitches splaying out in a registral diagram that is of later consequence to the precision of a time-capsule release toward resolution. C♭ is the privileged pitch, isolated in a metric position that exaggerates its mission: the paradox of the upbeat, the articulation of which argues that it is no such thing.

What sort of harmonic model might elucidate this C♭? To dismiss it as a minor ninth above the dominant is to trivialize it. In effect, we cannot know the dissonant implications of C♭ until it is shown to resolve, as flatted ninth, to B♭ at the downbeat of m. 2. Up to that point, the diminished seventh that unfolds about it seems in part controlled by a context established in the aftermath of *Die Krähe*: C♭ as B♮, suggesting that the true flatted ninth is the A♭ wanting resolution to G as dominant in C minor. Indeed, this implication of the opening measures is played out soon enough—hinted at in the fleeting F♯-G in m. 8 and exercised in the "lost-in-thought" music at mm. 11–13. Further, this striking dualism implicit in the opening dyad—dominant ninth on G, dominant ninth on B♭—is realized in the prolonged juxtaposition of just those harmonies across the entire second strophe, mm. 13–24.

The positioning of the A♭ at the downbeat of m. 1, and its "leading" through the labyrinth, competes with the C♭ for prominence. At first, in the distribution of the dominant ninth, it is deployed as seventh in the bass. In the echo of the motion C♭-B♭, it is absorbed into the inner voices, and its initial power is liquidated in the other chromatic inflection to the dominant—an inflection from the other side—approaching B♭ through its lower neighbor. The effect is of a delaying of the proper leading of A♭, *in the bass*, down to the third of a tonic triad. The waiting, apprehensively, for the A♭ to fall carries the music to its ultimate resolution.

In parallel, the poem plays on this element of suspended resolution. Again, the wanderer seizes simplemindedly on a commonplace of nature. In this idle staring, the single leaf becomes a gripping metaphor. When the leaf falls, it takes with it all hope—not, of course, that it does so literally, but that the wanderer's deluded mind wills it so. The image is charged with sardonic irony. First, the fall of the final autumn leaf is no predictable matter. The element of some inevitable, incalculable destiny enters in. Then there is the ironic reversal in impact: when the feather-light leaf touches down, it is made to symbolize a psychological cataclysm, the dashing of all desire. Actually, it is the fall itself—the measured time between the moment of detachment to the touching down—that is the signifier here: "Fällt das Blatt, fällt die Hoffnung ab" (*fallen*, *abfallen*; "to fall, to decay").

As a realization of both the dramatic scenario in its literal sense and the metaphoric implications of it, the music is beyond praise. Perhaps most astonishing of all is the grasp of a psychological twilight zone—the interminable flight of the leaf from the moment that it cuts loose from the tree to the moment of impact. What happens in the mind? The unfolding drama is calibrated to some sonata-like scene: the trembling of the leaf sets off an angst before the final act. The music teeters on the dominant. At the hint of a reprise, the splayed diminished seventh of the opening bars reduces to an obsession: C♭ and A♭ alone. The contoured phrases of the first strophe give way to a distracted music in which the voice struggles away from the falling octaves in the piano—octaves now, as the leaf grows to surreal dimension. Twice, in mm. 27 and 33, the music touches down to the lowest C♭, quadrupled, without harmony.

There are two resolutions. The first is routine enough: the loss of hope is set to a lugubrious cadential phrase in E♭ minor, "etwas langsamer," in a funereal dotted rhythm new to the song, but not to the cycle. The second is decidedly uncommon. The low C♭ is now given its head, and, for the first time, C♭ and A♭ are set in a linear descent the goal of which is the long-delayed resolution to G in the bass. Everything about m. 34 is calculated: the resolution is portrayed as a final gesture of reprise, the diminished seventh of m. 1 now set forth in some logical unfolding. The striking of the deep A♭ sets harmony loose once again: finally, a full dominant in which the A♭ sounds a seventh in the bass (see ex. 8.2).

Müller's third strophe is layered with oppositions.

> Ach, und fällt das Blatt zu Boden,
> Fällt mit ihm die Hoffnung ab,
> Fall ich selber mit zu Boden,
> Wein auf meiner Hoffnung Grab.

Three popular English translations destroy the syntax of the strophe. Decidedly not "Should the leaf fall, then hope falls. I too fall . . . ," the sense must dictate:

> Ah, and should the leaf fall to earth,
> and with it, should hope decay,
> *then* I myself shall fall to earth,
> and weep at the grave of hope.

Leaf falls, hope decays: I fall and weep. The shift in tense between the two couplets is not insignificant: the first couplet is the conditional clause, its two components contingent on the second, the apodosis. But German grammar

Example 8.2 *Letzte Hoffnung*, mm. 31–37

allows for some ambiguity here. On the face of it, the music separates off the two couplets, treating them not as contingencies, in any syntactic construct, but as sentences in tandem—as a parallelism with a rhetorical mission. At m. 35, the music breaks forth in a lamentation that puts to rest all the equivocation: the trembling on the brink that is the essence of the song is here grounded. As an expression of the poetic structure, the peroration plays forth on that constricted funereal cadence at mm. 29–30, answering its muffled tones and tight rhythms in the elegiac phrases of lament. In its contorted, sardonic self-pitying, Müller's final line has much in common with all those exit lines in Heine's lyrics.[4] It elicits in Schubert a song within a song—better, the

4. "Ich bin groß genug, Ihnen offen zu bekennen, daß mein kleines Intermezzo-Metrum nicht blos zufällige Ähnlichkeit mit Ihrem gewöhnlichen Metrum hat, sondern daß es wahrscheinlich seinen geheimsten Tonfall Ihren Liedern verdankt, indem es die lieben Müller'schen Lieder waren, die ich zu eben der Zeit kennen lernte, als ich das Intermezzo schrieb" (I am big enough to acknowledge openly to you that the similarity of the meter in my little intermezzo to your usual meter is not simple coincidence, but that it probably owes its innermost accents to your songs, for it was the beloved Müller songs that I got to know during just that time when I wrote the intermezzo), Heine confessed to Müller in a letter dated 7 June 1826 that was sent to accompany the gift of a copy of Heine's *Reisebilder*. "Wie rein, wie klar sind Ihre Lieder und sämmtlich sind es Volkslieder," Heine continued. "In meinen Gedichten hingegen ist nur die Form einigermaßen volksthümlich, der Inhalt gehört der conventionnellen Gesellschaft" (How pure, how clear are your songs, and yet collectively they are folk songs. In my poems, on the contrary, it is only the form that has to some extent the properties of folk song [*ist . . . einigermaßen volksthümlich*], while the content appertains to conventional society). (The letter is given in *Briefe 1815–1831*, ed. Fritz H. Eisner, vol. 20 of *Heinrich Heine: Säkularausgabe: Werke, Briefwechsel, Lebenszeugnisse*

song after the song—that again seems to establish a station in the cycle: a final outpouring of tears in memory of hope, the exhaustion of all feeling.

The stiff, funereal cadence at mm. 29–30, cast in a pointed rhythm new to the song but not to the cycle, calls up the opening phrases of *Auf dem Flusse* (see ex. 8.3). To posit that some deep musical relationship resides between the two phrases would be to strain reason. But context is everything. The ear casts about for some cognate. Those mute chords, *etwas langsam*, set a new tempo closer to the *langsam* (revised from the *mäßig* in the autograph) of *Auf dem Flusse* and bring to mind its similar accompaniment. The voice summons up the contour of its opening phrase. More compelling is how the E♭ minor of the cadence seems to play into the syntactic structure of the earlier song and particularly into the barren harmonies on A♯ at m. 45 in *Auf dem Flusse*, whose chilling emptiness lingers long after the song has been sung.

The lament of its closing measures is about earlier songs as well. Seeming to spring from the funereal cadence and, by association, from the friction in the opening phrases of *Auf dem Flusse*, it must also call to mind another lament, this one at the end of *Einsamkeit*—before its transposition to B minor. Just as the E♭ at the outset of *Die Post* seems to respond to that brazen, *sforzando* dominant seventh on B♭, so the lament in *Letzte Hoffnung* revives the fragmentary hymn, sung to the line ". . . war ich so elend nicht," that dissolves as the pedal B♭ gives way beneath the augmented sixth in D minor.

This is of course a relationship that vanishes once *Einsamkeit* is heard in B minor; in the version submitted for publication, it ceases to exist. Yet one gives it up with great reluctance. It persists in the ear, and the crucial (unanswerable) question is whether it persisted in Schubert's ear as well during the composition of *Letzte Hoffnung*, for it must be kept in mind that, while the transposition of *Einsamkeit* to B minor was clearly in deference to the *Fortsetzung* of the cycle into a part II, the moment at which, in the conceiving of part II, Schubert acted to transpose *Einsamkeit* cannot be established with any precision. That aside, one might still wish to entertain the view that, in its original conception, part I continued to haunt Schubert, even subliminally, during the composition of part II—that, while we are inclined, indeed obliged, to separate the two versions of part I categorically, the discrimination of the one from the other cannot have been so cut and dried for Schubert.

I am suggesting that we would do well to allow that, under certain conditions, the power of an original conception—*Einsamkeit* in D minor, in this instance—might continue to cast its spell in the mind of its conceiver and that, in the grasping of the whole, however that happens in the mind of a Schubert,

---

[Berlin and Paris, 1970], 249–51.) If the confession seems altogether uncanny, it must be said that the text of the letter survives in two accounts published by Müller's brother in 1845. The autograph has not survived. For a comment on the *Kommentar* (ed. Fritz H. Eisner and Fritz Mende [Berlin and Paris, 1975], 151), see the review by Alfred Estermann ("Die Gesamtausgabe des Heine-Briefwechsels: Zu den Bänden 20–27 der Heine-Säkularausgabe," *Heine-Jahrbuch* 17 [1978]: 251–59, esp. 254).

Example 8.3 *a*, *Auf dem Flusse*, opening measures. *b*, *Letzte Hoffnung*, mm. 29–31

some ambivalence in the recollecting of songs revised for whatever reasons seems altogether natural.

II

The musical introspection in *Letzte Hoffnung* is extreme. One wonders how Schubert can have regained composure after it. In what sense do the following songs—fully one-third of the twenty-four—complete a cycle? I think that there can be no question that for Schubert, if not quite so emphatically for Müller, *Letzte Hoffnung* is something of a watershed. What follows is the music of resignation. The old tensions have been played out. The wanderer continues, but by a kind of motor reflex, without feeling.

Still, this empty scenario needs to be reconciled with the charting of the music. Again, the music signals its moments of tonal significance. *Der Wegweiser* is perhaps the most suggestive in this regard. Much has been made of its relationship to *Gute Nacht:* the beginning of the journey and its end.[5] In the final strophe of *Der Wegweiser*, the outer voices, in graphic outline, converge inexorably toward the end of the road. The feel for closure is extreme: not in the Classical, structural sense of cadence, but as a "depiction" of closure in a metaphoric mode. All measure of time and distance ends here. The remaining songs are so many afterbeats, reflections on this condition of being without future. The road does not end; it disappears into a void.

Example 8.4 *Der Wegweiser*, mm. 28–34

Quite apart from all the obvious affinities with *Gute Nacht*, *Der Wegweiser* is rich in allusions to earlier songs. Its harmonic canvas is complex, and, because the song is situated at the end of the journey, its harmonic inflections will have a retrospective tinge. These lines at the end of the second strophe

Welch ein törichtes Verlangen
Treibt mich in die Wüstenein?

(What foolish yearning drives me into the wilderness?)

seem in particular to touch a raw nerve, eliciting a phrase that summons yet again the essence of *Auf dem Flusse* (see ex. 8.4). Poised on the dominant of E minor (a tonic never touched in the song), the incessant Bs give way under the harmony, slipping down to B♭—yet another flashback to a gesture by now symbolically keyed to *Auf dem Flusse* and, by extension, to all the other semitonal motion tied in with it.

The pointed juxtaposition of B minor (although only a passing harmony)

5. Youens, "*Wegweiser*," passim.

and G minor at mm. 35–37 seems to set in relief two principal tonal trajectories in the cycle (sketched out in ex. 8.5): the motion, on the one hand, along an axis of the minor subdominant and, on the other, along an axis of the dominant. This is the rub between *Rückblick* (song 8, G minor) and *Irrlicht* (song 9, B minor). In these trajectories is embedded as well the polarity between *Auf dem Flusse* and *Die Post.*

Example 8.5 *Winterreise*, pts. I and II, analytic sketch

The music for the fourth strophe is unique in its obsession with closure. From a strictly formal point of view, this is music for a coda: the structural cadence, its main accent, is at the downbeat of m. 55, resolving three full measures of dominant in root position. The harmony at m. 57, and all that follows, signifies that the music for *this* strophe is in elaboration of that cadence. The music is about closure to the exclusion of all else. Despite the acrobatics, subsequent cadences at mm. 67 and 77 only echo and enhance the principal cadence at m. 55.

The harmonic labyrinth between m. 57 and m. 65 is not what it seems. The $^{6}_{4}$s on D, F, and G♯ give the illusion of harmonic stations at G minor, B♭ minor, and C♯ minor. In point of fact, they are not triads at all, but so many passing tones in a focused prolongation of a single harmony, the dominant of the dominant. The graphing in example 8.6 displays some of the rhythmic complexity in the unfolding. No graphing can explain the illusory power of these emphatic $^{6}_{4}$s. Seductive distractions along the way, they mean to delude.

Example 8.6 *Der Wegweiser*, mm. 57–64, analytic sketch

The wanderer, sensing the ineluctable destiny in his journey, will have none of them. The repetition at mm. 67–77, no elegant variation, strips away any such distraction, reducing the journey to its linear essentials. In the final seven measures, the reduction is even more extreme—a distillation to a single essence.

These twenty-nine measures have a finality to them that is of a certain significance to the cycle. None of the remaining songs is about closure in any similar sense, nor do their tonalities point away from the G minor of *Der Wegweiser* along some teleological track. On the contrary, the F major of *Das Wirtshaus* evokes an otherworldly aura, no longer partaking of the journey.[6] *Mut!* is a strange poem. If its bluff show of courage sits uneasily as the penult in Müller's journey—perhaps it was this that prompted Schubert to set it back to the antepenult—the final couplet ("Will kein Gott auf Erden sein, sind wir selber Götter!") all of a sudden espouses a pantheism unprovoked in the texts of the twenty-two poems that precede it. For all its special beauties, *Die Nebensonnen* seems misplaced as well. After the catharses of *Letzte Hoffnung* and *Der Wegweiser*, the appeal to a lost love does not gain our sympathies.[7] If there is an inclination to understand A major in part I as a key on the dominant side (if not the dominant itself), the A major here seems rather to reinforce the mediant of F major—an overtone, not a root.

Der Leiermann, about neither past nor future, drones its mantic questions in a timeless present. "Wunderlicher Alter, soll ich mit dir gehn? Willst zu meinen Liedern deine Leier drehn?" We are not given to know the answers to such questions. The song itself is too well known in all its idiosyncrasies—perhaps the ultimate idiosyncrasy in the canon—to justify any detailed discussion of it here.[8] But its final strophe must give us pause. Set outside the formal repetitions of earlier strophes, it clings to the little tag whereby the organ-grinder articulates his threadbare cant (see ex. 8.7).

Everyone notices that, in these two final phrases, a different voice is heard: "Für die letzten Textzeilen . . . greift Schubert auf das Mittel einer Art rezitativischer Deklamation zurück, die er jedoch rhythmisch mit dem 'unmenschlich'-monotonen Dreier des Instrumentalparts verschränkt," writes Arnold Feil.[9] But there is another distinction to be made, for the two phrases at the

6. In a now famous argument, Georgiades suggests more than a general affinity with plainchant (*Schubert*, 379–83).

7. Yet the arcane imagery of the poem suggests a deeper significance for the cycle. And we now know that Schubert actually conceived much of this music, very likely in the summer of 1827, as a duet, crucially placed, in the opera *Der Graf von Gleichen*. On this point, see my "Posthumous Schubert," 209–11.

8. For Arnold Feil, the song "betokens the end of Western music, as defined by the thousand-year history of polyphonic composition. . . . In *Leiermann*, tonality as a fundament is ignored" (my translation) ("Schubert hier in gewisser Weise das Ende der abendländischen Musik . . . kennzeichnet. Im *Leiermann* ist die Tonalität als Grundlage ignoriert") (Feil, *Franz Schubert: Die schöne Müllerin; Winterreise*, 149 [Sherwin, trans., 128]).

9. "For the last text lines . . . Schubert falls back on the device of 'recitative' declamation, but interweaves it with the inhumanly monotonous triple meter of the instrumental part" (ibid., 148 [127]).

Example 8.7 *Der Leiermann*, closing measures

end are different *from one another* in this regard. The first is indeed declamatory, a desultory nonquestion put to a resigned phrase that asks no question in any of the obligatory rhetoric of conventional recitative: "Wunderlicher Alter, soll ich mit dir gehn?" The organ-grinder is unmoved.

But the second phrase sings. No performer can "speak" this question in quite the same way as the first. Here is a real question. It inspires real music—the only expressive phrase in the song and the only one to play on the complexities of interval, register, and harmony, of "thematic" dissonance: a phrase of substance. "Willst zu meinen Liedern deine Leier drehn?" What kinds of song are we to imagine might still be left to sing? If we suspect this wanderer to be composed out, Schubert's final phrase means to disabuse us. This phrase—these very pitches—summons up the extreme phrases of earlier songs. A final dominant ninth—the single harmony that, with eloquent parsimony, captures the sense of ♭6-5—a dying G-F♯ pitched where the singer must strain for articulation, brings to mind the final phrase in *Auf dem Flusse* and all the phrases that we have come to associate with it.

Inspired now, the organ-grinder reaches back for the most expressive of his familiar tropes. Altering it just enough to suggest some intimate response to the wanderer, he finds the sustenance to draw forth a *forte*, the single brief moment of affirmation in the song. The two are making music. If Schubert's notation invites no dynamic distinction in the voice, it is nevertheless contrary to imagine a performance in which the second phrase is not sung out in some way to distinguish it from the muted diction of the first. The *forte* argues for a *crescendo* on "drehn": here, too, the notation encodes signals toward its performance.

How could Schubert have acquiesced to a transposition of the song away from B minor? The key itself seems so profoundly a part of the topos of the song and so deeply bound in with the pitch world of *Winterreise.* Even the final F♯, crescendoing off into the void, seems to play on an acoustic first principle. The cycle ends not with any tonal resolve, for there is no "structural cadence" in this last song, but with a fifth—not of course literally so but rather, symbolically. The opening drone is in effect played out in the final simultaneities in m. 58. The F♯ is so overwhelming as to exert some acoustic pressure on the B to move down toward A♯—in one sense, to a dominant that never sounds and toward which all the song has been tending; in another, as a simple resolution that would render the F♯ consonant. Here, too, the powerful implication of a motion between B and A♯ conjures up that essential dissonance from which much in the cycle has drawn its inspiration.

The effect of B minor in *Der Leiermann* is of no orthodox kind. The song is hardly about B minor as a key in the usual sense; rather, it fixes on its barest essence. It means to stand apart, outside the main tonal argument in the journey, to be understood literally and in a metaphysical sense as an extreme harmony—its extremity defined in the unfolding of the journey. It reaches back to another point of extremity, to *Irrlicht*, with which it shares more than key.

In the transposition of the song to A minor, the eloquent place of *Der Leiermann* in the cycle is sorely compromised. As an extension of *Die Nebensonnen* (in A major), a false sense of closure is propounded: the opening drones of *Der Leiermann* now sound as afterbeats to the cadences in *Die Nebensonnen.* But the poems stand in no such intimate relationship to one another. The transposition of *Mut!* from an original A minor hopelessly confounds the sense of these last songs. No amount of speculation as to cause or effect can bring the matter right—can justify what is in effect a tampering with the critical essence of the cycle.

III

The original question returns. How is *Winterreise* a cycle? The center of gravity seems perceptibly to have shifted between part I and part II. When *Winterreise* was a cycle of twelve songs, D minor stood at the beginning and the end, criterion enough to propose it as a tonic in some conventional sense. In the conceiving of part II, this tidy sense of closure is obliterated: *Rast* and *Einsamkeit* are moved away from D minor. At the outset of part II, the tonal mission of the five songs beginning with *Die Post* and continuing through *Im Dorfe* is in the recasting of D as a dominant.

Consider again how *Letzte Hoffnung* closes (see ex. 8.8 below). The transposition to the tonic of the motive ♭6-5, a way of grounding the volatility of the motive and of stressing the cadential subdominant, has other implications as well. Every once in a while, Schubert writes a cadence of this sort. A Romantic appropriation of the antique plagal cadence, it exaggerates the stress

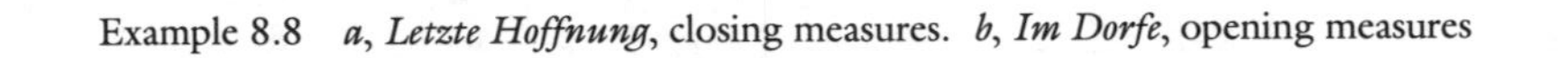

Example 8.8 *a*, *Letzte Hoffnung*, closing measures. *b*, *Im Dorfe*, opening measures

of the subdominant, *after* the final structural cadence, beyond the exigencies of any normal syntax. What is striking in this instance is the daring flirtation in these final measures with a tonic in need of further resolution. The minor seventh above E♭ is struck at the downbeat of three consecutive measures. The *decrescendo* in m. 45—the motive in dissolve—suggests less a sense of resolution of these dissonances than of a true disintegration of the tonic. The D♭ lingers, even in spite of the exquisite voice leading in the final measures.

If the ear seizes on this equivocation at the end of *Letzte Hoffnung*, it is encouraged by what follows. The opening bars of *Im Dorfe* play on the motive with which *Letzte Hoffnung* closes, reformulating its pitches and redefining its function. More emphatically, the power of redefinition lies in the implication of some tonal dynamic between the two songs and precisely in the tendency of the D♭—reheard as C♯, a member of an augmented-sixth chord—to resolve *up* to the D♮ of *Im Dorfe*. The ambivalence at the end of *Letzte Hoffnung* suggests more than an internal problem of cadencing. The dissolution in its final measures unseats E♭ in the tonal unfolding of the cycle—irradicates any sense of tonicity about it. The motion between *Letzte Hoffnung* and *Im Dorfe* is dominant defining, for, in retrospect, the initial D of *Im Dorfe* behaves like the resolution on the dominant that endows the function of the E♭ of *Letzte Hoffnung* as ♭VI (see ex. 8.8). It is the powerfully implicit *motion* between the songs that fixes this common cadential model in the ear. Having come to signify the remote in the close at hand, the region of the flat submediant is further endowed in Schubert's music: poetic distance, fantasy, dream, the romance of the "other," all are part of its mystique. This opposition between the actual and the illusory—the Romantic paradox—is captured in the paradoxical aspect of the augmented sixth in its enharmonic power to deflect away, as dominant seventh pro tem, to the most remote of keys against the tonic. Often enough, poetic meaning is lodged, not in the tonic, but in the negotiation between ♭VI and the dominant, in the slipping between illusion and reality, against which the tonic is mute. This is what is at issue in the motion between *Letzte Hoffnung* and *Im Dorfe*.

Augmented sixths are dominant defining—an axiom worth recalling yet again. Tonal focus sharpens at the instance of motion between the augmented sixth and its true dominant. In retrospect, then, the complex of songs at the outset of part II firms up a subdominant that forces the issue in the telling motion between the fading final measures of *Letzte Hoffnung* and the opening phrase of *Im Dorfe*. The motion must be perceived as the motion between subdominant and dominant—a structural move that finds resolution in *Der Wegweiser*.

The rich semiotic poetry of *Der Wegweiser* is seized in a music that flashes signals of the end. To understand Schubert's *Wegweiser* as a signal of the end—of complete exhaustion—is to read its sense of tonic both as the thing itself and as a signifier that extends beyond the song to the cycle. To put it that *Der Wegweiser* is the tonic member in a structural cadence that establishes the "key" of the cycle is perhaps to get at some grain of truth in the thing. But surely the idea of tonal centricity in *Winterreise* is too complex a phenomenon to be contained in that assertion. The narrative of *Winterreise* is effectively without end. The songs following *Der Wegweiser* neither confirm nor reinforce the sense of *Der Wegweiser* as a structural close but rather dissolve from it. This sense of tonic, perceived in *Winterreise* much as it is in the cycles in *Schwanengesang* and the fragmentary Goethe set from 1822, is an elusive quality, more an invisible magnetic force that, by association and implication, draws the poetry of the cycle into something cohesive. This is not the closed, "finished" tonal game of a Mozart quartet. The new poetic of absolute pitch—the attribution of poetic meaning to pitch itself—militates against the hierarchies of Classical tonal balances. The strict hegemony of tonic as formal beginning and end—as in effect "the piece"—is disenfranchised.

As the key of the last song in this ultimate song cycle, and as the key eternally associated with *Der Leiermann*, B minor has a complex mission, not easily fathomed. Freighted with affect and abstract symbolism, it figures prominently in each of the three cycles from 1827 and 1828. But, while B minor occupies a central position of considerable weight in the cycles by Heine and Rellstab, in *Winterreise* it seems to hover, an alter ego, alongside the main tonal thrust of the cycle. The final measures of *Der Leiermann* do not assert themselves in the manner of a tonic established and reaffirmed but rather echo as if in sympathetic vibration with some other, distant tonic. B minor, neither a tonic nor a dissonance—nor even an antitonic—continues to sound long after the cycle has run its course.

V

Mysticism, Ecstasy, and the Sublime

❄

Die Gebüsche

18
Au - - - - - gen. Es regt nur
22
ei - - - - ne See - le sich in des Mee - res
25
Brau - - - - - sen, und in den lei - sen
pp
28
Wor - ten, die durch die Blät - ter rau - schen, die
31
durch die Blät - ter rau - - - - - - schen.

34
So tönt in Wel - le Wel - - le wo Gei - - - ster

38
heim - lich trau - ren; so fol - gen Wor - te Wor - - ten, wo

42
Gei - ster Le - ben hau - - - - - - chen.

45
Durch al - - - - le Tö - ne tö -

49
- net im bun - ten Er - - den - trau - me
3

52
ein,
nur ein lei - ser
55
Ton ge - zo - gen, für den, für den, der
59
heim - - lich lau - - - - schet, für den, für
63
den, der heim - - - lich lau - - - - - schet.
67

9

Schlegel's *Abendröte* and the Failure of Cycle

Durch alle Töne tönet
Im bunten Erdentraume
Ein leiser Ton gezogen,
Für den, der heimlich lauschet.

As the epigraph inscribed by Schumann above his Fantasy for Piano, op. 17, Friedrich Schlegel's sonorous lines will forever evoke a shadowy subtext, the homage to Beethoven in the traces of *An die ferne Geliebte.* In the manner of such evocations, the traces are faint; the elusive "leiser Ton . . . für den, der heimlich lauschet" vanishes before it can be identified.[1] Schlegel's lines actually constitute the closing quatrain of *Die Gebüsche*, a poem set to music by Schubert in January 1819. An inspired song, it remained unpublished until Max Friedlaender offered it in a volume of *Nachgelassene (bisher ungedruckte) Lieder* in 1885.[2]

1. "Through the entire spectrum of sound in the many-colored dream of earth, one faint, attenuated tone sounds for him who listens privately." Schumann himself hinted at an identification of the "leise Ton" with Clara in the well-known letter to her of 9 June 1839, published in *Jugendbriefe von Robert Schumann*, ed. Clara Schumann, 3d ed. (Leipzig, 1898), 303. Here it must be recalled that the original version of the Fantasy, composed in 1836, was conceived as an "Obelisk" to the memory of Beethoven—this is explicit in the manuscript—and, further, that the reference to *An die ferne Geliebte* with which the first movement closes was made to return again, with some changes in harmony, at the very end of the third movement. On the original version, see Alan Walker, "Schumann, Liszt, and the C-Major *Fantasie*, Op. 17: A Declining Relationship," *Music and Letters* 60 (April 1979): 156–65.

2. For John Daverio, "the undulating sextuplet accompanimental figure that runs through Schubert's setting is called up in the last movement of Schumann's Fantasy, which, in addition, begins with a variant of the harmonic progression that opens Schubert's song" ("Schumann's 'Im Legendenton' and Friedrich Schlegel's *Arabeske*," *19th Century Music* 11 [Fall 1987]: 151). Can Schumann have known Schubert's song in 1836? A copy prepared for the Witteczek-Spaun collection was entered in a fascicle that Walther Dürr assigns to 1832 (see Dürr, *Franz Schuberts Werke in Abschriften*, 75, 79). It is thought that Witteczek had access to the acquisition of song autographs—the "Nachgelassene musikalischen Dichtungen"—that Diabelli purchased from Ferdinand Schubert early in 1830. On his visit to Ferdinand in the spring of 1839, Schumann wrote back to Leipzig, "This much I know for *certain*: he has not got one single song by his brother, as I asked him for one myself" (cited from Deutsch, *Memoirs*, 397). Further, the Schlegel motto appears to have been added during an editorial pass through the engraver's copy. The autograph date, 19 December 1838, seems to have been entered at the same time (see Walker, "Schumann, Liszt, and the C-Major *Fantasie*," 157).

The poem comes toward the end of *Abendröte*, a "Gedichtzyklus" of enticing complexity: twice ten poems, each run of ten prefaced with an untitled prologue.[3] The tenth poem in both parts is a sonnet: *Der Dichter*, each is titled, and the poet's elevated tone sets itself apart. The change in voice is perceptible. The opening lines of the second sonnet, a silent reflection on the various evocations of night in the poems preceding, are especially moving:

> Der schwarze Mantel will sich dichter falten,
> Die freundlichen Gespräche sind verschollen;
> Wo allen Wesen tief Gesang entquollen,
> Da muß die stumme Einsamkeit nun walten.

(The dark cloak folds itself tightly, the friendly conversations are missing; where deep song issued from all nature, mute loneliness must now prevail.)

Altogether, Schubert set no fewer than eleven poems from the cycle. But he did so at different times and, to judge from the piecemeal transmission of those manuscripts that have survived (reconstructed in table 9.1), in a frustrating sequence that on its face seems more haphazard than logical. Still, one is led to inquire whether the cyclic intimations of Schlegel's poems found any resonance in Schubert. Indeed, it was in the attempt to probe further into this very matter that Dietrich Berke was led to his notion of a "zyklische Verfahrensweise."[4]

Whatever else may be immanent in these data that tell of a Schlegel cycle, a provocative irony leaps out, for it seems very likely that *Die Gebüsche*—in Schlegel's ordering, the last of those that Schubert set—was the first to have been composed while, conversely, the prologue to the *erster Theil* was the last, if the "März 1823" entered by Schubert in the autograph is to be understood as the date of composition. That date will need further scrutiny. "Abendröthe. Erster Theil," Schubert's inscription at the head of the manuscript, establishes that the textual source here was some edition of Schlegel's poetry other than the *Musen-Almanach für das Jahr 1802* that evidently served him during the composition of *Die Gebüsche*, for the explicit division of the cycle into two parts first appears in the *Gedichte* published in Berlin in 1809 and Vienna in 1816, where the title *Abendröte* refers distinctly to the cycle as a whole. The first poem is in fact untitled. Unless Schubert was entirely oblivious of what he had copied, the inscription establishes as well an intent to compose a complete cycle.

It is of course conceivable that such a collection may have had its retrospective aspect; perhaps all the previously composed songs from *Abendröte*, reach-

3. The Schlegel poems first appeared in the *Musen-Almanach für das Jahr 1802*, ed. A. W. Schlegel and L. Tieck (Tübingen, 1802; facsimile reprint, Heidelberg, 1967), 133–57. A critical text showing variants in the *Gedichte* published in Berlin in 1809 and Vienna in 1816 is produced in the *Kritische Friedrich-Schlegel-Ausgabe*, vol. 5, *Dichtungen*, ed. Hans Eichner (Munich and Zurich, 1962), 179–91. Dietrich Berke evaluates the convoluted evidence for Schubert's source in "Schuberts Liedentwurf," 305–20.

4. Berke, "Schuberts Liedentwurf," 307.

TABLE 9.1
Friedrich Schlegel's *Abendröte* and Schubert's Settings

	A. *Abendröte*, Part I
"Tiefer sinket schon die Sonne"	D. 690, as *Abendröte*. Autogr. "März 1823"
Die Berge	D. 634. Autogr. (with D. 633) missing
Die Vögel	D. 691. "Reinschrift" without date. March 1820 in Witt-Spaun copy
Der Knabe	D. 692. Undated "Niederschrift." March 1820 in Witt-Spaun copy
Der Fluß	D. 693. Undated "Niederschrift." March 1820 in Witt-Spaun copy
Die Hirt	—
Die Rose	D. 745. Two undated autographs ("Reinschriften") in F. Published in 1822, in G, and as op. 73 in 1827, in G. The autographs seem to preserve a second version, the prints a first. Still, Hilmar dates one autogr. "gegen Ende 1820"
Der Schmetterling	D. 633. Autogr. (with D. 634) missing
Die Sonne	—
Die Lüfte	—
Der Dichter	—
	B. *Abendröte*, Part II
"Als die Sonne nun versunken"	—
Der Wanderer	D. 649. Autogr. undated (with D. 756, 778); Hilmar: 1822. Copy in Witt-Spaun, "Febr. 1819"
Der Mond	—
Zwei Nachtigallen	—
Das Mädchen	D. 652. Autogr. dated Febr. 1819. Witt-Spaun dated Febr. 1819
Der Wasserfall	—
Die Blumen	—
Der Sänger	—
Die Sterne	D. 684. Autogr. missing. "1820" in Witt-Spaun
Die Gebüsche	D. 646. Autogr. (with Tieck, *Abend*) dated January 1819
Der Dichter	—

ing back to January 1819, would have been gathered into it. Or, to view it from another angle, the composition of *Abendröte* was deliberately put off until some grander prospect on the cycle had come into view, so that it would be clear what sort of music might best allow entry into the cycle. But it is also possible, if not quite plausible, that the decision to compose *Abendröte* in March 1823 belonged to a new vision for a Schlegel cycle. Finally, one must consider whether the autograph of *Abendröte*, plainly a *Reinschrift*, was in fact a clean copy of a song actually composed some years earlier.

Each of these hypotheses is troubling in some measure. For one, the publication of *Die Rose* as early as 1822 might be taken as evidence that any notion of a complete Schlegel *cycle* had by that time been abandoned. Further, the array of dates between January 1819 and March 1823 does not square very well with what we know of other cases in which groups of poems were culled for a setting in some cyclic arrangement, where the integrity of the set seems to have been manifest from the outset. Witness this on-again, off-again pattern:

January 1819	*Die Gebüsche*, II:9
February 1819	*Der Wanderer*, II:1
	Das Mädchen, II:4
March 1820	*Die Vögel*, I:2
	Der Knabe, I:3
	Der Fluß, I:4
1820	*Die Sterne*, II:8
March 1823	*Abendröte*, I:prologue

Added to this, the transmission of *Die Berge* (I:1) and *Der Schmetterling* (I:7) in a single autograph (alas, among the missing) confirms no singleminded resolve to compose an integral work but suggests, rather, a lingering fascination with the Schlegel group, a passive flirtation with the notion of some cyclic arrangement that yet refuses to emerge.[5] Then, too, the setting of Schlegel's *Der Schiffer* in March 1820—an evocative poem redolent of (although written much earlier than) those mysterious sea poems in Heine's *Heimkehr*—is a puzzling intrusion. During a month that hints at a summoning of concentration on the *Abendröte* cycle, here is Schubert leafing ahead in the Schlegel *Gedichte* to a poem that stands outside the cycle.

But it is the earliest of these documents—or what we currently suppose to be the earliest—that is in many ways the most provocative. This is a manuscript that contains the autograph of *Die Gebüsche* (D. 646); it is of the kind that Deutsch would describe as an "erste Niederschrift." The manuscript contains as well a fragmentary setting, never completed, of Ludwig Tieck's *Abend* (D. 645), the third of four poems gathered in a cycle under the title *Der Besuch*.[6] Schubert set none of the others. Significantly, the lay of the manuscript, a pair of nested bifolios, allows that the two settings were composed contiguously, from which we might infer that Schubert was casting about for the project with which to engage his inclination toward cyclic process. And it is further significant that he is drawn in this instance to the poetics of the new Romantics; as Berke has established, Schubert will have found both these cy-

5. Because we know nothing about the autograph containing *Die Berge* and *Der Schmetterling*, and because these two songs were published together—along with Hölty's *An den Mond* (D. 193)—in 1826, it is at least conceivable that the autograph in question was a late *Reinschrift* prepared especially for this publication, *after* the decision had been taken to abandon a Schlegel cycle.

6. The autograph is now in private hands. I am indebted to Walther Dürr, Tübingen, for graciously providing a photocopy.

cles in the *Musen-Almanach für das Jahr 1802*, a volume edited by Tieck and A. W. Schlegel and containing the poetry of Novalis as well.[7]

The appeal of *Die Gebüsche* is immediate, and from the passionate sweep of the music one might even be led to suggest that the mysterious conceit in Schlegel's first quatrain held an allure for Schubert no less than for Schumann. The song gives the illusion of something fragmentary, improvised in the rapture of a reading, its phrases following on one another in the way that the elements of a telescope unfold. No orthodox formal archetype is put into play.[8] The suggestive harmonic gambit at the outset only hints at the bold sweep of its tonal spectrum, more a reaching for ecstatic cadences in remote keys than a reasoned charting of harmonic strategies.

The fragment as literary device had at the turn of the century become something of a banner, itself a metaphor for a new and innately Romantic mode of expression. In the writings of Friedrich Schlegel and Novalis in the late 1790s, the grouping together of aphoristic prose pieces, philosophical and critical, into "Fragmentensammlungen" in which undercurrents of sustained argument are at once obscured and illuminated, signals a new aesthetic: *Eisenfeile* (iron filings), Schlegel titled one such collection. Before 1819, examples of truly epigrammatic musical speech—of the spontaneity inherent in *fragment*—are rare. One thinks of the opening of Beethoven's Sonata in A, op. 101, the Bagatelles, op. 119 (*his* "Eisenfeile"), and very little else. In the 1820s, it was a quality pervasive in Beethoven's music. By the 1830s, it was a commonplace of style. The opening page of Schumann Fantasy, op. 17, is only the most characteristic example.[9]

Often, it is the intimation in the poem of some moment that might be taken as suggestive of return that Schubert will seize on. The idea of recapitulation—not in its conventional Classical sense but reinterpreted through some poetic model—is an especially fertile one in Schubert. Exquisite examples are legion: *An die Entfernte* (D. 765), *Nacht und Träume* (D. 827), and *Daß sie hier gewesen* (D. 775) are especially subtle in this regard. But the poetic idea of *Die Gebüsche* is of a different kind. Projected on the page in a single sustained strophe, its four quatrains grope toward some cosmic message. The marriage of *Ton* and *Wort*—better, the sublimation of word in tone—is conveyed in a convulsion of linguistic reverberation:

7. Berke ("Schuberts Liedentwurf," 309–11) was concerned to establish the sources of the literary texts that Schubert had before him and indeed succeeded in showing that, while the Schlegel poems set in 1819 were very likely known to Schubert in their earliest publication (in the *Musen-Almanach für das Jahr 1802*), others were clearly drawn from one or another of the later collections of Schlegel's *Gedichte*.

8. Perhaps in acknowledgment of its elusive "form," *Die Gebüsche* is one of very few songs to have drawn no comment at all from Mies in *Schubert: Der Meister des Liedes*. Mies's subtitle, *Die Entwicklung von Form und Inhalt im Schubertschen Lied*, gives only faint clue to the extremes of formal parsing applied methodically to nearly all the songs published in the old *Gesamtausgabe*—somewhere in excess of six hundred numbers!

9. See, e.g., Daverio, "Schumann's 'Im Legendenton,'" esp. 162–63.

7 Und in den leisen Worten . . .
9 So tönt in Welle Welle . . .
11 So folgen Worte Worten . . .
13 Durch alle Töne tönet . . .
15 *Ein* leiser Ton gezogen . . .

How does Schubert respond to a poem of this kind? If Schubert now and again takes his inspiration from some realistic detail in the poem, this cannot be an instance of that kind. Nor must we believe that composition necessarily begins at the beginning, that one phrase follows another, as though the composition were in effect a reading of the poem line by line. Common sense proposes that a moment of intense contemplation must follow a reading of the poem, a prerequisite to the first efforts to conceive it in music.[10] This in itself, we need to remind ourselves, gives grounds for suspecting that the conceiving of the song will grow from some inner place in the poem—from the crux of the poem or from an impalpable essence that invites Schubert to express it in tone.

In *Die Gebüsche*, it is the spontaneity of the music, symptom of an intuitive and therefore genuine response to the poetry, that is prized. That the idea expressed in Schubert's *Die Gebüsche* is somehow tied in with the cumulative swing of its language and the evocative imagery of its famous final quatrain—that the conceiving of the song begins and ends here—should need no tiresome argument. The music to that quatrain reaches for its moment of ecstasy at "*Ein* leiser Ton gezogen"—the "Ein" is *gesperrt*, typographically emphasized, in both the *Musen-Almanach* and the *Gedichte* of 1809 and 1816—and even provokes Schubert to an exceptional violation of Schlegel's text: "*Ein* leiser Ton" becomes "ein, nur ein leiser Ton." The tampering with Schlegel's language is merely a trace of what is at stake here: a typographic hieroglyph is translated into a phrase of sublime breadth. The climax at "nur ein" sets F♯ at the top of a $^6_4$ on A; in the following measure, the missing F♯ (structurally more significant even in its omission) is now understood as the root of a dominant, the high G a dissonant ninth. This in itself would not set the phrase apart from any number of ecstatic climaxes, even within a song given to several of them. But it is the context that astonishes, for the entire quatrain is set out as a protracted embellishment of the essential $^6_4$ on the dominant—a cadence whose resolution is put off beyond the limits of the poem. Resolution comes only with a repetition of the final line and, consequently, as an anticlimax. It is a necessary resolution, but clearly not the one that truly matters.

This confronts us again with the notion of reprise and, more broadly, with the problem of form in *Die Gebüsche*. If the setting of this final quatrain suggests something of the delicate task of the translator, the troubled approach to it, reaching back to the music beginning at "So tönt in Welle Welle," hints at

10. Joseph Spaun's famous description of Schubert pacing back and forth, Goethe's *Erlkönig* in hand, is vivid testimony to the rapture that might attend the act of reading (see Deutsch, *Memoirs*, 131).

a theory of Romantic form. Indeed, the reaching extends all the way back to the first measure. It is only that the music at "So tönt in Welle Welle" is meant to put us in mind of some recapitulatory device. The memorable phrase at "Und nur der Himmel lächelt" is echoed here: harmonic motion quickens, speaks with a fresh innocence in the immediacy of direct root-position confrontations, and moves off into exotic regions. Finally, D♭ major is tonicized at "Wo Geister Leben hauchen." On paper, the manipulation of tone between D♭ and the dominant of the dominant in G major is a simple exercise. But nothing in the exercise can account for all the nuances that contribute to the appeal of the music here, at once ambiguous, mystical, and inevitable. The music enacts Schlegel's script, capturing this impalpable, silent listening for the *Ton*. Indeed, it could be claimed that the singular image in the song is a perceptible threading of the "*Ein* leiser Ton" that sounds for the one who is tuned to listen. The inflection from D♭ major to C♯ minor has a spontaneous feel to it, yet the song has been flashing telltale signals of similar inflections almost from the beginning. Schlegel's curious title—there are no bushes in the poem—has its own cryptic message: the cosmic *Ton* is heard even here, in the base undergrowth.

And this is where a theory of Romantic form might be intimated. How to express "So tönt in Welle Welle"? In the poet's conceit for the essence of music, waves *sound* in waves.[11] Form is less a mapping of dramatic action—those temporal plottings through which we capture the play of sonatas—than the timeless evocation of some infinity of Being. But that is to define form itself, in any conventional sense, out of existence. The image of wave engendering wave—even of wave itself—is a counterformal one. The music of *Die Gebüsche* unfolds, unravels, reveals. Reveals what, exactly? How can we know that something is concealed at the outset? These are not questions with concrete answers, but, in the asking of them, we touch at some essence in the language of a song such as this.

Writing on the decision to approach Tieck's *Der Besuch* through a setting of what is the third poem in the cycle, Berke proposed that Schubert went directly to the most difficult of the four poems—and the least "poetic"—"and so Schubert may have viewed its setting as at the same time a test case for the possibility of a complete cycle."[12] The argument does not easily transfer to the case of the Schlegel poems, for *Die Gebüsche* exhibits none of the obstacles that seem to have impeded the setting of *Abend*. It is in some ways the most strikingly "musical" of the set and the most appealing as a problem in the setting of a text. Still, it too suggests itself "as a test case for the possibility of a

11. "It is more than a simile to call romanticism the wavelike ringing of a string or bell, in which the tone-wave fades into ever further distances, finally losing itself in us so that, while already silent without, it still resounds within." Thus, Jean Paul [Richter] in the *Vorschule der Aesthetik*. The passage is taken from the translation in Oliver Strunk, ed., *Source Readings in Music History* (New York, 1950), 746.

12. "Und so mag Schubert dessen Vertonung gleichsam als Testfall für die Möglichkeit des Gesamtzyklus angesehen haben" (Berke, "Schuberts Liedentwurf," 313).

complete cycle," but in this instance one has more the sense of an immediate response to what would be perceived as the ecstatic climax of the cycle, toward which the other settings would be subordinate. If that were the case, then the sporadic attempts to complete the cycle seem to testify to a lack of resolve, perhaps stemming from a perception that the spontaneous ecstasy of *Die Gebüsche* could not be made to follow in some integral rush from its antecedents.

The problem may have resided in *Die Gebüsche* itself. Schubert was evidently reluctant to let it out of his study—perhaps because the manuscript contained, as it does today, the fragmentary draft for Tieck's *Abend*, a project that Schubert may not have been prepared to condemn once and for all. No copies of the song are known to have circulated during his lifetime; the earliest known copy was prepared for Witteczek toward the end of 1832.[13] Even the autograph testifies that what has survived is in some measure an incomplete song. The *Langsam* at the top of the autograph is unpersuasive, even contrary to the effusive passions of the music. As he sometimes did, Schubert might well have tinkered with the tempo in the wake of some future performance—but that seems not to have happened.[14] The dynamic markings are no less enigmatic: a *piano* at the outset; a *pianissimo* in the keyboard part when the voice enters; and another *pianissimo* at "in den leisen Worten." The telling harmony at m. 2 (and again on its return in the postlude) is marked with Schubert's characteristic "hairpin."

All this signals a reluctance to be heard, as if the secrets of the poem were to remain concealed, unsung. The music itself, in its improvisatory feel, is as unconsciously revealing as anything in Schubert's portfolio. Yet the sweep of the music seems intentionally muted in these timid signs of evasion in the autograph. The contradiction hints at some deeper conflict, one that Schubert was unable to resolve.

This brings us round again to the setting of *Abendröte* as the prologue to part I. The date on the autograph is suspicious. Mysteriously, it had been read as March 1820—*not* 1823—until quite recently.[15] The earlier date is the more

13. On the dating, see Dürr, *Franz Schuberts Werke in Abschriften*, 75, 79.

14. Some will know Max Friedlaender's edition (*Schubert-Album* [Leipzig: C. F. Peters, 1887], 7:3–8), where the inscription is "Nicht zu langsam"—but on whose authority? Perhaps Friedlaender was working from a contemporary copy otherwise unrecorded in the literature. The case of *Frühlingsglaube* (D. 686)—not the only one—comes to mind. The earliest version (September 1820) is without tempo mark; an autograph dated 1820, and taken to be the second version, is marked "Mäßig"; a third version, undated, but very likely from November 1822, is marked "Ziemlich langsam," which is how the song was published in 1823.

15. Georg Kinsky, who had a careful look at the autograph in preparing a catalog of the Wilhelm Heyer collection, gives the date as "März 1820" (*Musikhistorisches Museum von Wilhelm Heyer in Cöln* [Cologne, 1916], 4:201). Whether Deutsch (*Schubert: Thematic Catalogue of All His Works in Chronological Order* [New York, 1951], 309) actually saw the autograph, which by that time had passed into the possession of Rudolf Nydahl in Stockholm, or depended rather on Kinsky's description is unclear. Mandyczewski, who based the text in the old *Gesamtausgabe* on Diabelli's posthumous edition, dated the work "March 1820," but he does not say how he comes to that date. The Nydahl collection is today at the Stiftelsen Musikkulturens främjande,

plausible, and, while the "März 1823" in the autograph is unambiguous, the autograph is a very clean document, perhaps copied from a rough draft or from an "erste Niederschrift" resembling the autograph of *Die Gebüsche.*

The song itself is even more or a puzzlement. Its opening measures, shadowy and tentative, have difficulty getting under way. If they miss that inaugural quality that Schubert will later find to set in motion a cycle of songs, they perhaps capture that moment of stasis between day and night from which the idea of the cycle is drawn. But the song does finally get under way, growing—the song seems actually to inflate, spatially—to memorable breadth in its final quatrain:

> Alles scheint dem Dichter redend,
> Denn er hat den Sinn gefunden;
> Und das All ein einzig Chor,
> Manches Lied aus einem Munde.

(Everything seems to apeak to the poet, for he has found its meaning; and the universe a single chorus, many a song from a single mouth.)

The closing music (shown in ex. 9.1) vibrates in motionless contemplation of Schlegel's cosmic revelation.

The opening measures of *Die Berge* dispel this meditative aura. The song was written in a manuscript together with *Der Schmetterling* (the manuscript itself was last seen around 1850); Mandyczewski, probably following the hint in the Witteczek *Verzeichnis,* which assigns both songs to the year 1815, printed them (without comment) directly after *Erlkönig* in the old *Gesamtausgabe.* It is easy to see how even a scholar of Mandyczewski's perspicacity might have been deceived by the superficial simplicity of these songs, a deception fed by their association, in the first edition (Weigl, 1826), with Hölty's *An den Mond,* a song verifiably from 1815. The dates assigned by Witteczek are for the most part reliable, so one wants a better argument for the "zwischen 1819 und 1823 (?)" in the new Deutsch than a presumption (implicit in Deutsch) that any undated setting from *Abendröte* must ipso facto fall within the span established by those settings that have been dated.[16]

The simplicity of *Die Berge* is of a sophisticated kind. Its opening phrases may seem nonchalant, but that is to miss their subtle inflections and the astonishing ease with which Schlegel's complex *senario,* alternating lines of seven and eleven syllables, is captured in a sustained paragraph the components of which follow from one another in no predictable pattern. These are not the conventions of phrase making that Schubert was working through in 1815.

Stockholm. I am indebted to Erling Lomnäs, of that institution, for his helpful description of the manuscript. The watermark is the two left quadrants of what appears to be Winter's type Ia (see "Paper Studies," 223–27), although the manuscript is not mentioned by Winter. Further, all Winter's examples of type I paper are lined with sixteen staves; *Abendröte* is on twelve-stave paper.

16. This is a refinement of the "(?) c. 1819" suggested for both songs by Deutsch (*Thematic Catalogue,* 280), who notes and tacitly refutes the date in the Witteczek Collection.

Example 9.1 *a*, *Abendröte* (D. 690), closing measures. *b*, *Die Berge* (D. 634), opening measures

Even the stark simplicity of its opening measures is unconventional: six measures of no harmony but tonic, in Alpine echo, capture a sense of Mountain, of expanse. One browses in vain through the offerings of 1815 for another song in which the subdominant is used with similar control—or used at all, in this pointedly evocative manner.

Schlegel's mountainscape, together with the sense of distance evoked in the subdominant music at "zu den Himmlischen oben," even to the pedal tone on G and the horn fifths, must call to mind the very similar, altogether striking effect in the second song of—yet again—*An die ferne Geliebte* (see ex. 9.2).[17] Beethoven's cycle was published in Vienna in October 1816; the *Wiener Zeitung* for 21 December announces it as having quite recently appeared ("ganz neu erschienen").[18] If we are prepared to believe that *Die Berge* owes something to Beethoven's "Wo die Berge so blau," then it cannot have been composed more than a month or two before the beginning of 1817.[19] Moreover, the allusion, conscious or not, to the second song in Beethoven's cycle, in the setting of a poem that stands second in Schlegel's *Gedichtzyklus*, holds a power of suggestion that even Schubert at his most distracted cannot have dismissed.

Why, in the end, did a Schlegel cycle never materialize? If there is a single theme that runs through the poetry of those cyclic projects that engaged Schubert from first to last, romantic love is very much a part of it. The appeal of the erotic as some deeply felt instinct is at the root of Schubert's music as well. But the eroticism in Schlegel's *Abendröte* is of an abstract kind. The entanglement of two lovers—of the poet/singer in love—is not engaged here. Rather, the two parts of the cycle contemplate an abstraction, explore the opposition between day and night at the very moment when the one becomes the other, a meditation on the paradoxical timelessness inherent in time. Here it would be good to recall that *Die Gebüsche*, the final poem before the closing sonnet in the second part, is a poem drenched in the aura of night. Its nocturnal shroud is consequently missed when the poem is taken in isolation, outside

17. Daverio ("Schumann's 'Im Legendenton,'" 151) claims to hear a reference to Beethoven's song in *Der Fluß*, but this suggests nothing more than a trivial and coincidental similarity in pitch contour. The sentiments expressed in *Der Fluß* would not have prompted Schubert to call forth "Wo die Berge so blau"; but if, for some arcane reason, a reference to Beethoven's song was intended, we must then ask why the song should have been cast in a key and in a rhythm that serve only to obliterate it. The dialectic of influence and anxiety, if that is what Daverio means to imply, is here unpersuasive.

18. George Kinsky, *Das Werk Beethovens: Thematisch-bibliographisches Verzeichnis seiner sämtlichen vollendeten Kompositionen*, completed and edited by Hans Halm (Munich and Duisburg, 1955), 275.

19. *Der Schmetterling*, too, wears a style familiar to other songs of 1817. *Liebhaber in allen Gestalten* (Goethe; D. 558) is very much like it, in the peculiar relationship of the opening strain in the piano to the tune and in its accompaniment. Again, Mandyczewski grouped it with songs from August 1815, but its autograph (which Mandyczewski did not know) dates it May 1817. A rather similar accompaniment, even closer in detail to *Der Schmetterling*, is to be found in *Die Einsiedelei* (Salis-Seewis; D. 563), which again dates from May 1817.

Example 9.2 *a*, *Die Berge*, mm. 11–21. *b*, Beethoven, *An die ferne Geliebte*, op. 98, "Wo die Berge so blau," mm. 18–30

the cycle, even if the language of the opening quatrain—"Und nur der Himmel lächelt / Aus tausend hellen Augen"—gives more than a hint of night.

Schlegel's cycle depends for its meaning on the passage of that infinitesimal instant between dusk and night—an "instant" indeed more metaphysical than real. The passing of time is essential to its plot. At the opening of the first part—

Tiefer sinket schon die Sonne,
Und es atmet alles Ruhe . . .

(The sun sinks deeper, and everything breathes peace.)

—we are witness to the setting of the sun. At the opening of the second part, time has passed. The sun is now a figure of memory:

Als die Sonne nun versunken,
Blühet noch der Abend rot.

(As the sun is now set, the evening yet blossoms red.)

The play of tenses—"sinket," "versunken"—plays up this sense of passage. How these fine but essential distinctions might be conveyed in a cycle of songs—of *Lieder* sung by convention in a *Volkston* perfected some forty years earlier in the service of the simple strophic narratives of lyric and ballad—would no doubt have given Schubert pause. Indeed, it is precisely the innocent, folk-like poems in the Schlegel group, and the bardic *Wanderer*, that drew an immediate response from Schubert and that have entered into the repertory.

Schubert's reluctance to touch the two closing sonnets is similarly troubling. These are not extraneous; they do not lie outside the cycle proper, as do the prologue and epilogue to Müller's *Die schöne Müllerin*, which Schubert wisely recognized as a stage device inessential to the argument of the cycle. To invoke *Der Dichter* himself is to speak to the sense of a heightened expression in which the various evocations in these two semicycles—the two sides of dusk—are brought to some poetic significance. To omit them is to lose the deeper meaning of the cycle. Contemplative poetry of this kind often enough inspired a deeply resonant music in Schubert. But in the direct language of *An die ferne Geliebte*, the cycle is conveyed in a single, discursive tone—a voice in which the narrative is invoked and sustained. One senses Schubert at a loss to reconcile the imagined music of these rich sonnets with the vernacular speech of the quaint poems that they frame. How these extremes of poetic language might be conveyed in a single narrative was not a problem that he was inclined to solve.

II

Apostrophes to night invariably call to mind Novalis. Of the six *Hymnen an die Nacht* that form the cycle published in *Athenäum*, Schubert set only the closing poetic fragment of the fourth hymn.[20] And he did so in January

20. The authoritative texts of the two versions of the *Hymnen an die Nacht* are given in *Novalis: Schriften*, vol. 1, *Das dichterische Werk*, ed. Paul Kluckhohn and Richard Samuel (Stuttgart, 1960), 130–57. The philological and critical measure of the work is taken in a monograph by Heinz Ritter (*Novalis' Hymnen an die Nacht: Ihre Deutung nach Inhalt und Aufbau auf textkritischer Grundlage ihre Entstehung*, 2d ed. [Heidelberg, 1974]).

1820—as the date on the autograph tells us—in the midst of his preoccupation with the Schlegel cycle.[21] In Schubert's repertory of settings, this Novalis fragment is perhaps the extreme example of that mystical, new-Romantic ecstasy in which the spiritual and the erotic are fused. Yet, for all the obvious reasons, the six *Hymnen an die Nacht*, a single, integral work, can hardly have inspired cyclic intentions in Schubert. For one, each hymn formulates an idiosyncratic diction special to its argument. The alternation of prose and poetry in the fourth hymn was still more complex in the manuscript version (which Schubert cannot have known); for the revision published in *Athenäum*, a long passage of some hundred lines of poetry is now camouflaged in a prose paragraph that nevertheless retains the epigrammatic style of the original language. More generally, the epic expanse of the six *Hymnen*, and the nature of its language, is simply inappropriate as sung text. There is no appeal here to the idea of song cycle.

In the fragment that Schubert chose to set, enigmas innate in the cycle of hymns as a whole are exacerbated. The "ich" in the fourth hymn shifts imperceptibly back and forth between the poet/lover and an unnamed Christ—less dialogue than a kind of "Selbstgespräch" in which the poet *becomes* Christ. The images of love are vivid:

O! sauge, Geliebter,	O draw me powerfully
Gewaltig mich an,	toward you, beloved,
Daß ich entschlummern	that I may find
Und lieben kann.	sleep and love.

Who is this "Geliebter"? In the larger context of the poem, it is difficult to dismiss Christ altogether. The fusion of Christ and carnal lover is absolute.[22] A Christ-like nimbus illumines the love. The fusion even has its homoerotic aspect. Schubert's setting, a fragment shorn of context, will be read differently. The paradox implicit in the fragment remains obscure and enigmatic.

It is instructive to read the earlier, handwritten version of the last lines of the fourth hymn—lines expunged in the *Athenäum* version. The lines corresponding to the closing lines in the printed version read:

21. The first page of the autograph, now at the Gesellschaft der Musikfreunde in Vienna, is shown in Walther Vetter, *Franz Schubert* (Postsdam, 1934), plate VIII. Elsewhere, Vetter reads meaning into a revision at the bottom of that first page, where the piano interlude finally placed between m. 23 and m. 26 was first inscribed after m. 13 and then vigorously deleted (*Der Klassiker Schubert*, 1:375).

22. Sara Friedrichsmeyer speaks of the "ambiguity between Christian and erotic forms of union" in her analysis of the lines beginning "O sauge, Geliebte, / Gewaltig mich an": "One should speak here of a deliberate role merging . . . in . . . the association of Christ and a sexual partner." Novalis, she claims, was "bringing to the work his own experience of mystic union and salvation" (*The Androgyne in Early German Romanticism: Friedrich Schlegel, Novalis and the Metaphysics of Love* [Bern, 1983], 97–98). John Neubauer speaks of "an inversion of Christian mystic eroticism. While mystics see Christ or the Madonna as a lover or bridegroom, Novalis reverses the relationship" (*Novalis* [Boston, 1980], 108).

Ich fühle des Todes
Verjüngende Flut,
Und harr in den Stürmen
Des Lebens voll Mut.

(I feel the rejuvenating tide of death, and in the storms of life, await it with courage.)

They are followed by this epilogue:

Von ihm will ich reden
Und liebend verkünden
So lang ich
Unter Menschen noch bin.
Denn ohne ihn
Was wär unser Geschlecht
Und was sprächen die Menschen,
Wenn sie nicht sprächen von ihm
Ihrem Stifter
Ihrem Geiste!

(For as long as I remain among men, I wish to speak of him and tell lovingly of his deeds. For without him what would our race be, and what would men talk about if not about him, their protector, their soul!)

Language such as this casts the entire passage—the fragment set by Schubert—in a rather different light. These lines were left behind in the manuscript when the poem was finally published. Schubert cannot have known them. They are offered here only in evidence that, for Novalis, the sublimation of life into a state of ideal love is a playing out of the mystery of the transsubstantiation of Christ. The two are parables for one another. As *text*, the passage set by Schubert is disencumbered of the fusion between sacred and profane love that is essential to Novalis. To read the fragment in isolation, in ignorance of the language that precedes it, is unwittingly to divest the poem of this layer of its meaning.

What does Schubert's setting mean to convey? Inexplicably dismissed, and even denigrated in more than one major study, the *Nachthymne* is an astonishing song and a central one in what we are now coming to see as a critical divide in Schubert's conception of himself—the winter of 1818–19 was the first of his "Jahre der Krise," to borrow from the title of an important symposium on the years 1818–23.[23] The opening music, hymn-like and strophic, in

23. The proceedings were published as *Franz Schubert: Jahre der Krise, 1818–1823: Arnold Feil zum 60. Geburtstag am 2. Oktober 1985*, ed. Werner Aderhold, Walther Dürr, and Walburga Litschauer (Kassel, 1985). In the introductory essay, "Franz Schuberts Wanderjahre," Walther Dürr recounts the events of Schubert's definitive break with the family on his return to Vienna in the autumn of 1818, at which point he took up lodgings with Johann Mayrhofer, with whom he shared a single room for more than two years. "Ten years his senior . . . eccentric, misogynist, deeply disturbed, and ultimately a suicide," in Maynard Solomon's description of the poet, Mayrhofer is a central figure in the argument for Schubert's homosexuality, which is the subject of Solomon's "Franz Schubert and the Peacocks of Benvenuto Cellini," *19th Century Music* 12 (Spring 1989): 193–206; the passage on Mayrhofer is on p. 198.

Schubert's devout, dactylic manner, hardly signals ahead to the crisis in the song, at mm. 26–36 (shown in ex. 9.3).

Example 9.3 *Nachthymne* (D. 687), mm. 25–36

Even in Schubert's expanding lexicon of harmonic neologisms, the passage of tones at mm. 33 and 34 stands apart. The composure of the phrase in B♭ major is a deception. The sense of B♭ as the root of a triad dissolves when the voice insists on E♮, not as an appoggiatura that will not resolve, but as a prominent, indeed decisive member of the harmony. For a moment, we take the aggregate to be a subdominant "sixte ajoutée" in the sphere of D minor. But the deep F♯s in the bass dispel all that (see ex. 9.4). Harmonic manipulation of this magnitude generally signals *Verklärung*—transfiguration, metamorphosis, and even, in this instance, transsubstantiation. The music pursues an opposition implicit in the poem:

A. Unendliches Leben Wogt mächtig in mir,	Eternal life surges powerfully in me
B. Ich schaue von oben Herunter nach dir.	I look down on you from above

This surging of eternal life sets loose a ponderous sequence the sheer weight of which suggests anything but ecstasy. At m. 31, a logical F♯ in the bass, parallel to the G♯ in m. 28, is avoided. Still, the ear clings to the first harmony in m. 31 as an incomplete dominant on F♯: the G is an unresolved ninth in the bass. So the taking of B♭ must be understood as a momentary tonicization of the leading tone in B minor, a point not realized until the pungent harmony at m. 34 converts the high D♮ into a hypersensitive tone with two functions: at once an appoggiatura that aims to resolve to C♯ and, in the end, a chromatic passing tone (C𝄪, actually) that moves *up* to the D♯ at m. 35. Overloading the *quality* of dissonance about D♮ is a way of charging the harmony, of isolating the moment. The sounding of F♯ in the bass signals a moment of transfiguration, and the singing of A♯ against the B♭ in the piano only clinches the point.

Example 9.4 *Nachthymne*, mm. 32–34, harmonic abstract

The configuration in m. 34, an augmented triad on the dominant, was very much in Schubert's ear at this time. Still rare, in 1820, as a harmony with its own credentials, it had become something of a code in the Schlegel settings (see ex. 9.5). This is the harmony underscored with that hairpin in m. 2 of *Die Gebüsche*. It stands in a similar position—the very same pitches, enharmonically

Example 9.5 *a*, *Die Sterne* (D. 684), opening measures. *b*, *Der Fluß* (D. 693), mm. 19–21

—at the opening of *Die Sterne* and peeks through in the middle of *Der Fluß*. Perhaps the most striking example is in the setting of the Petrarch sonnet "Nunmehr, da Himmel, Erde schweigt" (D. 630), which Schubert would have found, in the Gries translation, in August Wilhelm Schlegel's *Blumensträusse italiänischer, spanischer und portugiesischer Poesie* (Berlin, 1804). Composed in December 1818—a month before the *Nachthymne*—its arching phrases, in a vast stretch of sixths, compass Petrarch's celestial vision of night (see ex. 9.6).

But in *Nachthymne*, a reading of the poem seems altogether hinged to a reading of the harmony. More than an inconsequential passing chromaticism, the harmony at m. 34 virtually stops the song. The poem, too, is stopped. The harmony sounds *between* a repetition of the lines "Ich schaue von oben / Herunter nach dir," cranking up the pitch a notch: lines first heard in B♭ major are sung now in B major. Something more than simple parallelism is at issue here. The music *levitates* toward B major. Soaring arpeggiations in the piano left hand—a chorus of cellos in its best range—sing of apotheosis. In the broader harmonic context of the passage, the statement in B♭ major recedes, a parenthesis that explores the ambiguity of harmony in m. 31. The tracking of the bass to an ultimate F♯ is only strengthened in the delay (see ex. 9.7).

From here, the music dissolves in a chromatic labyrinth of touched-up diminished sevenths—"An jenem Hügel / Verlischt dein Glanz"—finding B again, now as dominant, and measuring the return through a circle of dominants to D major. The eros of these suggestive lines—"O! sauge, Geliebter, /

Example 9.6 *Sonett* ("Nunmehr, da Himmel, Erde schweigt"; D. 630), opening measures

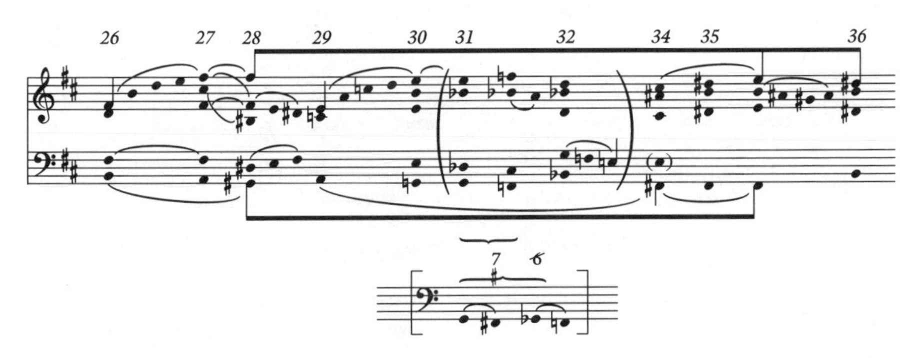

Example 9.7 *Nachthymne*, mm. 26–36, harmonic abstract

Gewaltig mich an,"—is captured in a palpitation, quivering into silence on the very harmony, an incomplete dominant ninth on F♯, left hauntingly unresolved at m. 31 (see ex. 9.8).[24] All this finds release in an *alla breve* finale, beginning "Ich fühle des Todes / Verjüngende Flut," that must bring to mind the liberating catharsis in Florestan's "Und spür ich nicht linde, sanft säuselnde Luft": to be sung, Beethoven instructed, "in einer an Wahnsinn grenzen-

24. Here translation is doomed. "Sauge, Geliebter, gewaltig mich an" is rendered "drink, beloved, powerfully of me" by Friedrichsmeyer (*The Androgyne in Early German Romanticism*, 97); "suck me with force toward you, beloved" by Neubauer (*Novalis*, 103); and "draw me, beloved, powerfully on" in *The Penguin Book of German Verse*, ed. Leonard Forster, rev. ed. (Baltimore, 1959), 304. Precisely what imagined action "sauge mich" would have inspired in Schubert is not given to us to know.

Example 9.8 *Nachthymne*, mm. 49–56

den, doch ruhigen Begeisterung" (in a rapture bordering on madness, and yet with composure), advice that Schubert's singer, too, might appropriate to good advantage.

But it is the ecstatic phrase in B major, the crowning moment in the song, that continues to sound. Is it the crowning moment in the poem as well? What in fact do these lines mean? Who is this "ich" who now looks *down*—and toward whom? The "Herunter auf Dich" in Novalis's manuscript is changed, in *Athenäum*, to "Herunter nach dir." The lowercase "dir" hints at a distancing in the discourse—less a passionate letter to the beloved than a poetic reflection, abstract and impersonal. But there is nothing abstract in this sensual invitation: "O! sauge, Geliebter, / Gewaltig mich an. . . ." "Herunter" and "hinüber" play into a dialectic of spiritual states.

Whether the phrase in B major is true to the poem, whether Novalis's obscure meaning is enhanced through this singing: these are tough critical questions that, to my mind, must be answered in the negative. Surely any sizing up of Schubert's *Nachthymne* must take a stance on this point. At the same time, the poem itself is so fraught with paradox and suspended dialectic—even its personae seem to melt into one another—that, given even the extremes of Schubert's style in 1820, it is hard to imagine a setting that might contrive to dignify the mysterious balances in the poem and not in some measure violate them. "Es gibt Mißverständnisse, die das höchste Einverständnis nur bestätigen," as it goes in Schlegel's memorable elegy to Novalis—misunderstandings that only confirm the highest understanding.

For all its problem with textual identity, the *Nachthymne* remains a telling work for Schubert. The setting of its ecstatic climax in the key of B major comes in response to what must count among Schubert's most sublime interruptions. Indeed, the centering of an opposition around B minor and B major as the extreme tonal outpost in the song—couching the gist of the poem here—will reverberate deep into the structure of the grand song cycles to follow.

The experience of *Nachthymne*, composed plumb in the midst of this preoccupation with the poems of *Abendröte*, cannot have failed to disturb whatever equilibrium Schubert might have managed to establish for himself in the conceiving of a Schlegel cycle. The *Nachthymne* is truer to the spirit of Romantic song cycle—to the Schlegelian sense of the work as fragmentary, disparate, yet innately one—than the songs of the Schlegel cycle, as they have come down to us. Only *Die Gebüsche* hints at a similar concept of form.

III

Schubert's engagement with the cyclic poetry of the new Romantics was a flirtation of sorts. In the end, however, the only intact, textually irrefutable cycles are those to the poetry of Wilhelm Müller. Here, in this simple fact, is some confirmation that Schubert felt a compatibility of style with Müller's naive, folk-like tone—that in the diction of his music and Müller's poetry is recognized a shared, common dialect. Even Heine's prickly lyrics, superficially similar to Müller's but touching some deeper vain of Romantic sensibility, seem to have provoked Schubert to a music that occasionally envelopes the poetry, smothering the simple diction that is at the seat of Heine's knife-like irony.[25]

In 1820, the *idea* of song cycle must have seemed infinitely promising to Schubert. *An die ferne Geliebte*, a lapidary model, modest and concise, was still fresh. New readings in the poetry of Friedrich Schlegel and Novalis, some acquaintance with the critical writings of the Schlegels, and renewed studies in Goethe—all no doubt lively topics for the *Lesegesellschaft* of poets and intellectuals into which Schubert had entered by 1818—will have challenged

25. Heine confessed his debt to Müller in a letter enclosed with a dedication copy of *Reisebilder: Erster Theil* (Hamburg, 1826): "Ich glaube erst in Ihren Liedern den reinen Klang und die wahre Einfachheit, wonach ich immer strebte, gefunden zu haben," he wrote, in a letter discussed in chapter 8 (n. 4) above. "In meinen Gedichten hingegen ist nur die Form einigermaßen volksthümlich, der Inhalt gehört der conventionnellen Gesellschaft," he continues, thus recognizing this disjunction between form and content that is one source of irony in his poetry (see *Heinrich Heine: Briefe 1815–1831*, 249–51).

Schubert to bold projects. That the boldest of them remained fragments—even that their identities were masked—speaks to deeper issues in the conceiving of song.

Reflecting on Schubert's setting of Goethe's *Wandrers Nachtlied* ("Über allen Gipfeln"), Thrasybulos Georgiades was led to these difficult insights:

> Musical structure is created when language is created as something real, when it is taken "at its word." Language understood in this way—as sentence structure, as the function of the verb, as the linking of images—is of a higher order than the music and (here is the essential point) the poem in its sense as work of art. It [language] appears as the primary phenomenon, the one which bestows life and makes art possible. . . .
>
> Schubert transformed the poem into composition as if penetrating through the poem and beyond it to the deeper level of language and creating directly from it. *Musical* structure replaces poetic structure. And yet his music, in which linguistic and poetic level interact with one another, permits the poetic work of art to shine through at the same time, and illuminates it anew.
>
> For both Goethe and Schubert, the linguistic fact is at bottom.[26]

Seeking more than an aphorism on the nature of song, Georgiades gropes for deeper truths. Separating out "Sprach" from "Gedicht" enables him to propose that language, as primary instinct toward speech, holds hierarchical priority over both poem and song. The poem is born of a language that it, the poem, must in turn reinvent. Schubert must somehow engage this process—must discover the *Urphänomen* from which the poem is born. The music, then, will spring from this deeper engagement with language. Yet even Georgiades's painstaking analysis—fifteen dense pages on Schubert's fourteen measures (and Goethe's twenty-four words)—only points up the imponderability of the marriage of word to tone. The essence of this quintessential Lied remains inviolable, beyond the reach of critical discourse.

It goes without saying that the dialectical balances between poem and language will differ from poem to poem, a fortiori from poet to poet. To imagine composition as this profound engagement with language—the composer as *Tondichter* in some literal sense—is yet to leave unsaid that a very similar di-

26. "Es wird musikalische Struktur dadurch geschaffen, daß die Sprache als Reales erfaßt, daß sie 'beim Wort' genommen wird. Die Sprache, so verstanden, als Satzgefüge, Funktion des Verbums, Verknüpfung von Vorstellungen, ist sowohl der Musik als auch—und darauf kommt es wesentlich an—dem Gedicht (als Kunstwerk) übergeordnet. Sie erscheint als das das Leben spendende, Kunst erst ermöglichende Urphänomen." "Schubert hat das Gedicht in Komposition verwandelt, indem er gleichsam durch das Gedicht und über es hinaus bis zu der tieferen, es tragenden Schicht, der Sprache, durchstieß und unmittelbar aus ihr schöpfte. Anstelle der dichterischen setzte er die *musikalische* Struktur. Doch läßt seine Musik—da sprachliche und dichterische Schicht in Wechselwirkung stehen—zugleich das dichterische Kunstwerk durchscheinen, und sie beleuchtet es neu." "Beiden, Goethe und Schubert, liegt das sprachliche Faktum vor." (Georgiades, *Schubert*, 24, 29; for Georgiades's text in a different translation, see his "Lyric as Musical Structure: Schubert's *Wandrers Nachtlied* ['Über allen Gipfeln,' D. 768]," trans. Marie Louise Göllner, in *Schubert: Critical and Analytical Studies*, 93, 100.)

alectic is set in motion in the conceiving of the *Tonstück*. It is a commonplace in theorizing about music to allege that, in the piece, both a special and, by induction, a general language of music are invented afresh.

It is the composer who must reinvent the poet. But then it happens that the poet, invoked in the imagining (in the image making) of the song, intrudes in the process, as if the poet had become the composer. Schubert, consciously or not, must compose as if Goethe—or Schlegel, or Heine—were dictating the poem from the language of the music.

If the process imagined here conjures up some impenetrable convolution of languages, the intention is merely to suggest that, for Schubert, the writing of the song is not so distant from the writing of a poem and that the engagement with the poem is an engagement with the poet. So it must not surprise us to find instances where an intimacy of this complexity simply fails to coalesce. Schlegel's *Abendröte* cycle is such an instance. The impediment resides not within the poem itself, as a sequence of special cases. Each would have appealed to some inner music in Schubert, and we can only regret that the two richest of them—the sonnets that punctuate the two halves of the cycle—were left unsung. The hesitation to engage them speaks, rather, to a problem of a higher order.

The problem might be expressed as an opposition to be reconciled. On the one hand, the veiled metaphors of poetic discourse are enhanced in a language empowered both to illuminate those salient relationships only hinted at in the poetry and to reify poetic abstraction with an expressive power given only to Romantic harmony. On the other, song cycle is narrative. The story unfolds in time. With a temporal accuracy unknown to poetry, music, in the rich texture of temporalities that is innate in it, realizes the motion of the narrative across its diachronic axis. How these two aspects of song maintain a balance, how the one (the synchronic, we might call it) would be constrained from violating the other (the diachronic), is the agon at the essence of song cycle.

Why Schlegel's *Abendröte* did not in the end inspire a song cycle in Schubert is a question without any verifiable answer. Still, to engage the question, to play out some answers, is to conjure the poet in the composer. It was given to Schubert—from those precocious settings of 1811 through to the last songs of 1828—to challenge the conventional limits of poetic discourse in a music of unequaled profundity. In a transference perhaps unique in art, Schubert *becomes* the poet—inhabits a poem that now becomes his. It is this rare sensibility that would induce Schubert finally to mask those conceptions, to reconfigure them for publication, and to retreat behind the bourgeois respectability of a publisher's imprint. In the end, it is not Cappi, Haslinger, and Diabelli who must be held responsible for the public imposture of those songs by Heine, Goethe, and Rellstab that ought to have survived with their cyclic infrastructures intact. The failure to complete the Schlegel cycle—in effect, the decision to dismantle it *as cycle* before it had been composed—is a symptom of that instinct that would later obscure the bold new conceptions into which groups of poems much less innately cyclic were forged. This is a sensibility that is at once cognizant of the power of music to remake poetry and of the responsibility of the singer to the poet. For while Novalis, Schlegel, and their literary colleagues understood music to be the mysterious agent for the conveying of Romantic sentiment—music as the embodiment of Romantic idea itself—Schubert, their closest contemporary, whose music comes nearest to proving their claim, would never quite divest himself of an earlier sense of the composer as singer, as minstrel, as the modest servant of the poem.

List of Works Cited

MUSIC

Collected Editions

Reichardt, Johann Friedrich. *Goethes Lieder, Oden, Balladen und Romanzen mit Musik.* Edited by Walter Salmen. Das Erbe deutscher Musik, vol. 58. Munich: G. Henle Verlag, 1964.

Schubert, Franz. *Franz Schuberts Werke: Kritisch durchgesehene Gesamtausgabe.* Ser. 20, vols. 1–10, *Lieder und Gesänge*, ed. Eusebius Mandyczewski. Ser. 21, *Supplement: Instrumental-Musik*, ed. Eusebius Mandyczewski. Leipzig: Breitkopf & Härtel, 1894–97. Reprinted as vols. 13–18 of *Franz Schubert: Complete Works.* New York: Dover Publications, 1965.

Schubert, Franz. *Franz Schuberts Werke: Revisionsbericht.* Edited by Eusebius Mandyczewski. Leipzig: Breitkopf & Härtel, 1897. Reprinted as *Editors' Commentary on the Critical Edition*, vol. 19 of *Franz Schubert: Complete Works.* New York: Dover Publications, 1969.

Schubert, Franz. *Neue Ausgabe sämtlicher Werke* (*NGA*). Edited by the Internationalen Schubert-Gesellschaft. Ser. 4, *Lieder*, ed. Walther Dürr. Kassel: Bärenreiter Verlag, 1970–.

Facsimiles

Beethoven, Ludwig van. *Vier Kompositionen aus den Jahren 1807–08: "Nur wer die Sehnsucht kennt" (WoO 134) aus Johann Wolfgang Goethes "Wilhelm Meister": Faksimile nach dem Autograph mit einer Studie von Paul Mies.* Bonn: Beethovenhaus, 1970. Reprinted as *"Nur wer die Sehnsucht kennt": Lied in vier Fassungen (WoO 134) nach einem Gedicht von Johann Wolfgang von Goethe: Faksimile des Autographs mit einer Studie von Helga Lühning.* Bonn: Beethoven-Haus, 1986.

Beethoven, Ludwig van. *Ludwig van Beethoven: Sechs Bagatellen für Klavier op. 126: Faksimile der Handschriften und der Originalausgabe mit einem Kommentar.* 2 vols. Edited by Sieghard Brandenburg. Bonn: Beethoven-Haus, 1984.

Schubert, Franz. *Franz Schubert: Die Winterreise: Faksimile-Wiedergabe nach der Originalhandschrift.* Kassel and Basel: Bärenreiter Verlag, 1955; reprint, 1966.

Schubert, Franz. *Franz Schubert: Der Graf von Gleichen: Oper in zwei Akten (D 918): Erstveröffentlichung der Handschrift des Komponisten aus dem Besitz der Wiener Stadt- und Landesbibliothek.* Text by Eduard von Bauernfeld. Edited with commentary by Ernst Hilmar. Vol. 2 of *Veröffentlichungen des Internationalen Franz Schubert Instituts.* Tutzing: Hans Schneider, 1988.

Schubert, Franz. *Franz Schubert: Schwanengesang: 13 Lieder nach Gedichten von Rellstab und Heine, D. 957: Faksimile nach dem Autograph.* Edited by Walther Dürr. Hildesheim: Gerstenberg Verlag, 1978.

Schubert, Franz. *Franz Schubert: Sonate für Klavier und Violine D-Dur Opus 137 Nr. 1, D 384: Faksimile nach dem Autograph und einer autographen Abschrift.* With commentary in English and German by Martin Bente. Munich: G. Henle Verlag, 1988.

Schubert, Franz. *Franz Schubert: Winterreise: The Autograph Score.* With an introduction by Susan Youens. New York: Pierpont Morgan Library / Dover Publications, 1989.

POETRY

Goethe, Johann Wolfgang von. *Goethe's Schriften.* 8 vols. Leipzig: Georg Joachim Göschen, 1787–90.

Goethe, Johann Wolfgang von. *Goethes sämmtliche Schriften.* Vol. 7, *Lyrische Gedichte.* Vienna: Anton Strauß, 1810.

Goethe, Johann Wolfgang von. *Goethe's Werke.* Vol. 1. Stuttgart and Tübingen: Cotta, 1815.

Goethe, Johann Wolfgang von. *Goethes Werke: Hamburger Ausgabe in 14 Bänden.* Vol. 1, *Gedichte und Epen*, ed. Erich Trunz. Hamburg: Christian Wegner Verlag, 1948. Reprint. Munich: C. H. Beck, 1981.

Hardenberg, Friedrich von [Novalis]. *Novalis Schriften: Die Werke Friedrich von Hardenbergs.* Vol. 1, *Das dichterische Werke*, ed. Paul Kluckhorn and Richard Samuel, 2d ed. Stuttgart: W. Kohlhammer Verlag, 1960.

Heine, Heinrich. *Briefe 1815–1831.* Edited by Fritz H. Eisner. Vol. 20 of *Heinrich Heine: Säkularausgabe: Werke, Briefwechsel, Lebenszeugnisse*, ed. Nationalen Forschungs- und Gedenkstätten der klassischen deutschen Literatur in Weimar and Centre National de la Recherche Scientifique. Berlin: Akademie-Verlag; Paris: Editions du CNRS, 1970. *Kommentar.* Edited by Fritz H. Eisner and Fritz Mende. Berlin: Akademie-Verlag; Paris: Editions du CNRS, 1975.

Heine, Heinrich. *Werke.* Edited by Stuart Atkins, in collaboration with Oswald Schönberg. Vol. 1. Munich: Beck, 1973.

Heine, Heinrich. *Historisch-kritische Gesamtausgabe der Werke* (*Düsseldorfer Ausgabe*). Edited by Manfred Windfuhr. Vol. 1, pt. 2, *Buch der Lieder*, ed. Pierre Grappin. Hamburg: Hoffmann & Campe, 1975.

Jacobi, Johann Georg. *Gedichte von Johann Georg Jacobi.* 3 vols. Meisterwerke deutscher Dichter und Prosaisten, vols. 16–18. Vienna: Chr. Kaulfuss & C. Armbruster, 1816.

Jacobi, Johann Georg. *J. G. Jacobi's sämmtliche Werke: Dritte, rechtmäßige Original-Ausgabe.* Zurich: Orell, Füßle & Co., 1819.

Müller, Wilhelm. *Gedichte von Wilhelm Müller: Vollständige kritische Ausgabe.* Edited by James Taft Hatfield. Berlin: B. Behr, 1906. Reprint. Nendeln, Liechtenstein and New York: Kraus Reprint, 1968.

Schiller, Friedrich. *Schillers lyrische Gedichte.* Edited by Heinrich Düntzer. Vol. 2. Leipzig: Ed. Wartig, 1874.

Schiller, Friedrich. *Schiller's Gedichte: Erläutert und auf ihre Veranlassungen, Quellen und Vorbilder zurückgeführt nebst Variantensammlung.* Edited by Heinrich Viehoff. Vol. 1, *Gedichte der ersten und zweiten Periode.* 5th ed. Stuttgart: Carl Conradi, 1876.

Schiller, Friedrich. *Sämtliche Werke.* Edited by Gerhard Fricke and Herbert G. Göpfert. Vol. 3, *Dramatische Fragmente; Übersetzungen; Bühnenbearbeitungen.* Munich: Carl Hanser, 1959.

Schiller, Friedrich. *Sämtliche Werke*. Vol. 3, *Gedichte, Erzählungen, Übersetzungen*, ed. Helmut Koopman. Munich: Winkler Verlag, 1981.

Schiller, Friedrich. *Schillers sämtliche Werke: Säkular-Ausgabe*. Vol. 1, *Gedichte I*. Edited, with an introduction and commentary, by Eduard von der Hellen. Stuttgart and Berlin: J. G. Cotta, n.d.

Schlegel, A. W., and L. Tieck, eds. *Musen-Almanach für das Jahr 1802*. Tübingen: Cotta'schen Buchhandlung, 1802. Facsimile reprint. Heidelberg: Lambert Schneider, 1967.

Schlegel, Friedrich. *Kritische Friedrich-Schlegel-Ausgabe*. Edited by Ernst Behler. Vol. 5, *Dichtungen*, ed. Hans Eichner. Munich: Ferdinand Schöningh Verlag; Zurich: Thomas-Verlag, 1962.

DOCUMENTS AND BIBLIOGRAPHIES

Albrecht, O. E., H. Cahoon, and D. C. Ewing, comps. *The Mary Flagler Cary Music Collection*. New York: Pierpont Morgan Library, 1970.

Deutsch, Otto Erich. *The Schubert Reader: The Life of Franz Schubert in Letters and Documents*. Translated by Eric Blom. New York: W. W. Norton & Co., 1947. Published in England as *Schubert: A Documentary Biography*. London: J. M. Dent, 1947.

Deutsch, Otto Erich. *Schubert: Thematic Catalogue of All His Works in Chronological Order*. In collaboration with Donald R. Wakeling. New York: W. W. Norton & Co., [1951].

Deutsch, Otto Erich. *Schubert: Die Erinnerungen seiner Freunde*. Leipzig: Breitkopf & Härtel, 1957.

Deutsch, Otto Erich. *Schubert: Memoirs by His Friends*. Translated by Rosamond Ley and John Nowell. London: Adam & Charles Black, 1958.

Deutsch, Otto Erich. *Franz Schubert: Die Dokumente seines Lebens*. Kassel: Bärenreiter Verlag, 1964. (= *NGA*, ser. 8: Supplement; vol. 5.)

Deutsch, Otto Erich. *Franz Schubert: Thematisches Verzeichnis seiner Werke in chronologischer Folge*. Kassel: Bärenreiter Verlag, 1978. (= *NGA*, ser. 8: Supplement; vol. 4.)

Dürr, Walther. *Franz Schuberts Werke in Abschriften: Liederalben und Sammlungen*. Kassel: Bärenreiter Verlag, 1975. (= *NGA*, ser. 8, Supplement; vol. 8: Quellen II.)

Friedlaender, Max. *Das deutsche Lied im 18. Jahrhundert: Quellen und Studien*. 2 vols. Stuttgart and Berlin: J. G. Cotta, 1902. Reprint. Hildesheim: Georg Olms, 1962.

Hilmar, Ernst. *Verzeichnis der Schubert-Handschriften in der Musiksammlung der Wiener Stadt- und Landesbibliothek*. Catalogus Musicus, vol. 8. Kassel: Bärenreiter Verlag, 1978.

Hilmar, Ernst, and Otto Brusatti, eds. *Franz Schubert: Ausstellung der Wiener Stadt- und Landesbibliothek zum 150. Todestag des Komponisten*. Vienna: Universal-Edition, 1978.

Kinsky, Georg. *Musikhistorisches Museum von Wilhelm Heyer in Cöln: Katalog*. Vol. 4, *Musik-Autographen*, ed. Frau Wilhelm Heyer. Cologne: W. Heyer, 1916.

Kinsky, Georg. *Manuskripte, Briefe, Dokumente von Scarlatti bis Stravinsky: Katalog der Musikautographen-Sammlung Louis Koch*. Stuttgart: Hoffmannsche Buchdruckerei Felix Kraus, 1953.

Kinsky, Georg. *Das Werk Beethovens: Thematisch-bibliographisches Verzeichnis seiner sämtlichen vollendeten Kompositionen*. Completed and edited by Hans Halm. Munich and Duisburg: G. Henle Verlag, 1955.

Mühlhäuser, Siegfried. *Die Handschriften und Varia der Schubertiana-Sammlung Taussig in der Universitätsbibliothek Lund.* Quellenkataloge zur Musikgeschichte, no. 17, ed. Richard Schaal. Wilhelmshaven: Heinrichshofen's Verlag, 1981.

Sotheby's. *Fine Printed and Manuscript Music including the Mannheim Collection: London, Friday 6th December 1991.* Auction catalog. n.p., n.d.

STUDIES

Abert, Hermann. *W. A. Mozart.* 7th ed. 2 vols. Leipzig: Breitkopf & Härtel, 1955. (*Index.* Prepared by Erich Kapst. Leipzig, 1966.)

Aderhold, Werner, Walther Dürr, and Walburga Litschauer, eds. *Franz Schubert: Jahre der Krise 1818–1823: Arnold Feil zum 60. Geburtstag am 2. Oktober 1985.* Kassel: Bärenreiter Verlag, 1985.

Allgemeine Musikalische Zeitung 31 (1829): 653–62.

Anderson, Emily, ed. and trans. *The Letters of Beethoven.* 3 vols. London: Macmillan; New York: St. Martin's Press, 1961.

Armitage-Smith, Julian. "Schubert's *Winterreise,* Part I: The Sources of the Musical Text." *Musical Quarterly* 60 (January 1974): 20–36.

Beck, Dagmar, and Grita Herre. "Anton Schindlers fingierte Eintragungen in den Konversationsheften." In *Zu Beethoven: Aufsätze und Annotationen,* ed. Harry Goldschmidt, 1:11–89. Berlin: Verlag Neue Musik, 1979.

Belart, Urs Wilhelm. *Gehalt und Aufbau von Heinrich Heines Gedichtsammlungen: Sprache und Dichtung.* Vol. 38. Bern: Paul Haupt, 1925. Reprint. Nendeln, Liechtenstein: Kraus Reprint Co., 1970.

Berke, Dietrich. "Schuberts Liedentwurf 'Abend' D 645 und dessen textliche Voraussetzungen." In *Schubert-Kongreß Wien 1978: Bericht,* ed. Otto Brusatti, 305–20. Graz: Akademische Druck- und Verlagsanstalt, 1979.

Brenneis, Clemens. "Das Fischhof-Manuskript: Zur Frühgeschichte der Beethoven-Biographik." In *Zu Beethoven: Aufsätze und Annotationen,* ed. Harry Goldschmidt, 1:90–116. Berlin: Verlag Neue Musik, 1979.

Brown, Maurice J. E. "Some Unpublished Schubert Songs and Song Fragments." *Music Review* 15 (1954): 93–102.

Brown, Maurice J. E. "The Posthumous Publication of the Songs." In *Essays on Schubert,* 267–90. London: Macmillan; New York: St. Martin's Press, 1966.

Brown, Maurice J. E. *The New Grove Schubert.* New York and London: W. W. Norton & Co., 1983.

Brusatti, Otto. "Zwei unbekannte Klavierwerke Franz Schuberts." In *Schubert-Studien: Festgabe der Österreichischen Akademie der Wissenschaften zum Schubert-Jahr 1978,* ed. Franz Grasberger and Othmar Wessely, 33–41. Vienna: Österreichische Akademie der Wissenchaften, 1978.

Capell, Richard. *Schubert's Songs.* 2d ed. New York: Basic Books, 1957.

Chusid, Martin. "Schubert's Cyclic Compositions of 1824." *Acta Musicologica* 36 (1964): 37–45.

Chusid, Martin. "Beethoven and the Unfinished." In *Franz Schubert: Symphony in B Minor ("Unfinished"): An Authoritative Score: Schubert's Sketches, Commentary, Essays in History and Analysis,* ed. Martin Chusid, 98–110. New York: W. W. Norton & Co., 1968.

Clifton, Thomas. "An Application of Goethe's Concept of Steigerung to the Morphology of Diminution." *Journal of Music Theory* 14, no. 2 (Winter 1970): 165–90.

Cone, Edward T. "Beethoven's Experiments in Composition: The Late Bagatelles." In *Beethoven Studies 2*, ed. Alan Tyson, 84–105. London, Oxford, and New York: Oxford University Press, 1977.

Daverio, John. "Schumann's 'Im Legendenton' and Friedrich Schlegel's *Arabeske*." *19th Century Music* 11 (Fall 1987): 150–63.

Dürr, Walther. "Schubert and Johann Michael Vogl: A Reappraisal." *19th Century Music* 3 (November 1979): 126–40.

Dürr, Walther. "Schubert's Songs and Their Poetry: Reflections on Poetic Aspects of Song Composition." In *Schubert Studies: Problems of Style and Chronology*, ed. Eva Badura-Skoda and Peter Branscombe, 1–24. Cambridge: Cambridge University Press, 1982.

Dürr, Walther. "Franz Schuberts Wanderjahre: Einführung in das Generalthema." In *Franz Schubert: Jahre der Krise 1818–1823: Arnold Feil zum 60. Geburtstag am 2. Oktober 1985*, ed. Werner Aderhold, Walther Dürr, and Walburga Litschauer, 11–21. Kassel: Bärenreiter Verlag, 1985.

Dürr, Walther. "Entwurf—Ausarbeitung—Revision: Zur Arbeitsweise Schuberts am Beispiel des Liedes 'Der Unglückliche' (D. 713)." *Musikforschung* 44 (1991): 221–36.

Enzinger, Moritz. "Franz von Bruchmann, der Freund J. Chr. Senns und des Grafen August v. Platen: Eine Selbstbiographie aus dem Wiener Schubertkreise nebst Briefen." *Veröffentlichungen des Museum Ferdinandeum in Innsbruch* 10 (1930): 117–379.

Feil, Arnold. *Franz Schubert: Die schöne Müllerin; Winterreise.* Stuttgart: Philipp Reclam, 1975. Translated into English by Ann C. Sherwin. *Franz Schubert: Die schöne Müllerin; Winterreise.* Portland, Oreg.: Amadeus Press, 1988.

Fischer-Dieskau, Dietrich, ed. *The Fischer-Dieskau Book of Lieder.* Translated by George Bird and Richard Stokes. London: Victor Gollancz / Pan Books, 1976. Originally published as *Texte deutscher Lieder.* Munich: Deutscher Taschenbuch-Verlag, 1968.

Fischer-Dieskau, Dietrich. *Auf den Spuren der Schubert-Lieder: Werden, Wesen, Wirkung.* 2d ed. Kassel: Bärenreiter Verlag, 1976.

Fischer-Dieskau, Dietrich. *Schubert: A Biographical Study of His Songs.* Translated and edited by Kenneth S. Whitton. London: Cassell & Co., 1976.

Forkel, Johann Nicolaus. *Musikalisch-kritische Bibliothek.* Vol. 1. Gotha: C. W. Ettinger, 1778. Reprint. 3 vols. in 1. Hildesheim: Georg Olms, 1964.

Friedrichsmeyer, Sara. *The Androgyne in Early German Romanticism: Friedrich Schlegel, Novalis and the Metaphysics of Love.* Stanford German Studies, ed. Department of German Studies, Stanford University, vol. 18. Bern: Peter Lang, 1983.

Frisch, Walter. "Schubert's *Nähe des Geliebten* (D. 162): Transformation of the *Volkston*." In *Schubert: Critical and Analytical Studies*, ed. Walter Frisch, 175–99. Lincoln and London: University of Nebraska Press, 1986.

Fux, Johann Joseph. *Gradus ad Parnassum, oder Anführung zur Regelmäßigen Musikalischen Composition: Aus den Lateinischen ins Teutsche übersetzt, mit Anmerckungen versehen und herausgegeben von Lorenz Mizler.* Leipzig: im Mizlerischen Bücherverlag, 1742. Reprint. Hildesheim and New York: Georg Olms, 1974.

Genette, Gérard. "Boundaries of Narrative." *New Literary History* 8, no. 1 (Fall 1976): 1–13.

Genette, Gérard. *Narrative Discourse: An Essay in Method.* Translated by Jane E. Lewin. Ithaca, N.Y.: Cornell University Press, 1980.

Georgiades, Thrasybulos G. *Schubert: Musik und Lyrik.* Göttingen: Vandenhoeck & Ruprecht, 1967.

Georgiades, Thrasybulos G. "Lyric as Musical Structure: Schubert's *Wandrers Nachtlied* ('Über allen Gipfeln,' D. 768)." Translated by Marie Louise Göllner. In *Schubert: Critical and Analytical Studies*, ed. Walter Frisch, 84–103. Lincoln and London: University of Nebraska Press, 1986.

Gerstenberg, Walter. "*Schubertiade*: Anmerkungen zu einigen Liedern." In *Festschrift Otto Erich Deutsch zum 80. Geburtstag*, ed. Walter Gerstenberg, Jan LaRue, and Wolfgang Rehm, 232–39. Kassel: Bärenreiter Verlag, 1963.

Goldschmidt, Harry. "Welches war die ursprüngliche Reihenfolge in Schuberts Heine-Liedern." *Deutsches Jahrbuch der Musikwissenschaft für 1972* (1974), 52–62.

Gottwaldt, Heinz, and Gerhard Hahre, eds. *Briefwechsel zwischen Johann Abraham Peter Schulz und Johann Heinrich Voss.* Vol. 9, *Schriften des Landesinstituts für Musikforschung Kiel.* Kassel and Basel: Bärenreiter Verlag, 1960.

Gräf, Han Gerhard. *Goethe ueber seine Dichtungen: Versuch einer Sammlung aller Aeusserungen des Dichters ueber seine poetischen Werke.* Vol. 9, *Dritter Theil: Die lyrischen Dichtungen.* Frankfurt: Rülten & Loeing, 1914.

Gruber, Gernot. "Romantische Ironie in den Heine-Liedern?" In *Schubert-Kongreß Wien 1978: Bericht*, ed. Otto Brusatti, 321–34. Graz: Akademische Druck- und Verlagsanstalt, 1979.

Hallmark, Rufus. "Schubert's 'Auf dem Strom.'" In *Schubert Studies: Problems of Style and Chronology*, ed. Eva Badura-Skoda and Peter Branscombe, 25–46. Cambridge: Cambridge University Press, 1982.

Heuß, Alfred. "Ein trunkenes Jünglingslied von Franz Schubert." *Zeitschrift für Musik* 95 (November 1928): 619–24, 679–82.

Hildesheimer, Wolfgang. *Mozart.* Frankfurt: Suhrkamp Verlag, 1977. Translated into English by Marion Faber. New York: Farrar, Straus, Giroux, 1982.

Hoorickx, Reinhard van. "An Unknown Schubert Letter." *Musical Times* 122 (May 1981): 291–94.

Hoorickx, Reinhard van. "The Chronology of Schubert's Fragments and Sketches." In *Schubert Studies: Problems of Style and Chronology*, ed. Eva Badura-Skoda and Peter Branscombe, 297–325. Cambridge: Cambridge University Press, 1982.

Johnson, Douglas, Alan Tyson, and Robert Winter. *The Beethoven Sketchbooks: History, Reconstruction, Inventory.* Edited by Douglas Johnson. Berkeley and Los Angeles: University of California Press, 1985.

Keiler, Allan. "On Some Properties of Schenker's Pitch Derivations." *Music Perception* 1, no. 2 (Winter 1983–84): 200–28.

Kerman, Joseph. "A Romantic Detail in Schubert's *Schwanengesang.*" *Musical Quarterly* 48 (January 1962): 36–49. Revised and reprinted in *Schubert: Critical and Analytical Studies*, ed. Walter Frisch. Lincoln and London: University of Nebraska Press, 1986.

Kerman, Joseph, "*An die ferne Geliebte.*" In *Beethoven Studies* 1, ed. Alan Tyson, 123–57. New York: W. W. Norton & Co., 1973.

Kinderman, William. "Beethoven's Symbol for the Deity in the *Missa Solemnis* and the Ninth Symphony." *19th Century Music* 9 (Fall 1985): 102–18.

Kramer, Lawrence. "The Schubert Lied: Romantic Form and Romantic Consciousness." In *Schubert: Critical and Analytical Studies*, ed. Walter Frisch, 200–236. Lincoln and London: University of Nebraska Press, 1986.

Kramer, Richard. "Schubert's Heine." *19th Century Music* 8 (Spring 1985): 213–25.

Kramer, Richard. "Distant Cycles: Schubert, Goethe and the *Entfernte*." *Journal of Musicology* 6 (Winter 1988): 3–26.

Kramer, Richard. "Posthumous Schubert." *19th Century Music* 14 (Fall 1990): 197–216.

Kreissle von Hellborn, Heinrich. *Franz Schubert: Eine biographische Skizze*. Vienna: L. C. Zamarski & C. D. Hmarsch, 1861.

Kreissle von Hellborn, Heinrich. *The Life of Franz Schubert*. Translated by Arthur Duke Coleridge. Vol. 2. London: Longmans, Green, & Co., 1869. Reprint. New York: Vienna House, 1972.

Kropfinger, Klaus. "Das Gespaltene Werk: Beethovens Streichquartett Op. 130/133." In *Beiträge zu Beethovens Kammermusik: Symposion Bonn 1984*, ed. Sieghard Brandenburg and Helmut Loos, 296–335. Munich: G. Henle Verlag, 1987.

Kruse, Joseph A., ed. *Heine Jahrbuch 1978: 17. Jahrgang*. Hamburg: Hoffmann & Campe Verlag, 1978.

Lewin, David. "Inversional Balance as an Organizing Force in Schoenberg's Music and Thought." *Perspectives of New Music* 6, no. 2 (Spring-Summer 1968): 1–21.

Lewin, David. "*Auf dem Flusse*: Image and Background in a Schubert Song." *19th Century Music* 6 (Summer 1982): 47–59. Reprinted, slightly revised, in *Schubert: Critical and Analytical Studies*, ed. Walter Frisch, 126–52. Lincoln and London: University of Nebraska Press, 1986.

Ley, Stephan, ed. *Beethoven als Freund der Familie Wegeler–v. Breuning*. Bonn: Verlag von Friedrich Cohen, 1927.

Lockwood, Lewis. "The Beethoven Sketchbook in the Scheide Library." *Princeton University Library Chronicle* 37 (Autumn 1975–76): 139–53.

Lord, Albert B. *The Singer of Tales*. Cambridge, Mass.: Harvard University Press, 1960. Reprint. New York: Atheneum, 1978.

Macdonald, Hugh. " ." *19th Century Music* 11 (Spring 1987): 221–37.

Marx, A. B. Review of *Nouvelles bagatelles, ou Collection de morceaux facils et agréables pour le pianof. par L. van Beethoven: Oeuvre 112. Cäcilia: Eine Zeitschrift für die musikalische Welt* 1 (1824): 140–44.

Mast, Paul. "Brahms' Study, Octaven u. Quinten u. A., with Schenker's Commentary Translated." In *The Music Forum*, vol. 5, ed. Felix Salzer and Carl Schachter, 1–196. New York: Columbia University Press, 1980.

Mies, Paul. *Schubert: Der Meister des Liedes: Die Entwicklung von Form und Inhalt im Schubertschen Lied*. Berlin: Max Hesses Verlag, 1928.

Mies, Paul. "'Sehnsucht von Göthe und Beethoven.'" In *Beethoven-Jahrbuch*, vol. 2, ed. Paul Mies and Joseph Schmidt-Görg, 112–19. Bonn: Beethovenhaus, 1956.

[Mizler (von Kolof), Lorenz Christoph.] "Sieben Schrifften [wegen der] Quinten und Octaven." In *Musikalische Bibliothek*, ed. Lorenz Mizler, vol. 2, pt. 4, pp. 1–95. Leipzig: Mizlerischen Bücherverlag, 1743.

Morgan, Robert P., "Dissonant Prolongations: Theoretical and Compositional Precedents." *Journal of Music Theory* 20 (Spring 1976): 49–91.

Müller-Blattau, Joseph. "Schuberts 'Unvollendete' und das Problem des Fragmentarischen in der Musik." In *Von der Vielfalt der Musik: Musikgeschichte, Musikerziehung, Musikpflege*. Freiburg i. Br.: Verlag Rombach & Co., 1966.

Neubauer, John. *Novalis*. Twayne's World Authors Series: A Survey of the World's Literature, ed. Ulrich Weisstein, no. 556. Boston: Twayne Publishers, 1980.

Newcomb, Anthony. "Structure and Expression in a Schubert Song: *Noch einmal* Auf dem Flusse *zu hören.*" In *Schubert: Critical and Analytical Studies*, ed. Walter Frisch, 153–74. Lincoln and London: University of Nebraska Press, 1986.

Overbeck, Gertrud. "Goethes Lehre von der Metamorphose der Pflanzen und ihre Widerspiegelung in seiner Dichtung." In *Publications of the English Goethe Society*, n.s. 31 (1961): 38–59. (Papers read before the society, 1960–61, ed. Elizabeth M. Wilkinson.)

Reed, John. *Schubert: The Final Years*. London: Faber & Faber, 1972.

Reed, John. *The Schubert Song Companion*. Prose translations by Norma Deane and Celia Larner. New York: Universe Books, 1985.

Rellstab, Ludwig. *Aus meinem Leben*. Berlin: J. Guttentag, 1861.

Richter, Jean Paul. From the *Vorschule der Aesthetik*. Translated in *Source Readings in Music History: From Classical Antiquity through the Romantic Era*, ed. Oliver Strunk, 744–63. New York: W. W. Norton & Co., 1950.

Ritter, Heinz. *Novalis' Hymnen an die Nacht: Ihre Deutung nach Inhalt und Aufbau auf textkritischer Grundlage ihre Entstehung*. Beiträge zur neueren Literaturgeschichte, 3d ser., vol. 17. 2d ed. Heidelberg: Carl Winter Universitätsverlag, 1974.

Rosen, Charles. "Romantic Originals." *New York Review of Books*, 17 December 1987, 22–31.

Salm, Peter. *The Poem as Plant: A Biological View of Goethe's Faust*. Cleveland and London: Case Western Reserve University Press, 1971.

Schenker, Heinrich. "Schubert: *Ihr Bild*." *Der Tonwille: Flugblätter zum Zeugnis unwandelbarer Gesetze der Tonkunst einer neuen Jugend dargebracht* 1, no. 1 (1921): 46–49.

Schenker, Heinrich. *Das Meisterwerk in der Musik: Ein Jahrbuch*. Munich: Drei Masken Verlag, 1925–30. Reprint. 3 vols. in 1. Hildesheim: Georg Olms, 1974.

Schenker, Heinrich, ed. *Johannes Brahms, Oktaven und Quinten u.A.* Vienna: Universal-Edition, 1933.

Schenker, Heinrich. *Harmony*. Edited by Oswald Jonas. Translated by Elisabeth Mann Borgese. Chicago and London: University of Chicago Press, 1954.

Schenker, Heinrich. *Free Composition* (*Der freie Satz*). 2 vols. Edited and translated by Ernst Oster. New York and London: Longman, 1979.

Schochow, Maximilian, and Lilly Schochow. *Franz Schubert: Die Texte seiner einstimmig komponierten Lieder und ihre Dichter*. 2 vols. Hildesheim and New York: Georg Olms, 1974.

Scholes, Robert. "Language, Narrative, and Anti-Narrative." *Critical Inquiry* 7, no. 1 (Autumn 1980): 204–12.

Solie, Ruth. "The Living Work: Organicism and Musical Analysis." *19th Century Music* 4 (Fall 1980): 147–56.

Solomon, Maynard. "Schubert and Beethoven." *19th Century Music* 3 (November 1979): 114–25.

Solomon, Maynard. "Franz Schubert's 'My Dream.'" *American Imago* 38 (1981): 137–54.

Solomon, Maynard. "Franz Schubert and the Peacocks of Benvenuto Cellini." *19th Century Music* 12 (Spring 1989): 193–206.

Steglich, Rudolf. "Das romantische Wanderlied und Franz Schubert." In *Musa-Mens-Musici: Im Gedenken an Walther Vetter*, ed. Institut für Musikwissenschaft der Humboldt-Universität zu Berlin, 267–76. Leipzig: VEB Deutscher Verlag für Musik, 1969.

Stein, Jack M. "Schubert's Heine Songs." *Journal of Aesthetics and Art Criticism* 24 (Summer 1966): 559–66.

Stein, Jack M. *Poem and Music in the German Lied from Gluck to Hugo Wolf.* Cambridge, Mass.: Harvard University Press, 1971.

Sulzer, Johann Georg. *Allgemeine Theorie der schönen Künste.* 4 vols. New enlarged 2d ed. Edited by C. F. Blankenburg. Leipzig: Weidmannschen Buchhandlung, 1792–94. Reprint. Hildesheim: Georg Olms, 1967.

Tovey, Donald Francis. *Essays in Musical Analysis.* Suppl. vol., *Chamber Music.* London: Oxford University Press, 1944.

Turchin, Barbara. "The Nineteenth-Century *Wanderlieder* Cycle." *Journal of Musicology* 5 (Fall 1987): 498–525.

Vetter, Walther. *Franz Schubert.* Potsdam: Akademische Verlagsgesellschaft Athenaion, 1934.

Vetter, Walther. *Der Klassiker Schubert.* 2 vols. Leipzig: C. F. Peters, 1953.

Walker, Alan. "Schumann, Liszt and the C-Major Fantasie, Op. 17: A Declining Relationship." *Music and Letters* 60 (April 1979): 156–65.

Weber, Gottfried. *Versuch einer geordneten Theorie der Tonsezkunst zum Selbstunterricht, mit Anmerkungen für Gelehrtere.* Vol. 1. Mainz: B. Schott, 1817.

White, Hayden. "The Value of Narrativity in the Representation of Reality." *Critical Inquiry* 7, no. 1 (Autumn 1980): 5–27.

Wiese, Benno von. "Friedrich von Schiller: Die Götter Griechenlandes." In *Die deutsche Lyrik: Form und Geschichte*, 2 vols., ed. Benno von Wiese. Düsseldorf: August Bagel Verlag, 1956.

Winter, Robert. "Paper Studies and the Future of Schubert Research." In *Schubert Studies: Problems of Style and Chronology*, ed. Eva Badura-Skoda and Peter Branscombe, 209–75. Cambridge: Cambridge University Press, 1982.

Wolff, Christoph. "Schubert's 'Der Tod und das Mädchen': Analytical and Explanatory Notes on the Song D 531 and the Quartet D 810." In *Schubert Studies: Problems of Style and Chronology*, ed. Eva Badura-Skoda and Peter Branscombe, 143–71. Cambridge: Cambridge University Press, 1982.

Youens, Susan. "*Winterreise*: In the Right Order." *Soundings*, no. 13 (Summer 1985): 41–50.

Youens, Susan. "*Wegweiser* in *Winterreise*." *Journal of Musicology* 5, no. 3 (Summer 1987): 357–79.

Zeman, Herbert. "Franz Schuberts Teilhabe an der österreichischen literarischen Kultur seiner Zeit." In *Schubert-Kongreß Wien 1978: Bericht*, ed. Otto Brusatti, 285–304. Graz: Akademische Druck- und Verlagsanstalt, 1979.

Index of Names and Works

(*numbers in boldface refer to music examples*)